US FOREIGN POLICY

Domestic Roots
and International Impact

Richard Johnson

BRISTOL
UNIVERSITY
PRESS

First published in Great Britain in 2021 by

Bristol University Press
University of Bristol
1-9 Old Park Hill
Bristol
BS2 8BB
UK
t: +44 (0)117 954 5940
e: bup-info@bristol.ac.uk

Details of international sales and distribution partners are available at bristoluniversitypress.co.uk

British Library Cataloguing in Publication Data
A catalogue record for this book is available from the British Library

ISBN 978-1-5292-1535-9 hardcover
ISBN 978-1-5292-1536-6 paperback
ISBN 978-1-5292-1537-3 ePub
ISBN 978-1-5292-1538-0 ePdf

Cover design: Liam Roberts
Front cover image: Liam Roberts

To my students

Contents

List of Tables and Figures

Tables

Figures

Acknowledgements

This book is based on various undergraduate and graduate United States Foreign Policy courses I have taught at Lancaster University, the University of Cambridge and Queen Mary University of London. I view teaching and research as dynamically related, and this book is no exception. Teaching is one of the most enjoyable aspects of my job, and it has been a pleasure to teach such interesting, enthusiastic and capable groups of students across these three institutions, as well as my other US politics students through courses at the University of Oxford, the University of Virginia and Beijing Foreign Studies University. This book is dedicated to them all.

The majority of this book was written while I was lecturer in US Politics and International Relations at Lancaster University. I want to express special thanks to wonderful colleagues at Lancaster, especially those in the Department of Politics, Philosophy and Religion who came to be a tremendous source of support and encouragement during challenging times. I acknowledge in particular Gavin Hyman, Christopher Macleod and Rachel Cooper, who have been dear friends throughout my time at Lancaster and afterwards. I also acknowledge many other wonderful colleagues who helped to form a special community at Lancaster, including, but not limited to, the following: Sunita Abraham, Rahaf Aldoughli, Patrick Bishop, Brian Black, Darren Bowes, Andrew Chubb, Sam Clark, Sheila Constantine, Erica Consterdine, Clare Coxhill, Karolina Follis, Mark Garnett, Brian Garvey, Robert Geyer, James Groves, Julie Hearn, Anderson Jeremiah, Koko Kawanami, Kim Knott, Anna-Sophie Maass, Kathryn MacKay (and Drew Countryman), Simon Mabon, Neil Manson, Sarah Marsden, Christopher May, Tom Mills, Kunal Mukherjee, Shuruq Naguib, Astrid Nordin, Laura Premack, Chakravarthi Ram-Prasad, Alison Stone, Joe Thornberry, Linda Woodhead and Katherine Young. Wendy Francis is much missed. I feel fortunate to have known and worked with her, even for a relatively short period of time.

The rest of this book was written during the COVID-19 pandemic as I began my new position as lecturer in US Politics and Policy at

Queen Mary University of London. I would like to thank my new colleagues in the School of Politics and International Relations who welcomed me in such unusual circumstances. Although the pandemic has meant we have not yet been able to meet socially, I look forward to getting to know you all better in time.

I am very grateful to the team at Bristol University Press for being so enthusiastic about this project from the start. Chief among these has been my editor Stephen Wenham, as well as the production and editing team. Stephen's forbearance was much appreciated. My thanks, too, to Caroline Astley and Dawn Rushen. I am also grateful to all those anonymous reviewers who read this book in various forms, from proposal to final manuscript. Your feedback has improved the work.

I have been given great support throughout this period by Lee Evans. He is someone who doesn't take easily to compliments, but he has, quite simply, been my strength and stay all these months, and I and his group of friends, in this and many other countries, owe him a debt greater than he would ever claim or we shall ever know.

Finally, my love and thanks to my parents Ruth and Tony and my other family members, especially my grandmother Christine and my uncles Jeff, David and Peter.

Introduction

At 10:07 on Wednesday, 16 October 2019, in Room HVC-304 at the US Capitol Visitor Center in Washington, DC, Ambassador Michael McKinley began seven hours of closed-door interviews with members of the House Intelligence, Oversight, and Foreign Affairs Committees. McKinley had been a diplomat and served four times as a US ambassador since 1982. Until his resignation the previous week, he had held a unique role as senior adviser to Secretary of State Mike Pompeo. McKinley descended to the conference room below the US Capitol that day to testify about Donald Trump's attempt to solicit information from the Ukraine about former Vice President Joe Biden for political advantage in his re-election campaign.

McKinley first introduced himself by emphasizing that his work as a State Department official was non-political. He abhorred the idea that politics should enter into his advice about the role of the US abroad. He told the interrogators:

> I'm going to be very direct on this. I'm a career Foreign Service officer. This [administration] has been, as many administrations have been – there's [sic] many moments that are highly political that spill over…. The one thing I knew above anything when I accepted this job was I wasn't going to sit and become part of the political environment. So I didn't sit and have discussions with Secretary Pompeo about what was happening with White House politics, you know, White House approaches. (US House of Representatives Permanent Select Committee on Intelligence, 2019: 44)

McKinley's testimony reflected the view that US foreign policy operates separately from domestic policy matters. Foreign policy, it has often been argued, is about the pursuit of national interests. It is best handled by non-partisan experts. Given the high stakes, foreign policy requires neutral expertise – like that provided by Ambassador McKinley. In contrast, it is thought that domestic policy is more open to be shaped by the demands of interest groups, parties and voters. In this vein, John F. Kennedy once remarked, 'Domestic policy can only defeat us; foreign policy can kill us' (quoted in Schlesinger, 1973: 401). For this reason, many people believe that 'neutral' concepts about the 'rules' of the international system, developed by scholars of international relations (IR), must be sheltered from considerations of partisan advantage or constituent interests. Republican Senator Arthur Vandenberg famously captured these sentiments when he warned after the Second World War, 'It will be a sad hour for the Republic if we ever desert the fundamental concept that politics shall stop at the water's edge' (Haas, 2016: 255).

In this perspective, Donald Trump deserted this 'fundamental concept' by making choices about foreign policy on the basis of domestic political factors, in particular trying (unsuccessfully) to secure his own re-election. David Adler and Ben Judah wrote in *The Guardian* newspaper two months after McKinley's testimony, 'in the US, foreign policy – and its notion of a national interest protected by the executive – became a cherished ideal behind which the founders promised to lead their city on the hill. Trump has laid waste to this worldview' (2019).

Ambassador McKinley's words were transcribed as evidence in the House impeachment investigation against President Trump. The following day, at 12:39 pm, Acting White House Chief of Staff Mick Mulvaney took charge of the White House's daily press briefing. Mulvaney brought up McKinley's testimony, which had not yet been declassified. Attempting to diminish McKinley's standing by apparently forgetting his name, Mulvaney told the White House press corps:

> I heard this yesterday and I can never remember the gentleman who testified. Was it McKinney [sic], the guy – was that his name? I don't know him. He testified yesterday…. Well, McKinney [sic] said yesterday that he was really upset with the political influence in foreign policy. That was one of the reasons he was so upset about this. And I have news for everybody: Get over it. There's going to be political influence in foreign policy. (Shear and Rogers, 2019)

Mulvaney's words were roundly criticized in the press. In one major respect, these criticisms were justified. Mulvaney was trying to defend President Trump's solicitation of a foreign government to assist directly in his re-election effort. The House of Representatives considered this attempt to subvert the democratic process worthy of articles of impeachment, which were passed on 18 December 2019.

Yet many commentators also attacked the general point that Mulvaney had proffered: 'there's going to be political influence in foreign policy'. In *Foreign Affairs*, a house journal of the foreign policy establishment, Timothy Naftali argued that Trump had 'shattered the traditional wall between domestic politics and foreign policy' (2020). In *The Washington Post*, Josh Rogin wrote, 'Trump's foreign policy is all politics' (2020). In this assessment, Trump inappropriately and dangerously poured domestic politics into foreign policy. Soliciting a foreign power to take part in a US election is obviously wrong, corrupt and illegal, but can the same be said about making foreign policy decisions based on domestic political considerations?

Even a cursory review of recent US history suggests that Donald Trump was not the first recipient of such criticism. Trump's predecessor Barack Obama was also criticized for subsuming foreign policy to domestic political considerations. In 2015, Colin Dueck wrote that Obama made decisions about foreign policy in order to maximize domestic political benefit, even if they were not objectively the best decisions in the national interest. Dueck wrote, 'Since Obama's greatest ambitions are within the domestic policy arena, he is very reluctant to risk them through international or military policies that might shatter his center-left coalition.... [F]oreign policy decisions are often delayed or avoided in order to minimize domestic political risk', a strategy which, in Dueck's view, endangered US national interests and 'allowed numerous threats to germinate internationally' (Dueck, 2015: 6, 38). Vali Nasr, a State Department adviser between 2009 and 2011, was scathing of Obama's supposedly political approach to foreign policy. He wrote that President Obama's tendency to leave 'major foreign policy decisions [to] a small cabal of relatively inexperienced White House advisers whose turf was strictly politics was truly disturbing'. Reflecting on his specialist region of the Middle East and Afghanistan, Nasr lamented that 'American actions in that region of the world were reshaped to accommodate partisan political concerns unimaginable a few decades ago' (Nasr, 2013).

Obama was not as much an historical outlier as Nasr supposed. His predecessor, George W. Bush, was also accused of pouring domestic politics into his foreign policy. Kevin Fullam and Alan Gitelson argued that soon after 9/11, 'The war on terror was quickly adopted as a tool for partisan advantage' (2009: 246). *The Economist* (2008) claimed that Bush 'did something that was new in foreign policy: he turned the war on terror into an instrument of partisan advantage with the aim of building an enduring Republican majority'. Jon Herbert took the same view, arguing that Bush 'exploited the crisis after September 11' (2011: 269). Other scholars argued that Bush designed his foreign policy in response to appeals by evangelical Christian lobbying groups (Milkis and Rhodes, 2007; Peterson, 2004: 252).

Likewise, Bush's predecessor Bill Clinton was accused of making foreign policy decisions to suit domestic political considerations. Stephen Walt wrote in a critical assessment of Clinton's foreign policy that the 1999 World Trade Organization (WTO) Ministerial Conference was a failure because Clinton 'sought to appease a variety of domestic interest groups by calling for tougher labour standards' (Walt, 2000: 75). Clinton was also accused of engaging in military adventurism to distract from political difficulties at home. Dick Morris, one of Clinton's political advisers, wrote in his memoirs that he encouraged Clinton to 'use foreign policy situations to demonstrate your strength and toughness to the American people' (Morris, 1997: 38).

Clinton's predecessor, George H.W. Bush, came under similar accusations of using the military to boost domestic perceptions of the president's strength. A failed coup in Panama in October 1989 convinced US policymakers that the military leader Manuel Noriega was unlikely to be removed from power through internal politics. The Bush Administration used the pretext of a murdered US officer to launch the largest-scale US intervention since Vietnam to remove Noriega from office. Patrick Haney believes that Bush was motivated to remove Noriega in part to dispel perceptions that he was a 'wimp' (Haney, 2002: 105).

Taking a wider view of history, a pattern emerges. Nearly every modern president has been accused of making foreign policy calculations based on domestic political considerations rather than on some neutral or scientific assessment of the 'national interest'. In a retrospective of the Nixon presidency, Thomas Schwartz argues that Richard Nixon 'undertook steps in foreign policy ... with a strong sense of their impact on Nixon's domestic standing. Although these moves could be justified for foreign policy reasons, it is clear that their timing and choreography was designed for maximum domestic political effect' (Schwartz, 2017: 205). Even Nixon's visit to China, while momentous in geopolitical terms, was 'carefully timed' and 'its political and electoral significance at home was not lost on the president' (Johnstone and Priest, 2017a: 9–10).

This book argues that, far from being the exceptions, these behaviours are the norm. Indeed, *all* foreign policy decisions are ultimately subject to domestic political factors. While many commentators draw a distinction between foreign policy and domestic policy, this book argues that such a division is an illusion. There are important reasons why domestic factors will always shape foreign policy considerations. First, the institutions that produce US foreign policy are not fundamentally different from the institutions that produce other policies. Second, the people who construct foreign policy are largely the same collection of individuals who construct domestic policy: politicians and the bureaucrats who serve them. Brian Rathbun observed that foreign policymakers think about foreign affairs similarly to how they approach domestic political considerations. He concluded, 'if domestic and foreign policies are inspired by common core values, it makes little sense to study domestic and foreign policy in isolation' (Rathbun, 2007: 403).

Third, while foreign policy often entails a wider number of relevant subjects (heads of foreign governments, international organizations, citizens of other countries), the population who ultimately hold American policymakers accountable for their decisions on foreign policy is the same population who hold them accountable for their decisions on other policy matters: the American electorate. The usual political influences still apply in foreign policy: money, partisanship, the media, interest groups, demographic cleavages and ideological divisions. Foreign policy consists ultimately of actions carried out to meet a collection of aims and objectives specified by elected politicians. Because these principals cannot remove themselves from the domestic political world they inhabit, all foreign policy contains domestic political considerations.

Summary of this book

This text analyses the construction and application of US foreign policy in the modern era, with close attention to its domestic roots. It is organized around four broad themes: the languages and ideologies of US foreign policy, the institutions of US foreign policymaking, the actors who influence and shape the content of US foreign policy, and the policy goals and ideas that motivate US foreign policy.

By way of introduction, readers will first be exposed to the ideologies and languages of US foreign policy. The book introduces readers to the main currents of academic debate by entering into a discussion about some of the methodologies and ideological assumptions that pervade the scholarly literature. Readers are then introduced to the institutions that make US foreign policy, in particular the White House, the State Department, the Department of Defense, the intelligence agencies and Congress, with an explanation of the institutional processes of making foreign policy. There is also an analysis of the constitutional and statutory framework that enhances (and sometimes limits) different institutions' foreign policy decision-making autonomy.

The book then analyses the role of different 'publics' who exercise influence through these institutions. The public's views on foreign policy matter, but it is often argued that in broad terms the American public's knowledge about foreign affairs is limited and that interest in world affairs is typically low. The media play a role as both a conduit of information and as a set of autonomous actors seeking to influence both the public and policymakers. Readers will learn not just about the role of public opinion but also about the role of many relevant foreign policy 'publics': think tanks, business lobbies and unions, religious groups, immigrant diasporas, racial and ethnic groups, and others who seek to influence foreign policy. This section also takes seriously the role of electoral politics and partisanship in shaping US foreign policy, factors that were de-emphasized in many 20th-century accounts of politics stopping 'at the water's edge'. It also emphasizes the importance of money and race, two factors we know to be crucially important in other areas of US policymaking but that are too often undervalued in US foreign policy accounts.

Finally, the book will study the broad goals of US foreign policy – security, trade and democracy. What is the priority placed on these objectives by different presidential administrations? To what extent do they cohere? What are the tensions between them? The goals of foreign policy, this book argues, are strongly shaped by domestic pressures.

While the book draws from sources analysing the broad history of US foreign policy, readers are encouraged to think in particular about how these ideas, institutions and goals have been at work in the foreign policy of recent presidential administrations, including those of George W. Bush, Barack Obama, Donald Trump and Joe Biden. The book brings US foreign policy to the readers through different lenses, informed not just by the theories of international relations but also by politics, history and communications studies. The book places domestic institutions and actors at the heart of the study of US foreign policy, rather than 'grand strategy', international actors or elaborate theoretical IR concepts. While the text is not silent on these concepts, the book's aim is to bring both the American state and different publics into the heart of the study of US foreign policy.

PART I

The Ideologies and Languages of US Foreign Policy

1

The Study of US Foreign Policy

This book differs from many texts on US foreign policy in two key respects. First, unlike books written by many historians, it is organized thematically rather than chronologically (McDougall, 1997a; Ambrose and Brinkley, 2012 [1971]; Young and Kent, 2013). A chronological organization is well suited to providing an historical overview of how different events unfolded over time, but such an approach also has its drawbacks. Simply telling the 'story' of US foreign policy as a series of events and decisions, one after another, obscures patterns of practice. It also militates against cross-case comparison and theoretical abstraction, which can be useful in identifying relevant sets of actors and institutions. A thematic organization is more consonant with a book emerging from a political science tradition.

The second way in which this book differs from other studies of US foreign policy is that it decentres the paradigms and concepts that have dominated international relations (IR) scholarship in the post-war period. These paradigms constitute a 'language' of IR in which scholars and policymakers converse. Yet, as this chapter will explain, the mainstream paradigms of IR also have major gaps in their conceptual vocabulary, especially with respect to race.

A study of US foreign policy from a political science approach, however, does not entail a wholesale rejection of historical and IR perspectives. Indeed, it is important to be conversant with these perspectives, not least in order to be able to critique them. This chapter provides readers with an overview of the academic scholarship on US foreign policy from an IR perspective. The first section familiarizes the reader with the 'languages' of US foreign policy scholarship. It focuses on the debate between proponents of realism and liberal idealism in IR theory, as to whether the US has an interest- or values-based approach to foreign policy. The second section assesses what can be rescued from this well-rehearsed debate, as well as exposing some of its core empirical, epistemological and ethical shortcomings. The third section outlines alternative 'languages' of IR scholarship, such as constructivism, Marxism and postcolonialism.

International relations languages: realism and liberalism

Realism and liberalism (sometimes called 'idealism' or 'liberal idealism') are the two major paradigms of IR scholarship. They are attempts to describe the behaviour of individuals and states in the so-called 'international system'. Patrick Porter describes them as 'the theoretical floor on which the rest of us dance' (2020: viii). Realism and liberalism are part of the everyday parlance of foreign policy commentary. You might read in a newspaper that a particular policymaker was 'a hard-headed realist' or a 'dyed-in-the-wool' liberal (*The Economist*, 2008). They are also terms that foreign policymakers themselves use to describe their own worldviews. Each is an **ideal type**; individuals and states are closer to one approach than the other but do not necessarily match it perfectly. In this sense, realism and liberalism can serve as important ways to think about foreign policy without needing to be a 'perfect fit'.

Liberalism refers to a values-based approach to foreign policy. Liberalism sees it as important to improve overall global conditions, rather than simply focus on one state's interests. Liberal IR theory regards liberal, capitalist democracy as an inherent good. It asserts that it is important for countries to embrace a liberal constitutional and economic model for the benefit of their own citizens and humanity as a whole. The theory's high priest, John Ikenberry, argues that open markets, international institutions, democratic values and commitment to 'progressive change' foster 'collective problem solving' delivered through 'shared sovereignty and the rule of [international] law' (2009: 71).

Most variants of liberal international theory accept that the international system is, by default, 'anarchic'. That is to say, the antecedent condition of global affairs is a kind of international 'state of nature' with no clear sovereign or governing structure. Liberal IR theory purports that such anarchy can be overcome – not through **power** and conquest, but through ideas, values and processes. Order in liberal internationalism is built on treaties, institutions and trade agreements. In the language of game theory, liberals believe that the international system is a 'non-zero sum' (Grieco et al, 1993). In plainer language, all countries benefit from the peace and stability that can be achieved through a liberal internationalist framework.

Jimmy Carter is often said to have pursued the closest to a liberal idealist foreign policy of any US president (Skidmore, 1993; Schmitz and Walker, 2004). Carter ran for president in 1976 on the theme of making US foreign policy compatible with what he saw as the basic goodness of the American people. He argued that the US needed to 'stand for something' and that its foreign policy should be guided by integrity and morality, with an emphasis on human rights (quoted in Drezner, 2018). Several months after becoming president, Carter declared at the University of Notre Dame, 'I believe we can have a foreign policy that is democratic, that is based on fundamental values, and that uses power and influence, which we have, for humane purpose' (1977).

A characteristic liberal move was Carter's announcement within a day of becoming president that he would be moving nuclear weapons off the Korean peninsula. Carter had not consulted the Pentagon in advance, and nor had he made demands for reciprocal action from the USSR. He removed the weapons because he believed it to be the morally right thing to do (Carter, 2005). Carter had originally toyed with the idea of withdrawing US troops from the peninsula entirely. Ultimately, Carter's foreign policy legacy ended in tatters as 52 Americans were held hostage in the final 444 days of his presidency by a group of Iranian student revolutionaries in Tehran. The hostage crisis was perceived as the inevitable outcome of Carter's liberal approach to foreign policy, which Stephen Ambrose and Douglas Brinkley (2012 [1971]: 289) call 'waffle'.

There are several critiques of the liberal approach to foreign policy. Some would argue that, as in the case of Carter, it is hopelessly naive and ultimately a form of weakness (Tiewes, 1987; Skidmore, 1996; Kraig, 2002; Sneh, 2008). Others would suggest that America's liberal idealism has led the country to pursue an almost messianic, crusading agenda, which is quite dangerous (Lieven, 2005: 67; Berggen and Rae, 2006). Other commentators argue that liberalism is a rhetorical mask worn by foreign policy actors to hide their realist motivations (explained below). The Iraq War was originally said to be a war to remove dangerous weapons of mass destruction from Saddam Hussein (a realist motivation), but after no weapons were found, the war was post facto justified in liberal terms: as a war to bring democracy and freedom to the Iraqi people and to remove a brutal dictator (Freedman, 2005; Lieven, 2005; Heinze, 2008; Porter, 2018). Such cynicism may be unmerited, however. The evidence from confidential memoranda written by US foreign policy actors – unearthed through archival research – suggests that what policymakers say in private often does not differ substantially from the types of arguments they make in public (Khong, 1992).

The competing theory to liberalism is realism. The fathers of American realist theory are generally agreed to be Hans Morgenthau and George Kennan, although the British diplomat and academic E.H. Carr also played an instrumental role in realism's theoretical development. Kennan had been a career diplomat in the 1930s and 1940s. His experiences informed his 1951 book *American Diplomacy, 1900–1950*, which set out the view that American foreign policy was too sentimental and moralistic. Kennan believed that the mass public had driven policymakers to pursue 'high-minded' and 'idealistic' goals that did not serve US interests (Hunt, 2009). Worse, he believed that too many of the foreign policymakers in the US had been lawyers, which meant that they had inappropriately applied legal principles and practices such as contract or adjudication to the international arena, for which they were poorly suited. Kennan argued that the US needed to construct its foreign policy according to well-defined national goals, responsive to the realities of global affairs. He called his concept 'realism', which, as Michael Hunt describes, has become something of a 'buzzword ... dear to undergraduates and armchair strategists' (2009: 6).

Realism is based on several key assumptions. First, the nation-state is the primary actor in world politics. Second, the national interest is the key concern that states must address and protect. Third, security is the primary national interest. Fourth, other states' security implications – not their internal politics, economics or human rights record – should be what matters to foreign policymakers. As with liberalism, realism imagines that states exist in an international system that is defined by the antecedent condition of anarchy, where it is the responsibility of each individual state to secure itself from the others. A paradox known as the **security dilemma** arises when each state's pursuit of its own security can lead to greater instability in the overall system (Jervis, 1978; Snyder, 1984; Schweller, 1996; Glaser, 1997; Booth and Wheeler, 2007). A kind of 'balance of power' politics, then, becomes the way to mitigate this dilemma (Walt, 1987; van Evera, 1999).

Since the 1970s, realist theorists have de-emphasized the particular individual psychologies of world leaders and instead emphasized empirical measures of power, such as the size of a military, as well as geopolitical factors, such as alliances and natural resources. This form of realism is sometimes called 'neorealism' or 'structural realism'.[1] Structural realism has two main postures: defensive and offensive.

Defensive realism discourages unnecessary engagement and finds security from a fortified posture (Snyder, 1991; Grieco, 1997; Tang, 2010). **Offensive realism** contends that security comes through power, and power comes through maximizing control over or relative to other countries (Mearsheimer, 2001).

President Donald Trump described his foreign policy approach as 'principled realism'. He claimed to have shorn ideology for hard-headed foreign policy pragmatism, organized around the principle of respect for each state's sovereignty. He told the United Nations (UN) General Assembly in 2018, 'America's policy of principled realism means we will not be held hostage to old dogmas, discredited ideologies, and so-called experts who have been proven wrong over the years, time and time again'.[2] Michael Anton, one of Trump's national security advisers, described the **Trump Doctrine** as the view that liberal internationalism 'is now well past the point of diminishing returns. Globalism and transnationalism impose their highest costs on established powers (namely the US) and award the greatest benefits to rising powers seeking to contest US influence' (2019). One commentator observed that Trump's foreign policy vision 'is consistent with a realist vision of statecraft and is notably free of the grand ideational commitments to democracy, human rights, and human freedom which characterized post-Cold War foreign policy' (Ettinger, 2019: 415).

In spite of their differences, all types of realism emphasize the need for a pragmatic, power- and security-oriented approach to foreign policy. While Kennan's work has been hugely influential, a few notes of caution need to be sounded. First, there is reason to think that Kennan was overly sceptical about the dangers of ideology. As an American diplomat in the USSR in the 1930s, Kennan had observed Joseph Stalin's Great Purge, which led to more than half a million counter-revolutionaries being killed due to their insufficient commitment to communist ideology (Hunt, 2009). Kennan's distrust of ideology was deeply informed by these events – but perhaps overly so. Second, it is fair to say that Kennan had too much trust in foreign policy technocracy. He believed that foreign policy bureaucrats carried little cultural baggage or prejudices, unlike the American public. But Kennan's view entailed overlooking some very serious cultural biases and ethnocentric assumptions within the State and Defense Departments. Third, in decrying liberal ideology, Kennan was, of course, ironically promoting an ideology of his own. Rather than seeing realism as bereft of ideology, it is, in reality, just another set of ideological claims.

Critical perspectives on realism and liberalism

The realism–liberalism debate has shown remarkable durability since the mid-20th century, but these theories alone tell us remarkably little about the US foreign policymaking process discussed in subsequent chapters. Even in the field of international relations, realism and liberalism have serious flaws. Namely, there are key empirical and ethical concerns that limit their value.

Empirically, the paradigms are difficult to 'test'. As Aaron Ettinger has written, 'Reading US foreign policy history through the IR lenses of realism and liberalism/idealism can become an act of confirmation bias' (2019: 417). Foreign policymakers' motivations are hard to pin down, as the unresolved debate over the 'realist' or 'liberal' reasons for the Iraq War shows (Lieberfeld, 2005; Nuruzzaman, 2006; Yordan, 2006; Heinze, 2008; Schmidt and Williams, 2008; Miller, 2010; Dodge, 2010; van Rythoven, 2015; Deudney and Ikenberry, 2017; Porter, 2018). This empirical and methodological imprecision results in commentators coming to diametrically opposed descriptions about US foreign policy, depending on which pieces of evidence they choose to emphasize. Some scholars portray the US as the world's 'last best hope', a phrase Abraham Lincoln used in an 1862 address to Congress. Daniel Deudney and Jeffrey Meiser (2012) celebrate the US as 'the most powerful, appealing, and successful form of political, economic, and social organization in modern times'. They contend that 'over nearly twenty-five decades it has relentlessly progressed ... in turning the abstract and lofty Enlightenment goal of a fully free society into a practical working arrangement' (Deudney and Meiser, 2012: 22). Other commentators view the history of US foreign policy as a series of unforgiveable, tragic interventions. The genocide of Native Americans, the predatory war that seized thousands of kilometres of Mexican land, the death of over 100,000 Filipinos under American colonial administration, the use of nuclear weapons on civilian populations, and the wars in Vietnam and Iraq paint a grim picture of a country motivated purely by realist priorities of power, wealth and resources, with little regard to humanitarian or liberal values.

Most scholars embrace the battling contradictions. Arthur Schlesinger (1986) described US foreign policy as an internal warfare between 'realism and messianism'. Michael Kammen (1972) said that US foreign policy was a form of 'utopian pragmatism'. Michael Hunt (2009) highlighted multiple paradoxes of US foreign policy: a country that promoted liberty but believed in racial hierarchy; a country that shunned popular revolution but itself was formed through revolution.

Such indeterminacy leaves the reader none the wiser. Does America have an interest- or values-based approach to foreign policy? Is it nationalist or internationalist? Leftist or rightist? Presidential adviser Eugene Rostow gave a plausible answer: perhaps it is 'all of the above' (1993: 22).

Indeed, the divergence between realism and idealism may be overdrawn. Walter McDougall (1997b) argues that all US foreign policy actions have contained elements of realism and liberalism. He argues that US political actors for the last century have tended to believe that US security interests were best served when other countries were prosperous and democratic. This 'liberal realism' was the logic underlying acts of humanitarian generosity which, in practice, helped to keep America safe, such as the **US Food Administration** (1917–20),[3] the American Relief Administration (1919–23), the Marshall Plan (1948) and John F. Kennedy's international agencies for peace and development (for example, the US Agency for International Development, the Alliance for Progress and the Peace Corps) (McDougall, 1997b).

The Clinton Administration, in this vein, pursued a strategy called 'democratic enlargement' that focused on strengthening and expanding capitalism and liberal democracy around the world, especially in post-Soviet countries (Brinkley, 1997; Ambrose and Brinkley, 2012 [1971]; Sondergaard, 2015). The idea was that as more countries embraced the American political and economic model, the US would face fewer security threats. Clinton's strategy was partly premised on this notion of **democratic peace theory** – that democracies tend not to go to war with each other (Layne, 1994; Rosato, 2003; Kinsella, 2005; Doyle, 2005). Democratic peace theory depends on the notion that voters restrain military adventurism through electoral sanction because it is ultimately they (the public) who must bear the costs with their taxes and their lives. In an autocracy, ordinary citizens have no formal mechanism to punish leaders who lead them to unnecessary wars.

Some liberal theorists have gone further to argue that democracy is not a necessary condition for such peace. A shared economic system can generate the same dynamic. Namely, political leaders will be constrained from going to war against a country whose economic system is so intimately bound with their own that war would impose economic costs on both parties. This was the logic behind the creation of the European Coal and Steel Community, the forerunner of the European Union (EU). If France and Germany's economies were closely bound, then war between them would be irrational because there would be no resources to 'conquer' from the other. Economic

integration was seen as key to security. Clinton told Congress in his 1994 budget speech, 'We have put our economic competitiveness at the heart of our foreign policy' (1994: 9). One commentator put it slightly differently. Ronald Steel argued that after the Cold War, the US secured itself by moving from a nuclear standoff with Russia to subsidizing them (Steel, 1995).

Globalization, it was thought, satisfied the goals of both liberalism and realism. In a playful rift on democratic peace theory, *The New York Times* columnist Thomas Friedman offered his own 'McDonald's peace theory'. Friedman wrote in his 1999 book *The Lexus and the Olive Tree*, 'No two countries that both had McDonald's had fought a war against each other since each got its McDonald's' (Friedman, 1999: 248).[4] Friedman's logic underlay Bill Clinton's approach to the People's Republic of China. Clinton predicted (wrongly) that China's economic integration in global capitalism would diminish the likelihood of conflict with the US and spur internal democratic reforms. Clinton said in 2000, 'Bringing China into the World Trade Organization on the terms we have negotiated will advance all these goals. It will open a growing market to American workers, farmers, and businesses. And more than any other step we can take right now, it will encourage China to choose reform, openness, and integration with the world'. Clinton's prognostication has not been borne out. As China has grown richer, it has not become more democratic or more supportive of US strategic security interests. This is consistent with the academic research that shows that increased economic and institutional contact helped to sustain and prop up communist regimes in Eastern Europe during the Cold War rather than undermining them (Sarotte, 2001: 169–78; Garton Ash, 1993: 367–8).

There are also ethical questions that need to be raised about the epistemological assumptions of realist and liberal theories. Both are said to draw heavily from **contractarian political theory**. The main forebears of this tradition include the 17th-century English philosophers Thomas Hobbes (see, for example, Williams, 1996; Malcolm, 2002; Yurdusev, 2006) and John Locke (see, for example, Ward, 2006; Chadwick, 2009), the 18th-century Genevan theorist Jean-Jacques Rousseau (see, for example, Hoffmann, 1963; Riley, 1973; Williams, 1989; Knutsen, 1994; Roosevelt, 2006; Falaky, 2014), and the 19th-century Prussian thinker Immanuel Kant (see, for example, Hurrell, 1990; Archibugi, 1995; Franke, 2001; Harrison, 2002; Wilkins, 2007; Molloy, 2017). IR scholars often attribute to these thinkers the core concepts of their theories. Locke and Hobbes are thanked for the concept of the natural state of anarchy. Kant is credited with ideas of democratic peace.[5] Michael Desch writes that Locke and Kant have 'had the greatest influence on US foreign policy', even though he admits that he cannot find evidence that they have been read by many US foreign policymakers (2007: 11–12). Even pre-modern writers, such as the Athenian historian Thucydides (see, for example, Doyle, 1990; Clark, 1993; Forde, 1995; Welch, 2003) and the medieval theologian Augustine of Hippo (see, for example, Loriaux, 1992; Brown et al, 2002) are cited by some scholars as providing great insight into 21st-century international relations. Recently, the work of Thucydides, who lived in the 5th century BC, is said to be able to help policymakers determine whether or not the US and China will go to war in the 2020s (Allison, 2017).

Realism and liberalism are 20th-century concepts, developed by IR scholars after the Second World War. So why do so many IR theorists attribute these paradigms to long-dead, renowned political theorists? The answer may be that these canonical theorists are viewed as more 'credible' than the theories' more proximate intellectual forbears from within the IR field itself. The language of IR theory has been carefully constructed to mask the field's dubious intellectual beginnings. International relations began in the early 20th century as a study of 'world races'. It was dominated by white scholars who were increasingly anxious about the threat posed to white nations by anti-colonial movements and non-white nations (Anievas et al, 2015; Vitalis, 2015). The influential journal *Foreign Affairs* began its life as the *Journal of Race Development* (1910–19). As Julie Reeves writes, 'the choice of the journal's title tells us something of what early IR scholars considered the subject of international relations to be about' (2004: 707). The defeat of Russia by the Japanese in 1905 was described by prominent IR academic Alfred Zimmern in 1926 as 'the most important historical event which has happened or likely to happen in our lifetime: the victory of a non-white people over a white people' (1926: 82). These anxieties were voiced in leading IR texts of the time, such as Oswald Spengler's 1918 *The Decline of the West* and Lothrop Stoddard's *The Rising Tide of Color Against White World Supremacy* (1920). The alarm was further raised when the Turks defeated the Greeks in 1922, an event that drove Prince Philip of Greece (later the Duke of Edinburgh) into exile.

Explicit study of race-based hierarchies was discredited by the horrors of the Second World War and the Holocaust, but the Cold War – and the technological possibility of global annihilation – gave international relations fresh purpose. Rational choice research was prioritized to provide a state-centred study of strategic calculations

(Amadae, 2003; Acharya, 2018). Research that 'demonstrated' the superiority of US capitalist democracy was prioritized. Critical and subaltern voices were silenced (Shilliam, 2011). Research agendas were shifted, and language was subtly massaged (Isaac, 2007). Scholars were more likely to speak of American 'interests' in the Pacific rather American 'colonies' or 'imperialism' in the Pacific. In this context, it was important for IR not to be associated with its earlier doctrines of racial supremacy. Scholars repurposed classic texts to present 20th-century concepts such as the 'security dilemma' as race-blind and timeless. They concocted a false genealogy of IR ideas. But it is naive to think that the paradigms developed by IR scholars in the Cold War had been purged of racist and imperialist biases simply because they did not mention race explicitly. As Errol Henderson writes, 'a racist latticework undergirds major theoretical frameworks that inform research and policy in IR' (2013: 90).

Specifically, both realism and liberalism rely on concepts and assumptions about world politics that have historically treated non-white people as being of 'second order' importance. International anarchy, a core concept in mainstream IR theory, is particularly problematic in this regard. Anarchy is the bedrock on which realism and liberalism is premised. It is presented as an analytical, race-neutral concept. Yet, by asserting that the international system is anarchic rather than hierarchical, theorists are making a normative claim, which fails to acknowledge unequal power within the international system (Kazmi, 2019). Henderson goes so far as to argue that liberalism and realism 'are oriented by racist – primarily, white supremacist – precepts' (2013: 71).

John Ikenberry, one of the leading proponents of liberalism, implicitly embraces international inequality in his theoretical framework. He uses terms such as 'advanced democracies', 'advanced economies', 'weak countries' and 'the periphery' to build out his theory of America's liberal grand strategy, yet Robert Vitalis (2015: 178) has trenchantly argued that this conception is neocolonialist. Ikenberry writes:

> ... the notion of [an American] empire is misleading – and misses the distinctive aspects of the global political order that has developed around US power. The United States has pursued imperial policies, especially toward weak countries in the periphery. But US relations with Europe, Japan, China, and Russia cannot be described as imperial, even when "neo" or "liberal" modifies the term.... This is not empire; it is a US-led democratic political order that has no name or historical antecedent. (Ikenberry, 2004a)

Ikenberry's theory of international relations is only plausible if some countries are treated as equals while others are not. When anarchy was first introduced to IR by G. Lowes Dickinson in 1916, the concept was limited to European states as a way of explaining the causes of the First World War (Dickinson, 1916). The supposed race-blind equality of the anarchic international system crumbles at first inspection. Racist IR scholarship in the pre-Second World War decades undoubtedly shaped subsequent research, yet international relations' genuine origins are too rarely discussed.[6] Scholars are more comfortable torturing the fragmentary Melian Dialogue of Thucydides' *History of the Peloponnesian War* than confronting the explicit racism of the first few decades of 20th-century IR theory.

Even when IR scholars cite early 20th-century actors, the racist dimensions of their ideas are often concealed. US President Woodrow Wilson is celebrated as a hero of liberal internationalism for his 'Fourteen Points' and his commitment to national self-determination (Heater, 1994; Neuberger, 1995; Ambrosius, 1996; Manela, 2007; Throntveit, 2011; Miller, 2020). In *America Right or Wrong*, Anatol Lieven holds up the Clinton Administration as a triumph of Wilsonian principles (apparently a good thing), while George W. Bush's alleged rejection of them was an embarrassing sign of the American president's failure to support international organizations and multilateralism (Lieven, 2005: 14). Yet the fact that Wilson was a virulent white supremacist, who segregated the federal government and rejected black equality (King, 2007 [1995]), seems to be an important omission. Wilson did *not* believe that all national groups had equal capacity for self-determination. Even the term 'national self-determination' meant something quite different in its 1910s context than it does in the 2020s (Lynch, 2002). Not all people were fit for nationhood, in Wilson's analysis.

In academic scholarship, we must pay attention to not just what is said but also what goes unsaid. It is convenient for academics who teach IR to present the field as a scientific study of interactions between states, following timeless laws of peace, stability and conflict that can be traced back to the writings of the ancients. The language of IR today might be purged of race, but this does not mean that it lacks racial – and even racist – grammar. As Robert Vitalis (2000) has written, there is 'a norm against noticing' race in IR. Similarly, Randolph Persaud and R.B.J. Walker write that race 'has been given the epistemological status of silence' (2001: 374). It is time to break that silence.

Other languages

Realism and liberalism are the dominant paradigms of IR, but they are not the only ones. This section explores three major alternative languages of IR: constructivism, Marxism and postcolonialism. All three take a 'critical' look at realism and liberalism, drawing from many of the observations about their intellectual history outlined in the previous section.

Coined by Nicholas Onuf in 1989, **constructivism** (or 'social constructivism') operates as a loose catch-all for a variety of alternative approaches, but at its core it is influenced by postmodern scholarship, which rejects the notion of 'objective' or 'final truth' (Onuf, 1989; Jackson et al, 2016: 241). While constructivists do not make claims that are devoid of facts or truth, they 'admit ... that their claims are always contingent and partial interpretations of a complex world' (Price and Reus-Smit, 1998: 272). Constructivism emphasizes the importance of the construction of a 'self-image' in relation to others. These ideas, with different social weight and import, are the currency of IR.

Constructivism makes a valuable point that the international system is not some kind of concrete phenomenon that exists separate from existing relations between states and peoples. It is made; it does not have an existence on its own. According to constructivist theory, the US possesses a self-image as a global guardian of democracy and acts accordingly (Dueck, 2006). The notion of the US as a 'nation of immigrants' is another example of the US self-image that is socially and politically constructed.

There is some question, however, as to whether constructivism is a substantive theory of IR or simply a kind of ontological position. It's perfectly possible for a liberal IR theorist to accept that international norms, like contract and the rule of law, are socially constructed without jettisoning their commitment to liberal IR theory (Finnemore, 1996; May, 2017). Likewise, a realist could accept that the international state system or even the idea of security is socially 'constructed' and, nonetheless, believe that the primacy of security and power relations between states are the main components of IR. Indeed, constructivism has much to add to realist IR. Five hundred British nuclear weapons are less threatening to the US than five North Korean weapons because of the nature of the relationships between the US and those two countries (Wendt, 1995: 73) As Alexander Wendt, one of the pioneers of constructivism, explained, constructivism does not claim that 'ideas are more important than power and interest, or that they are autonomous from power and interest. The claim is rather that power and interest have the effects they do in virtue of the ideas that make them up' (Wendt, 1999: 135–6). More nuanced constructivist approaches 'acknowledge ... the partial validity' of realism and liberalism, without succumbing to 'the sterility' of one or the 'naiveté' of the other (Katzenstein, 1996: 537).

In contrast to constructivism, a **Marxist theory** of IR is materialist. It regards foreign policy as a product of the economic needs of those who control its means of production. Marxists believe that economic production is the basis of all human activities. Marxist scholars do not regard the state as an autonomous entity, but one that is run in the interests of its ruling class (Miliband, 1969). In the case of the US, a Marxist scholar would argue that American foreign policy simply serves the economic interests of the elites who occupy the offices of power in Washington and capitalists on Wall Street and in American industry. According to Robert Cox, the father of critical international political economy, non-territorial power has become increasingly important for capitalist state actors (Cox, 2002), which means the American state extending its power beyond traditional geographic boundaries to secure the global means of production on behalf of its ruling class, as demonstrated by US dominance of global technology, finance, trade and services.

Some Marxist scholars take a system-based approach and think critically about the role of the US in a world economy defined by unequal exchange (see, for example, Wallerstein, 1993). For these scholars, class conflict manifests itself in the form of developed states plundering and exploiting less developed states (and indeed, keeping them deliberately underdeveloped). Andre Frank argued that while it was widely believed that the US contributed more capital in the form of investment and aid to underdeveloped countries than it received from them, the US (and more specifically, its businesses) enjoyed a net capital outflow from many poorer parts of the world (Frank, 1971). Famous Marxist scholars of US foreign policy include William Appleman Williams (1959) and Perry Anderson (2017).

A third alternative language of US foreign policy study is the language of postcolonialism. Postcolonial theorists point out that IR theorists are integrated into the world they study. They are insiders; they do not stand outside the systems they write about. Therefore, it is important for IR theorists to be reflective on their own position, and for multiple voices, perspectives and backgrounds to be represented among their cohort. IR theory has often been criticized for reflecting a certain white, Western perspective to the exclusion of other voices. Historically, heterodox viewpoints in the field have been marginalized for racial or ideological reasons. Written in 1915, W.E.B. Du Bois's essay, 'The African roots of war', identified competition for colonial dominance as a major cause of the First World War, but this essay is largely forgotten. To the extent that colonialism as a source of the First World War was recognized, it was usually through Vladimir Lenin's *Imperialism: The Highest Stage of Capitalism* (1917 [2010]) to which constructivist scholars still turn rather than to Du Bois's article, which came out first. Equally, Ralph Bunche's *A World View of Race* (1936) rejected the alarmist inclinations of his IR contemporaries. These writers were part of the **Howard School of International Relations**, a loose grouping of African-American scholars at the prestigious Howard University in Washington, DC. They include Alain Locke (head of the Foreign Policy Association), Ralphe Bunche (who won the Nobel Prize), E. Franklin Frazier, Rayford Logan, Eric Williams and Merze Tate (Henderson, 2013; Vitalis, 2015). A quick review of many IR texts and reading lists will show the continued marginalization of scholars of colour from the field. IR is still overwhelmingly dominated by white, male perspectives.

As will be discussed in Chapter 9, the US was (and in some ways remains) a colonial power (Immerwahr, 2019). Taking the legacies of its colonialism into accounts of the study of US foreign policy can help to shed fresh light on the US's role in global affairs. Mark Laffey and Jutta Weldes demonstrate the advantages of this postcolonial framework in their article 'Decolonizing the Cuban Missile Crisis' (2008). The nuclear crisis of 1961, which is widely regarded as the closest the world has come to full-scale conflict between nuclear powers, is almost always recounted from the perspectives of the US and the USSR, standing 'eyeball to eyeball' before 'heroic' statesmanship persuaded the USSR to back down and for the peaceful *status quo ante* to be restored (Laffey and Weldes, 2008: 564). The position of Cuba itself is almost always ignored, as if the country was some kind of empty floating island that had foolishly 'vacated its sovereignty' to the Soviet Union. Yet, as Laffey and Weldes show, Cuba's alliance with the Soviet Union cannot be understood separately from the years of US colonial influence on the island, which involved the wide-scale exploitation of the Cuban economy and interference in its domestic politics that ultimately produced the Castro revolution of the mid-1950s. By taking the Cuban perspective more seriously, it is clearer that the Cuban Missile Crisis was not merely a potential tragedy imposed on the US, but one whose origins lie in US colonial behaviour in the Caribbean.

Conclusion

Some scholars argue that 'international relations' and 'foreign policy' must be analysed separately. The former is said to refer to interactive systems of states whereas the latter tries to explain individual countries' patterns of behaviour (Waltz, 1996). According to Brian Schmidt, such accounts regard the 'international system' as an autonomous, external variable on the US's foreign policy choices (Schmidt, 2012). In this way, 'realism' and 'liberalism' often escape the domestic level of analysis. It also enables IR theory to proclaim a false neutrality or scientism. The field's methodological pathologies, as well as its epistemological and ethical shortcomings, are blithely overlooked. This chapter has taken seriously the languages of US foreign policy scholarship that stem from a variety of IR theories, but also treated them critically. It is important for students of US foreign policy to be conversant in the theories, not least because they furnish the vocabulary of US foreign policy scholarship and practice.

Yet, while they will be present in the background of the forthcoming chapters, this book does not align itself with any of these approaches. Instead it draws much more from the tradition of historical institutionalism, which centres the state and domestic political actors and interests (Levi, 2002). One of the seminal works from this tradition was Peter Evans, Dietrich Rueschemeyer and Theda Skocpol's 1985 volume *Bringing the State Back In*. In this volume, Skocpol (1985) made an important call for 'bringing back' political institutions into the heart of political analysis, seeking out how they form and shape political identities, hierarchies, actions and strategies. In this book, an historically informed understanding of American state structures and the actors who inhabit and place demands on these institutions will be used to shed light on the foreign policymaking process and policy outcomes. Through this approach, patterns of practice become clearer and enable us to form general inferences about recurring features of the US foreign policy process. As Karen Orren and Stephen Skowronek write, 'Pattern identification is the *sine qua non* of the enterprise' (2004: 7).

2

The Ideology of American Exceptionalism

In April 2009, while attending the NATO summit in Strasbourg, President Barack Obama was asked the following question by the *Financial Times* journalist Edward Luce, 'Could I ask you whether you subscribe, as many of your predecessors have, to the school of American exceptionalism that sees America as uniquely qualified to lead the world, or do you have a slightly different philosophy? And if so, would you be able to elaborate on it?' Obama replied, 'I believe in American exceptionalism, just as I suspect that the Brits believe in British exceptionalism and the Greeks believe in Greek exceptionalism', before hastily adding, as if catching himself, 'the United States remains the largest economy in the world. We have unmatched military capability. And I think that we have a core set of values that are enshrined in our Constitution, in our body of law, in our democratic practices, in our belief in free speech and equality, that, though imperfect, are exceptional.'[1]

Obama's comments hit on a central problematic in the discussion of American exceptionalism. Does American exceptionalism imply that America is 'special', or does it simply mean that the US is 'different'? Are all countries exceptional, in that they are distinctive? As one commentator put it succinctly, 'American democracy is unique, but so are all other national democracies' (Fabbrini, 1999: 466). Does exceptionalism imply some kind of higher, normative frame? Does a country being exceptional suggest it has a greater purpose? A unique mission?

In order to understand how Americans view their country's role in the world, it is first essential to get a sense of how Americans view themselves. Polling evidence, discussed below, suggests that large majorities of the American public believe that their country is the greatest in the world as a consequence of some unique factors about its founding, history and values. Ultimately, this chapter argues that this thesis of American exceptionalism as a signal of American 'greatness' and its unique world 'mission' should be rejected because it is unfalsifiable. But, as a matter of empirical comparison, the US is different in many respects from other countries, including other advanced industrialized democracies. American difference, in the domestic realm, shapes its unique role in the foreign policy arena.

Defining exceptionalism

Core to many Americans' self-understanding is the ideology of American exceptionalism. Studied from a range of scholarly perspectives, the conclusion that the US is somehow 'different' is largely accepted, but there is substantial disagreement about what American exceptionalism actually means. Claims of the US as being 'exceptional' often assume a normative, even providential, framework. They can even border on the messianic – commentators and political actors alike have spoken of America's 'mission for liberty'. Conceptions of cultural superiority find their way into these claims. They have been instrumental in liberal[2] rationalizations of US foreign policy interventions, such as justifying the US occupation of Iraq and Afghanistan on the basis of the US's uniquely endowed responsibility of spreading democracy around the world.

The 19th-century French writer Alexis de Tocqueville is usually credited as the forefather of the thesis of 'American exceptionalism' in his two-volume study of American politics and society, *Democracy in America* (1835/40). Tocqueville's use of the term 'exceptional', however, bears little similarity to its present-day usage. Tocqueville did declare that the 'situation of Americans is thus entirely exceptional'.[3] However, few note that in the preceding paragraph Tocqueville had also remarked, 'I cannot consent to separate America from Europe, in spite of the Ocean which divides them'.[4] What Tocqueville meant by these statements requires some contextualization.

Alexis de Tocqueville was the product of an aristocratic, Norman background whose family members had been victims of the Terror during the French Revolution. In spite of the tragedies that his family experienced, Tocqueville did not call for a reprisal on democrats or restoration of the old order. Tocqueville accepted that the march to equality could not be stopped, and so, it had to be managed. Although the Revolution was a startling event, Tocqueville reasoned that it was 'the result of a very long process, the sudden and violent climax of a task to which ten generations had contributed. If it had not taken place, the old social structure would nonetheless have collapsed' (de Tocqueville and Mélonio, 2001 [1856]). Tocqueville believed that equality was the trend of history. Writing in his first volume of *Democracy in America*, he stated that 'the gradual development of the principle of equality is, therefore, a providential fact' (de Tocqueville, 1835/40: 6). To stop its progress would be to 'resist the will of God'; however, its development was 'not yet so rapid that it cannot be guided' (de Tocqueville, 1835/40: 7). Tocqueville was a 'reluctant democrat' who was far more comfortable playing the role of the 'enlightened aristocrat, preaching to the stupid, nostalgic, and rancorous' mob (Kelly, 1992: 234, 231).

It is intellectually misconceived to read Tocqueville's *Democracy in America* (1835/40) as stand-alone work celebrating America's unique greatness. The book was as much a commentary about Orléaniste France as it was about Jacksonian America. Tocqueville had, after all, been commissioned to write his study by the French government. For Tocqueville, while America and France had vast differences in origins, they were drifting towards similar destinations. Tocqueville predicted that the movement of modernity was towards equality of conditions – in both Europe and the US. The differences in their geographic and historical conditions were not interpreted by Tocqueville as implying American greatness. If anything, Tocqueville feared the levelling tide that he believed was approaching.

Many public commentators, politicians, and even some academics in the US add a normative significance to American difference. They claim that America's difference makes it 'special' or 'great'. 'Special' implies not just uniqueness, but also higher status by virtue of such uniqueness. It goes beyond empirical findings to assert a normative claim. The familiar account, summarized critically by Rogers Smith, is that America has been made great because of the absence of feudalism and socialism and due to the pervasiveness of bourgeois liberalism and republicanism (Smith, 1993). According to the so-called 'liberal tradition', the US's origins as a nation have uniquely disposed the US to be, as President Ronald Reagan echoed, 'a shining city upon a hill' (1989). Proponents of this account argue that the US was founded by hard-working Protestant dissenters, who saw no class differences and valued religious liberty from state oppression. Boundless, supposedly 'empty' or undeveloped land enabled high levels of geographical mobility, which, in turn, supported social mobility. This 'classless' society, undergirded by a sturdy Protestant work ethic, ensured that the US became a highly literate and prosperous society, but without the social strife and class tensions that characterized the nations of

Europe (Myrdal, 1944; Hartz, 1955). Ironically, the British Prime Minister Margaret Thatcher summarized this view crisply when she told the Hoover Institution in 1991, celebrating 'two great victories: President Reagan's victory over communism in the Cold War, and President Bush's victory over aggression in the Gulf':

> Americans and Europeans alike sometimes forget how unique is the United States of America. No other nation has been created so swiftly and successfully. No other nation has been built upon an idea – the idea of liberty. No other nation has so successfully combined people of different races and nations within a single culture. Both the founding fathers of the United States and successive waves of immigrants to your country were determined to create a new identity. Whether in flight from persecution or from poverty, the huddled masses have, with few exceptions, welcomed American values, the American way of life and American opportunities. And America herself has bound them to her with powerful bonds of patriotism and pride. The European nations are not and can never be like this. They are the product of history and not of philosophy. (Thatcher, 1991)

This account of American political development often takes on a kind of quasi-religious aspect to it. In earlier periods of American history, white American settlers declared that it was their 'manifest destiny' to appropriate lands belonging to indigenous peoples and Mexicans. Messianic or providential claims of American greatness can still be found in some academic scholarship. University of Virginia professor James Caesar (2012) forwards the view that America has been charged with a special 'mission'. He believes that the US has embraced a 'mission for liberty', which has changed the world to such an extent that the mission must be taken for a 'historical fact'. On the matter of religious liberty, for instance, Caesar argues that 'its survival may owe much to what takes place in this nation [the USA], which at times has seen fit to extend an outstretched arm and to offer protection with its mighty hand'. Caesar adds defiantly, 'To ignore or deny this fact is to close one's eyes utterly to reality' (Caesar, 2012: 26, 21).

Factually, these accounts of American exceptionalism are narrow and of dubious validity. The liberal tradition's description of America's establishment erases the experiences of Native Americans, African Americans and the poor. For them, America was not a tolerant society, free from feudal vassalage. It was a country that drove them from their lands, threatened their lives, broke up their families and exploited their labour for little or no compensation. To say that their experiences are (tragic) 'exceptions' to American development is to imply that the experience of white Protestant middle-class men was the 'norm', and that everyone else experienced something other than the 'true' American experience.

Consequently, the view that American difference is tantamount to American greatness is heavily laden with a nationalistic chauvinism that has little place in serious scholarly analysis. The former Speaker of the US House of Representatives, Newt Gingrich, implied in a 2011 book that to deny American exceptionalism on these terms was itself un-American. Gingrich wrote, 'There is a determined group of radicals in the United States who outright oppose American Exceptionalism ... these malcontents struggle to reduce American power and transform our political and economic systems into the kind of statist, socialist model that is now failing across Europe' (Gingrich, 2011: 7). The title of former Massachusetts Governor (and later Utah Senator) Mitt Romney's book, released in advance of his 2012 presidential campaign, *No Apology: The Case for American Greatness*, is indicative of this mindset (Romney, 2010). While Mitt Romney dissented from President Donald Trump presentationally, they shared this feverish view of a 'special' American project. In his final months as president, Donald Trump signed an executive order to establish the Advisory 1776 Commission that would ensure a 'patriotic education' and 'defend the legacy of our exceptional Nation's founding along with its extraordinary Founders' (White House, 2020). Neither is it a partisan distinction. Joe Biden, in his final speech as vice president, spoke of the US as an 'exceptional democracy for more than 200 years' (World Economic Forum, 2017). When Biden was nominated for the presidency at the 2020 Democratic Convention, former Secretary of State John Kerry pronounced, 'Joe Biden knows we aren't exceptional because we bluster that we are; we are exceptional because we do exceptional things'.[5]

Regardless of the scholarly value of the claim of exceptionalism as 'greatness', it is undeniable that such views are widely held in the American public. Many Americans subscribe to a kind of creed that takes for granted the superiority of the American constitutional system and the American liberal capitalist economic system. These twin elements, many Americans think, set the US apart from the rest of the world. It makes the US, as Bill Clinton's Secretary of State Madeleine Albright put it, 'the indispensable nation'.[6] A 2012 Chicago Council Survey found that 66 per cent of Americans agreed with the

Figure 2.1: Public attitudes on American exceptionalism

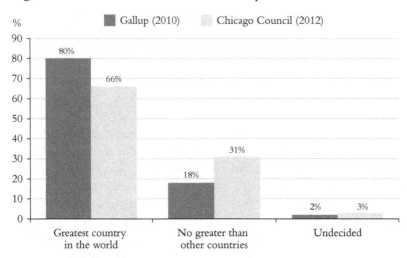

Source: Based on data from Forsythe and McMahon (2016, Table 1.3)

statement, 'the United States has a unique character that makes it the greatest country in the world' (see Figure 2.1). A similar question asked by Gallup two years earlier found that agreement was widely held by both Republicans and Democrats, with 91 per cent of Republicans and 73 per cent of Democrats professing a belief that the US is the greatest country on the planet.

These attitudes have serious implications for US foreign policy. Writing during the Second World War, the Swedish sociologist Gunnar Myrdal observed that 'The American Creed is identified with America's peculiar brand of nationalism, and it gives the common American his feeling of historical mission of America in the world – a fact which now becomes of global importance' (Myrdal, 1944: 5). It was on this myth that the US-led liberal order is premised. Most Americans have, as Anatol Lieven puts it, 'an absolutist faith' in their national myths (Lieven, 2012: 73). This, of course, does not stand them out from most other countries. All countries possess certain myths. But Americans' solipsism, it might be argued, is more dangerous and impactful, given the strength and influence of its military, economy and culture. After George W. Bush's second inauguration, the German newspaper the *Frankfurter Allgemeine Zeitung* ran with the headline, 'Bush threatens: even more freedom!' This hubristic, exceptionalist perspective has cost the US dearly. American foreign policymakers have often ignored the advice or experiences of those who do not take America's superiority for granted. For example, Bernard Fall's

1961 *Street without Joy* was a perceptive account of France's failures in Vietnam, which could have served US foreign policymakers well, but it was viewed as largely irrelevant by the defence establishment because the French were perceived to be inferior soldiers and administrators to the Americans. Nearly 60,000 American soldiers died in the years to follow in Vietnam.

American difference

American exceptionalism can be interpreted more dispassionately, merely to refer to the fact that the country is an empirical outlier on a variety of social and political measures. Compared to peer countries, the US has stood out for its weak socialist movement; its strong military; the small size of its government; its very high level of religious profession; its high levels of political gridlock; its high birth rates; its very high incarceration rates; its lack of universal healthcare; its persistent use of the death penalty; its high levels of gun ownership and gun-related violence; high levels of wealth inequality; high overall living standards; high levels of residential segregation; and low levels of union membership. Some scholars have identified currents in popular American ideology that set it apart from many other countries (Hartz, 1955; Huntington, 1981). Sociological accounts have tended to emphasize (the absence of) class consciousness (Gerber, 1997). Numerous scholars have also focused on political institutions, such as the US Constitution or the strength of the American state (Howe, 1985 [1977]; Dahl, 2003; Lipset and Marks, 2000; Gonzalez and King, 2004). Quite simply, therefore, exceptionalism can refer to the recognition of a characteristic that is not shared with some other unit.

Another source of confusion in discussions about American exceptionalism stems from a lack of agreement over a comparative framework. Byron Shafer (1991: vi) writes in the introduction to *Is America Different?*, 'the problem is that all societies, observed closely enough, are distinctive, while all societies observed with sufficient distance, are simultaneously similar'. The US has been compared against a variety of units – all countries, old democracies, consolidated democracies, Western Europe, federal systems, and so on – without much discussion justifying the choice of sample. Many commentators have made the mistake of jumping into the content of their analysis without taking into serious consideration their methodological approach or comparative case selection.

One mistake is to rely on an unspecified sample, which may result in impressionistic comparisons lacking intellectual rigour. Larry

Gerber's study of the US labour movement fell foul of this selection bias. Gerber rightly criticized portrayals of American workers as 'monolithically apolitical' (1997: 258). For example, in 1906 Werner Sombart famously declared that the ship of American socialism had crashed on the 'reefs of roast beef and apple pie' (1962 [1906]: 277). Yet, while Gerber framed his comparative study as one between the labour and socialist parties of 'Western Europe' and the US labour movement, his work relied overwhelmingly on the experience of just one country – the United Kingdom – to make his comparison. Although this approach could lead to a perfectly valid two-country comparison (see, for example, Shergold, 1983), it is difficult to make the claim that the US is different *in general* based on a comparison with only one country. Gerber's findings contrast with the work of Seymour Martin Lipset and Gary Marks (2000), who also showed that late 19th-century America possessed a unionized, industrial working class and labour movement which was not dissimilar from labour movements in the rest of the industrialized world at the time. By drawing comparisons with a number of different cases within their clearly specified sample (industrial democracies), Lipset and Marks were able to make more nuanced comparisons within the sample (for example, federal systems, ex-British colonies, agricultural economies, and so on) without risking selection on the dependent variable. As a result, Lipset and Marks pinpointed essential, yet subtle, points of difference the US had with similar countries (for example, strong judiciary, party primaries, doctrinaire socialist leaders, anti-statist labour leaders).

Sometimes the sample has been well chosen, but the analysis falls back to unfocused, unreflective statements. In his study of the US Constitution, Robert Dahl (2003) contended that the US should be compared and evaluated by the standards of long-standing democracies, which he defines as democracies that have continuously existed for more than 50 years. This generated a sample that included most of Europe, a few Commonwealth countries, Costa Rica, Israel and Japan. In order to justify his viewpoint about American difference, however, Dahl sometimes ignored, downplayed or glossed over similarities the US political system has with other countries. For example, he only paid lip service to the existence of first-past-the-post (FPTP) single-member constituencies in the UK and Canada, yet he dwelled on the system's inadequacy in the US. Had Dahl taken the next step and shown that the existence, practice or effect of FPTP in the US was somehow *different* than that of the UK and Canada, he might have been able to draw stronger conclusions than he was otherwise able.

Dahl is not the only guilty actor in this regard. Theodore Lowi's work (1984) on federalism and socialism underplayed the success of socialist/labour parties in other federal systems such as Australia, Germany, Switzerland and Canada. Similarly, Louis Hartz (1955) famously claimed that socialism did not develop in the US due to the early granting of white manhood suffrage, but a number of countries granted universal male suffrage before the development of a socialist/ labour party: Switzerland (1848), Australia (1850s), France (1875) and Canada (1885). These empirical anomalies were – more often than not – overlooked. Countries with early working-class (white male) suffrage nonetheless produced viable labour and socialist parties years after the initial granting of working-class suffrage. In New Zealand, suffrage was granted to (European-origin) men in 1879, but the New Zealand Labour Party was founded only in 1916.

In addition to careful consideration of the format of cross-national variation, it also worth considering whether it is always appropriate to treat the US as a single unit. Lipset and Marks (2000) also found value in using the explanatory power of varying context across national contexts *and* within the US. The US is a large, diverse and regionally divided country. Noting both American geography and a reasonably strong federal tradition, it sometimes makes a great deal of sense to compare differently the various regions of the US. Failure to account for regional variation can lead to wildly differing claims. Goran Therborn (1977) declared that the US was one of the last industrialized countries to grant universal suffrage; Louis Hartz (1955) declared that it was among the first. Both claims were wrong *in toto* because the former was true only about the South; the latter was true only about the North and West (if at all) (Rueschemeyer et al, 1992).

Sometimes the level of comparison can be dropped even lower, analysing distinct social groups rather than simply the sum of the individuals in a particular region or country. Rogers Smith has wisely pointed out that much of the commentary on American exceptionalism has been based on accounts that focus on the narrow relationship patterns of 'white men, largely of northern European ancestry' (Smith, 1993: 549). The treatment of whites may reveal that the US was quite similar to other advanced, industrialized democracies, but the exclusion of African Americans, Native Americans and (to a lesser extent, relatively speaking) women may have set America apart from other industrialized contemporaries.

Some commentators have also seriously underevaluated the importance of temporal variation in studying cross-national difference. By using the ratification of the US Constitution as his year 0, Sergio

Fabbrini ignored the state institutions and structures that preceded the US Constitution and, indeed, the independent United States of America. In an otherwise informed article, Fabbrini demonstrated a remarkable lack of awareness of European history in an article that claimed to be analysing the US from a 'European perspective'. Casting aside the 17th- and 18th-century constitutional struggles in England, Fabbrini declares, 'constitutional politics – that is the politics of constitutional change – was born in America' (Fabbrini, 1999: 483–4). Temporal cut-off points, at both ends, can distort research.

Fundamentally, the question of whether America is 'different' has suffered not from a lack of study but from a lack of conceptual clarity and organization. By defining more plainly what we mean by 'different' and by identifying the units by which we are measuring such difference, the important question of American difference may be answered meaningfully. The study of American difference should be rooted in cross-national comparisons, using empirical data guided by where America falls as an outlier. With this framework in mind, it is possible to rescue the study of American difference from the potential embarrassment of falling into a realm of dubious causal and comparative premises.

Conclusion

The thesis of American exceptionalism – as a claim about a special national 'mission' or 'special providence' – should be rejected, at least as a tool of analytical inquiry. The belief in some unique American 'mission' rests mainly on superstition about providence and destiny, subjects beyond the pay grade of political scientists. It is a 'complex of myth and ideology, sentiment and prejudice' (Howe, 1985 [1977]: 136). Yet, understanding the ideology of American exceptionalism is an essential element in any study of the US. It is the cultural foundation on which the edifice of American politics and government has been built. Few actors or institutions operate on a different set of core assumptions, especially in mainstream politics, policy and law. Ultimately, then, observers cannot ignore that there is a core assumption that undergirds most of American policymaking: that people everywhere around the world admire (or are envious of) the US and that, given the chance, people would gladly choose to be Americans (or at least have their 'freedoms'). We do not need to accept this worldview in order to take it seriously as one that shapes US foreign policy.

PART II

The Domestic Institutions of US Foreign Policy

3

The Executive Branch:
The President, Defense and State

The president of the United States is the pre-eminent actor in US foreign policy. Ceremonies in the White House Rose Garden, grand summits in foreign capitals, bilateral exchanges in the Oval Office – these are the public face of executive branch diplomacy. High-profile appearances on the international stage – Richard Nixon's visit to China, Ronald Reagan's insistence on tearing down the Berlin Wall, Donald Trump's meetings with North Korea's Kim Jong-un – are easily accessible in popular memory. Numerous treatises have been written about presidents' personal relationships with foreign leaders, such as Reagan and Margaret Thatcher (O'Sullivan, 2006; Aldous, 2012) or George W. Bush and Tony Blair (Naughtie, 2004; Shawcross, 2004). Moments of crisis, in which the president's 'call' is required, once more give the impression of presidential domination over US foreign policy: John Kennedy and the Bay of Pigs crisis, Bill Clinton and the 'Black Hawk Down' affair, Barack Obama's instruction to kill Osama bin Laden on the territory of a US ally.

Attention to these situations of great diplomatic intensity can leave an impression that the president is the *sole* actor in the executive branch. While individual presidents matter, we should be mindful of the fact that the executive branch is an institution, led by the president, but by no means only made up by him (or, one day, her). While it is interesting to focus on the personal trivia of individual presidents, it is important not to overlook the structural features of the executive branch and the many other actors who inhabit it (Burke, 1992). To the extent that presidents' particular styles and strategies matter, one must consider how they intersect with enduring structural features of the executive branch. Indeed, on a visit to Washington, DC, it soon becomes clear that the executive departments and agencies are extremely important players on their own terms, exercising a degree of governing autonomy (Carpenter, 2001; Johnson, 2007). They are, this chapter argues, essential to understanding the institutional machinery of US foreign policymaking.

This chapter is divided into four sections. The first discusses the 'civilian' side of the executive branch when it comes to foreign affairs. The most eminent foreign policy actor in the executive branch besides the president is the secretary of state.[1] The State Department is the major department that constructs and coordinates US foreign policy, and it is where the US diplomatic corps is located. State Department officials carry out a range of vital functions on behalf of the US government abroad, and provide information and policy suggestions for the president and secretary of state back home. When the president informs himself about foreign affairs, however, he does not rely on State Department bureaucrats alone. Presidents frequently look to close advisers, who provide guidance and insight on foreign developments and national security matters. This advice is inevitably filtered, at least partially, through a political lens. The second section of this chapter examines the military side of the executive branch, specifically, the Department of Defense and the intelligence agencies, discussing what has sometimes been termed the **military–industrial complex**, the intimate relationship between US policymakers and those who have a material interest in the perpetuation of the outsized US defence budget.

The last two sections address the role of the president more directly. While the Constitution makes no explicit mention of parties, any analysis of the modern presidency is incomplete without taking seriously the president's partisan context.[2] The third section contends that the president's role in foreign policy must also be understood in partisan terms. The last section addresses the nature of presidential power within the constraints of the US constitutional system. The president's leadership over the executive branch may give him a reasonably high level of administrative power, but the power of the president to act autonomously on foreign policy matters depends, to some extent, on deference from other branches of government. It has often been argued that the US has two presidents: one who is extremely powerful in foreign affairs and a second who is relatively weak in domestic politics. This theory is known as the 'two presidencies' thesis. This final section weighs up the evidence and offers some possible criticisms of this much-discussed theory.

The State Department, civilian advisers and presidential diplomacy

The executive branch is much bigger than the president and his aides in the White House. The president, in fact, oversees 15 cabinet-level departments, a dozen or so administrative agencies that support the president's work within the executive office, and nearly 30 other policy-based federal executive agencies, that together employ roughly 2 million full-time employees. Below the president are powerful cabinet departments (for example, State, Treasury, Defense, Homeland Security and Agriculture), and within each of these departments is an enormous bureaucracy of agencies and sub-agencies. There are also important semi-autonomous specialist agencies (for example, the US Agency for International Development [USAID], the CIA [Central Intelligence Agency], the Export–Import Bank), which assist the president directly or advance particular policy goals.

For much of US history, the president was highly dependent on these bureaucratic departments for resources and information. The executive branch had reasonable administrative capacity, but the president was relatively weak within it. Until the 1930s, the president had virtually no support within the White House, whereas from the mid-19th century, executive branch departments were powerful and penetrated the day-to-day lives of ordinary Americans (Johnson, 2007). This image of a weak president surrounded by strong executive departments is not the popular rendering of executive power, especially from commentators who promote the image of an 'imperial presidency' (Schlesinger, 1973). Yet studies of the federal bureaucracy have shown that executive branch agencies never had total loyalty to the president and often developed their own sense of mission, separate from the president's policy agenda (Carpenter, 2001). Such bureaucratic autonomy could make it difficult for the president to steer his own agenda clearly.

For decades, presidents lacked a set of officials whose sole job was to support the president and his policy agenda directly. Until the mid-19th century, presidents were given no staff at all. If they wanted even a secretary to sort through their letters or arrange their diaries, they needed to pay for someone out of their own pocket. It wasn't until 1857 that Congress gave the president a budget to hire his own staff: one clerk. Abraham Lincoln fought the Civil War with the assistance of just two secretaries in the White House. By 1900, President William McKinley had 13 members of staff. By 1920, President Warren Harding had 31 members of staff. By the time Franklin Roosevelt became president in 1933, he had just 33 people working for him.

Roosevelt, finding the situation intolerable as he tried to push through his ambitious New Deal agenda, called for a commission to recommend ways of reforming the executive branch. The result was the Brownlow Committee, comprising some of America's leading political scientists: Charles Merriam, Luther Gulick and Louis Brownlow. The Committee concluded in 1937, 'the President needs help. His immediate staff assistance is entirely inadequate' (The President's Committee on Administrative Management, 1937). Based on the Committee's proposals, Congress passed the Reorganization Act of 1939, with its most significant creation being the executive office of the president (EOP), which now has 4,000 members of staff who support the president directly.

Today the president has the benefit of numerous agencies that provide foreign policy input. They include agencies within the EOP (for example, the National Security Council and the US Trade Representative), members of the president's cabinet (such as the secretaries of State, Defense, Energy, Homeland Security), and members of independent military and civilian federal agencies (for example, the CIA, the Maritime Commission, the International Trade Commission and the Joint Chiefs of Staff). From these bodies presidents typically draw a number of key advisers, who form the president's inner circle when responding to foreign policy dilemmas. As Patrick Haney (2002) describes, some presidents have preferred a rigid hierarchy and formalistic policymaking structure (for example, Dwight Eisenhower). Others (for example, John F. Kennedy) have preferred a less structured and more collegial organization. Each form has its own advantages and disadvantages. Presidents who have preferred a hierarchical structure have the advantage of clarity and minimize the possibility of advisers speaking past each other. However, presidents can sometimes find themselves 'locked into' decisions without canvassing a full range of options. Presidents with collegial styles can enjoy exposure to a wide range of ideas, but they can also suffer from a lack of specificity with regard to goals and objectives. It has also been argued that a collegial style is by no means a guarantee that a president will hear a wide range of views, especially if the colleagues on whom the president relies to give advice think in a similar way to the president and to each other.

Irving Janis (1972) argued that the fiasco at the Bay of Pigs in Cuba in 1961 was the result of President Kennedy having chummy advisers who didn't challenge each other enough and became victims of 'group think'. He concluded that too often Kennedy's foreign policy advisers, sometimes called 'the whizz kids', were driven by their own need for self-esteem that they got from being an accepted member of this socially important 'insider' group. Fears of shattering the warm feelings of perceived unanimity kept some of Kennedy's advisers from objecting to the Bay of Pigs plan until it was too late. David Halberstam (1972) argued that Kennedy's and Lyndon Johnson's reliance on these bright, young advisers led to a blindness caused by arrogance. Their hubris resulted in the tragedy in Vietnam where the president's advisers were too clever by half to realize that there was no possible way that the US could win a ground war in Vietnam.

One of the most important 'whizz kids' was Walt Rostow, who served as a State Department bureaucrat under Kennedy and national security adviser under Johnson. Rostow was widely viewed to be a brilliant mind. He was admitted to Yale at the age of 15, was a Rhodes Scholar at Oxford, and completed his PhD before he was 24. He was a professor at MIT in the 1950s and was brought in by Kennedy and later retained by Johnson to provide advice on foreign affairs. It was Rostow who encouraged President Kennedy to invest troops in Vietnam, telling him that 'clean-cut success in Vietnam' was likely and would help ease the political tension back home caused by the Bay of Pigs fiasco. Presidents Kennedy and Johnson became blindsided by Rostow's putative expertise, and Rostow's reputation for brilliance shielded him from scrutiny (Buzzanco, 1996). One scholar called Rostow 'America's Rasputin' (Milne, 2008), a reference to the malevolent spiritual adviser to Tsarina Alexandra who is blamed for contributing to the collapse of the Russian monarchy with his bad advice.

After the president, the most important person in American foreign policy decision-making is the secretary of state. Stephen Krasner writes, 'For US foreign policy, the central state actors are the President and the Secretary of State, and the most important institutions are the White House and the State Department' (1978: 11).[3] Presidents have been known to delegate a large amount of autonomy to their secretaries of state (for example, Richard Nixon and Gerald Ford with Henry Kissinger, Barack Obama with Hillary Clinton), especially when the president's focus is directed on domestic affairs (Dueck, 2015). The secretary of state, not the president (although his consent is implicit), is the designated official to sign off on all foreign agreements made by US public officials, according to the Case-Zablocki Act of 1972.

The secretary of state is nominated by the president and confirmed by the Senate. Once in office, the secretary of state is in charge of a large bureaucracy of his or her own. The State Department consists of nearly 70,000 employees working in Washington and around the world. At the beginning of the Obama presidency, Congress appropriated funds to increase State Department staff by 1,108 and added 1,200 new international development officers in USAID (Clinton, 2012). These officials engage in a wide range of tasks. Some are matters of 'high diplomacy': top-level relations with governments around the world. Others are more mundane, but still important, matters of 'low diplomacy'. American missions abroad sometimes employ hundreds of staff who are involved in the domestic affairs of other countries of interest, providing assistance in a range of policy fields: health, energy, communications, finance, agriculture, justice and security. These efforts are not purely benevolent acts of goodwill; they serve US interests. For example, by helping 'energy-poor' countries in Central America and the Caribbean develop their own biofuels, the US lessens their dependence on imported oil from Venezuela, a US adversary. Diplomatic staff are also often located in areas of key military interest. The US Embassy in Islamabad has 800 members of staff. One in five members of the US diplomatic corps work in Pakistan, Afghanistan or Iraq (Clinton, 2012: 248).

State Department officials also engage in **public diplomacy**, which refers to the outreach efforts of American diplomats in the countries in which they are stationed. These efforts aim to promote America's image abroad and to engage with local populations in order to help explain the work that the US is doing in their country and to educate citizens of other countries about the foreign policy mission of the US. 'Public diplomacy' can involve doing television interviews, going to schools, organizing community meetings or hosting student exchange programmes. Often overlooked is the wide range of services that US State Department officials deploy, which has little to do with the types of 'diplomacy' just discussed. State department officials are involved in providing medical assistance (for example, pandemic relief and family planning), educational services (such as literacy, job and skill training), agricultural advice (for example, irrigation and crop management), environmental expertise (for example, energy self-sufficiency), legal guidance (such as drafting constitutions and electoral systems), technical support (for example, IT systems) and developmental assistance (for example, economic planning and loans).

Alongside the State Department, a number of executive branch agencies also promote US interests abroad through civilian power. These include USAID, the Millennium Challenge Corporation, the Overseas Private Investment Corporation (OPIC), the Peace Corps and the Export–Import Bank. Many of these were created during the Cold War to fight communism by providing US-backed economic assistance to developing countries. Leaders such as Kennedy were concerned that the Soviet Union would try to use economic assistance to incline countries towards communism. Today, these agencies have a wide remit and offer assistance to some of the poorest countries in the world.

Krasner believed that what distinguishes the secretary of state is 'their high degree of insulation from specific social pressure and a set of formal and informal obligations that charge them with furthering the nation's general interests' (1978: 11). This view of an insulated, politically neutral State Department is not credible today, if it ever was. In the 19th century, the secretary of state position was sought by those with presidential ambitions – or was viewed as a legitimate consolation prize for election losers. Of the first 42 secretaries of state, 11 were candidates for the US presidency (about one in four).[4] Hillary Clinton and John Kerry's tenures as secretary of state under Barack Obama revived this link between aspiring (or failed) presidential candidates and the State Department, which had fallen into neglect in the mid-to-late 20th century.

In the modern era, State Department activities are regularly directed towards meeting the policy objectives of domestic constituencies. Even State Department agencies that do important work, such as help fight disease and malnutrition, can still be deployed to advance domestic political goals. As will be discussed in Chapter 6, the State Department's Center for Faith-Based and Community Initiatives within USAID has proven to be an important agency by which Republican Presidents George W. Bush and Donald Trump ensured the placement of high-profile evangelical leaders in their administration, as well as saw federal money flow to Christian charities popular with their important Christian evangelical voter base.

The Department of Defense and the military-industrial complex

In contrast to the secretary of state, whose role has existed since George Washington's first cabinet in 1789, the 'secretary of defense' is a relatively young cabinet position. It was the creation of a major reorganization of the defence bureaucracy during the presidency of Harry Truman following the Second World War. While in a technical sense the secretary of defense replaced the position of secretary of war, which had existed since Washington's presidency, the new post was not just a name change. It represented a transformation of the military bureaucracy, with a much higher degree of centralization around the secretary of defense than the secretary of war had enjoyed.

At the end of the Second World War, the Eberstadt Report of 1945, officially known as the Taskforce Report on National Security Organization, recommended a dramatic reorganization of the executive branch bureaucracy to protect the US from external threats. The attack on Pearl Harbor in 1941 had exposed the vulnerabilities of the US military. The recommendations of the Eberstadt Report were sometimes called the 'Pearl Harbor System' in recognition of these origins. The Eberstadt Report led to the National Security Act of 1947, which Douglas Stuart calls 'the second most important piece of legislation in modern American history', second only to the Civil Rights Act of 1964 (Stuart, 2008: 2). The Act created nearly all of the major institutions of the national security bureaucracy, including the Department of Defense (initially called the National Military Establishment), the National Security Council and the CIA. President Harry Truman later wrote in his memoirs, 'To me, the passage of the National Security Act and its strengthening amendments represented one of the outstanding achievements of my administration' (quoted in Geselbracht, 2019 [1955]: 408). It is hard to disagree with Truman substantively. The National Security Act is one of his most durable and consequential policy legacies, yet the Act is little known today, and Truman is not closely associated with its progeny, such as the CIA.

The National Security Act faced some initial teething problems. James Forrestal, the first secretary of defense, felt constantly undermined by the three military chiefs, especially the secretary of the Navy, who also served in the cabinet. Forrestal pleaded for greater unification and centralization than even the National Security Act had allowed. Forrestal also clashed with President Truman, who disagreed with Forrestal's calls for more funding. Truman sacked Forrestal in March 1949, and Forrestal committed suicide two months later, throwing himself out of the 13th floor window of Bethesda Naval Hospital. A few months after Forrestal's death, the National Security Act was amended to bring about some of the changes that Forrestal had recommended, not least removing the secretary of the Navy from cabinet and instead, formally sublimating the post to the secretary of defense. In addition, the 1949 amendments created the chairman of the Joint Chiefs of Staff, a position that would be nominated by the president and take precedence over all other military personnel. The chair acts as the president's and secretary of defence's principal military adviser.

The US Department of Defense is a vast executive branch department, which contains not only three military departments (the Army, Navy and Air Force) but also intelligence and other services such as the National Security Agency (NSA), the Defense Advanced Research Projects Agency and the Defense Logistics Agency. In December 2019, President Donald Trump added the US Space Force (USSF) as a special service branch under the US Air Force. This is now one of the eight uniformed services of the US military.[5] The Department of Defense has 750,000 non-military employees, 1.3 million active-duty soldiers and 825,000 reserves.

The Department of Defense has an annual budget of well over $600 billion, dwarfing every other country's military spending. In fact, the total spending of the next eight countries on defence added together would not match that of the US (see Figure 3.1). The budget is so vast that services that might ordinarily be associated with other government departments end up being wrapped into the Department of Defense appropriation bill. For example, administration of overseas voting is run through the Federal Voter Assistance Program (FVAP), which is funded by the Department of Defense. Some international aid money is channelled through defence. Infrastructure spending in politically sensitive areas is typically funded through the defence appropriations bill rather than the foreign operations bill, which funds the State Department and USAID. If you want a programme to be funded by Congress, it's not a bad strategy to claim it has a defence dimension, however tenuous. Unlike in other areas of public policy,

Figure 3.1: Military spending, by country (top 10 spenders in US$), 2018

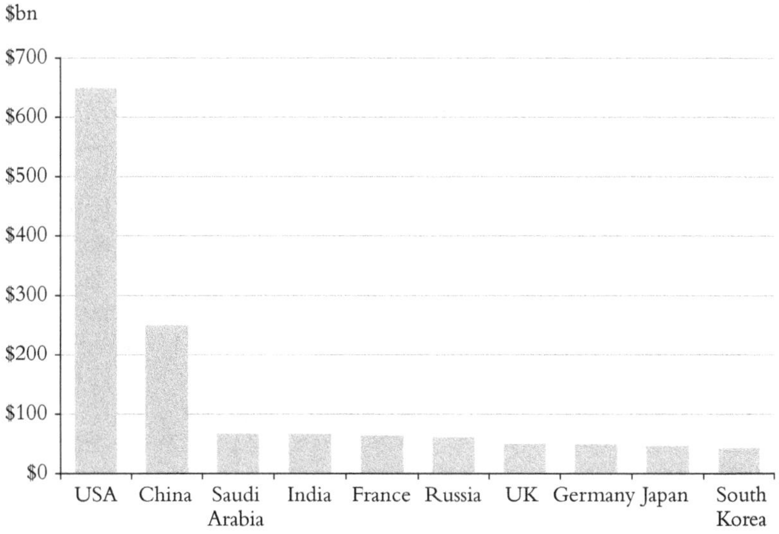

Source: Based on data from the *SIPRI Yearbook* (2018)

Congress members' fiscal conservatism seems to take a temporary leave of absence when the defence appropriations bill is up for a vote.

Given the size of the US defence budget, it should not come as a surprise that some people have questioned what influence the military has had on American politics and society. One of the long-held principles of the US military is that it is led by civilians. The subordination of military officials to the decisions of political masters is seen as a prerequisite of liberal democracy. An example of this is the fact that applicants to US military academies are required to receive a letter of recommendation from their member of Congress in order to be trained as a military officer. President Harry Truman remarked that each American military officer 'learns of his dependence on "politics" from the moment he solicits his first application blank for a service academy' (Raymond, 1964: 174–5).

However, commentators have long been concerned over the extent to which there truly is civilian control over the military. President Donald Trump in particular put this principle under strain when he appointed numerous retired generals to positions that had long been considered to be for civilians. Trump's Chief of Staff John Kelly was a retired general, as were his Secretary of Defense James Mattis and two of his National Security Advisors, Michael Flynn and H.R. McMaster. Joe Biden did not reverse this pattern, nominating retired General Lloyd Austin to be his secretary of defense (Golub, 2020). Yet, even before the Trump presidency, many observers worried that the US military had too much control over civilian politics.

President Dwight Eisenhower, a former general himself, famously expressed concern in his 1961 Farewell Address about the unwarranted influence of the 'military–industrial complex'. The military–industrial complex refers to the intimate relationship between military officials and civilian policymakers. Eisenhower worried that the military could hold sway over the American political process because of its size, prestige and material resources. The term itself was coined by Ralph Williams and Malcolm Moos, political science academics who served as speechwriters for Eisenhower. Williams recorded in his planning notes that the two men wanted to raise 'the problem of militarism…. We must be very careful that the merchants of death do not come to dictate national policy' (quoted in Ledbetter, 2011: 110–11). It is worth quoting Eisenhower's warning in its context:

> Our military organization today bears little relation to that known by any of my predecessors in peacetime, or indeed by the fighting men of World War II or Korea. Until the

latest of our world conflicts, the United States had no armaments industry. American makers of plowshares could, with time and as required, make swords as well. But now we can no longer risk emergency improvisation of national defense; we have been compelled to create a permanent armaments industry of vast proportions. Added to this, three and a half million men and women are directly engaged in the defense establishment. We annually spend on military security more than the net income of all United States corporations.

This conjunction of an immense military establishment and a large arms industry is new in the American experience. The total influence – economic, political, even spiritual – is felt in every city, every State house, every office of the Federal government. We recognize the imperative need for this development. Yet we must not fail to comprehend its grave implications. Our toil, resources and livelihood are all involved; so is the very structure of our society.

In the councils of government, we must guard against the acquisition of *unwarranted influence, whether sought or unsought, by the military-industrial complex*. The potential for the disastrous rise of misplaced power exists and will persist. We must never let the weight of this combination endanger our liberties or democratic processes. We should take nothing for granted. Only an alert and knowledgeable citizenry can compel the proper meshing of the huge industrial and military machinery of defense with our peaceful methods and goals, so that security and liberty may prosper together. (emphasis added)[6]

In order to understand Eisenhower's warning, we must revisit the context in which he was making his speech. As president, Eisenhower had embarked on the 'New Look' defence strategy, in which he increased nuclear and air force spending but cut the overall military budget by 20 per cent. Historians, such as Robert Buzzanco (1996), accuse military leaders of teaming up with Democrats in Congress in the 1950s to undermine the Eisenhower Administration. It was an easy way for Democrats to score points against Eisenhower, a Republican, and military leaders were upset about their budgets being cut. Senator Lyndon Johnson was chair of the Senate subcommittee on military preparedness at the time, and he regularly paraded military leaders before the committee to decry Eisenhower's 'New Look'. A reporter said to one general that his testimony 'had probably helped the Democrats more than several speeches by their candidates'. The general replied with a grin, 'Ah you get the idea, don't you' (Davis, 1967: 228).

Eisenhower felt stung by the collusion of congressional Democrats with military officials and the defence industry. Martin Medhurst (1997) argues that Eisenhower's farewell speech was a veiled attack on the incoming Kennedy Administration. Kennedy had run for president as a 'cold warrior', painting the Republicans as weak on defence. When he was inaugurated, Kennedy offered a blank cheque on defence:

> Let every nation know, whether it wishes us well or ill, that we shall pay any price, bear any burden, meet any hardship, support any friend, oppose any foe to assure the survival and the success of liberty. This much we pledge – and more.[7]

The notion that the US would 'pay any price' alarmed Eisenhower. Eisenhower thought that this was hopelessly naive and gave the military far too much power. Indeed, soon after Kennedy became president, his Secretary of Defense Dean Rusk discovered that the US Air Force had misrepresented data to claim that the USSR had more weapons than the US when, in fact, the reality was the other way around (Ledbetter, 2011). The so-called 'missile gap' controversy had been a major point of contention between Kennedy and his Republican rival, Eisenhower's Vice President Richard Nixon, in the 1960 election. Indeed, given the closeness of that election (Kennedy won the electoral college by a margin of just 18,953 votes across three states[8]), it is possible that these inaccurate data could have tipped the election to Kennedy (Amadae, 2003).[9] Kennedy's election was initially welcomed by the Pentagon as 'the consummate cold warrior' (Buzzanco, 1996). In his post-presidency, Eisenhower's farewell speech made him an unlikely hero of the anti-militarist left. An editorial in left-leaning magazine *The Nation* remarked, 'It can be said, quite without irony, that nothing became Mr Eisenhower's career in office like the leaving of it' (Pach and Richardson, 1991: 230).

Reputationally, there are few organizations in the US with higher esteem than the military. Having served in the military carries high political capital. Politicians who haven't served sometimes need to compensate. Bill Clinton's manoeuvres to avoid serving in the Vietnam War came under heavy criticism during his 1992 election campaign. As president, Clinton would turn to actors with military experience to bolster the credibility of his initiatives. He even asked the recently retired General Colin Powell to endorse his North American Free Trade Agreement, even though there were no evident implications for the military (Buzzanco, 1996). Fellow draft avoider Donald Trump similarly surrounded himself with retired military officials. It is also telling that even when Donald Trump proposed massive cuts to the federal budget, the only departments for which he proposed increases were Defense, Veterans Affairs and Homeland Security.

While American presidents often seek to drape themselves in the flags of the armed services, it is important not to see the military as purely passive vessels of their political masters. The military is political: it has interests and goals and depends on public resources to achieve them. These goals do not always accord with the mission of the incumbent presidential administration. Democratic President Bill Clinton learned this lesson to his political misfortune early on. In 1992, Clinton campaigned for president on the promises that he would reduce Department of Defense spending and allow gay men and women to serve openly in the US military. Soon after his election, the Joint Chiefs of Staff blocked Bill Clinton's proposal for allowing gay soldiers, claiming that the change would undermine military morale. Many commentators believe that the military did not have a legitimate reason to block this initiative and that Clinton had the authority to change the rule as commander-in-chief. But Clinton's generals knew that this was a policy where Clinton lacked broad public support. They knew that they could flex their muscles and give Clinton a black eye politically on the controversial subject of gay soldiers. In doing so, they made Clinton a less credible actor of military matters when he sought to subsequently reduce the defence budget (Buzzanco, 1996).

The military's vast budget has implications beyond day-to-day politics. It enables the US military to have enormous penetration into various aspects of American society (Engerman, 2004). This was perhaps most acute in the post-war expansion of America's research-intensive universities. Between 1940 and 1960, the research budget of US universities increased by one hundredfold to $1.5 billion (or $12.5 billion in 2017 value). Three-quarters of university research funds came from the federal government, and 40 per cent of this came from the Department of Defense and Atomic Energy Commission alone (Ledbetter, 2011). Additionally, ostensibly private companies, that relied heavily on Department of Defense funding, such as Douglas Aircraft Company, provided funding for research projects, set up research institutes at American universities and funded think tanks. US government-funded social science research bodies based at

US universities included American University's Special Operations Research Office, MIT's Center for International Studies and Harvard's Russia Research Center. Partly a result of student activism and protest, the Mansfield Amendment in 1973 finally restricted direct Department of Defense spending on university research, leaving the US military establishment to draw on scholars based outside the academy and funding 'independent' research institutes, such as the Institute for Defense Analysis, the Human Resources Research Center and the RAND Corporation, which Sonja Amadae calls the 'quintessential American Cold War institution' (2003: 11). RAND was the source of the flawed 'missile gap' projections between the US and USSR during the Eisenhower presidency.

American military funding actively shaped research through the proliferation of individualistic and computational methodologies (Solovey, 2001). It also directed research to study areas of strategic interest (see, for example, Trager, 1960). Academics were funded by the Department of Defense to investigate the political and social causes of communism, the 'laws' of human behaviour, the psychology of warfare and rational choice theory (Amadae, 2003; Rohde, 2009). The projects often had a specific military purpose. For example, a research project to understand how information travels through illiterate people was used to strengthen the production of US military propaganda directed at illiterate and semi-literate societies. Latin American specialists were enlisted to give courses on Cuba to high-level government officials (Rohde, 2009). One of the most dramatic examples was Michigan State University's Vietnam Advisory Group, which used federal funding (USAID grants and CIA support) in the 1950s and 1960s to build a multi-million dollar nation-building programme in South Vietnam to support the regime of Ngo Dinh Diem (Scigliano and Fox, 1965; Ernst, 1998). Michigan State University's project helped bolster a corrupt dictator and, as one historian put it, played a key role in 'the making of a police state in South Vietnam' (Kuzmarov, 2012: 141). It was a grim example of academic 'impact' at any cost.

At the same time, this link between military, industry and university led to the repression of certain research: suspicion of Keynesian and left-wing academics; a repression of teaching Marxist theory; a retreat from cultural political studies; and a discouragement of studies that were critical of the functioning of democracy in the US (Schrecker, 1986; Isaac, 2007). University academics were even fearful to work for the Eisenhower brothers (Dwight and Milton)'s centrist Republican Critical Issues Council because they feared reprisals from the military establishment in the form of reduced grant capture (Ledbetter, 2011).

The academics who worked on Michigan State's Vietnam project had to sign contracts that stated that they would not write books or articles reflecting poorly on the Diem regime (Scigliano, 2018).

The Cold War political scientists claimed that their research was universally valid, impersonal, factual and technical (Amadae, 2003). Because the positions taken by these researchers were not 'partisan' in the sense that they did not advocate for one party over another, they were wrongly viewed as apolitical. Earl DeLong at American University's Special Operations Research Office defended his institute's reliance on Pentagon funding, stating that because their research was scientifically based, it was beyond reproach. 'Facts are beyond propaganda', wrote De Long.[10] In fact, this research was deeply infused with normative content, especially a political commitment to the American model of capitalist, liberal democracy and an expectation of progress (Chomsky, 1997; Lewontin, 1997). Rational choice approaches were, as Amadae puts it, rescued from 'academic oblivion' by the Department of Defense in the 1950s. Ultimately, this research approach became privileged as 'rigorous' and reverberated throughout the academy, influencing numerous fields in the social sciences, including sociology, psychology, anthropology (Price, 2016), economics and political science (Isaac, 2007). For example, 'public choice' theory in political science, associated with William Riker and the University of Rochester's Department of Political Science, sought to provide 'objective' and 'rational' calculations about democratic decision-making. Even Harvard's John Rawls endorsed the characteristic premises of Cold War rational choice theory in his works of philosophy promoting as neutral, universal and objective the idea that 'justice' could be computationally identified through the actions of fair-minded individual agents. It is not an exaggeration to say that the modern American research university was built by the Cold War US military establishment. Stuart Leslie proposed modifying Eisenhower's term to acknowledge this expanded nexus: the **military-industrial-academic complex** (Leslie, 1993).

The president as party leader

In recent decades, the president's role as party leader has assumed great importance. Presidents shape the party in their own image, pronouncing on party policy, mobilizing grassroots supporters and providing support to party initiatives and infrastructure. This is more than simply a cult of personality around the president. Sidney Milkis and his collaborators have identified a phenomenon that they call

executive-centred partisanship (Milkis and Jacobs, 2017; Milkis and York, 2017). This refers to the tendency of modern presidents to use their powers of the executive branch to advance political and policy goals on behalf of their party. As a result, national party organizations (such as the Republican National Committee and the Democratic National Committee) have increasingly ceded control over party messaging and policy development to the White House.

Executive-centred partisanship is the product of two institutional reforms, as well as some broader secular changes in the nature of American politics. The first reform was the aforementioned Executive Reoganization Act of 1939 that gave the president a bureaucratic infrastructure loyal to his personal policy initiatives and priorities. The EOP has proved to be exceptionally useful in providing thinly veiled partisan messaging and policy development. Second, in the mid-20th century, the two main parties disempowered their hitherto highly decentralized, patronage-based structures, stripping power from state and local party bosses. Party power bases consequently became much more nationally situated than before. Concurrently, the news media in the US has nationalized, as local papers have diminished in their output and public focus has increasingly been directed towards Washington (Hopkins, 2018). Together, these changes have resulted in a nationalized political culture, with the president enjoying a sophisticated political machinery that no has no serious rival within the party.

The president has unique power to shape the party's policy direction, but must also be attentive to the party's core electoral constituencies. Presidents who pursue policies that offend their party's base can rarely do so without electoral risk (Milkis and Tichenor, 2019). Fortunately for them, presidents have found that they can use foreign policy to deliver to domestic electoral constituencies, while avoiding congressional blockages encountered in some areas of domestic policy. Many of these moves are symbolic, such as moving and opening embassies, honouring historic events or granting official recognition to countries and their capitals. Donald Trump's decision to move the US Embassy from Tel Aviv to Jerusalem was a significant signal to his evangelical support base, who believe that the Jewish state's capital must be the ancient Biblical city, in spite of claims to the contrary from the local Palestinian population.

One of the most vivid examples of this is the 'Mexico City Rule', a presidential executive order that prohibits US international aid funding from going to charities that provide or support abortion services. The rule also prohibits federal money being used to fund groups that campaign for the legalization of abortion in countries where it is currently prohibited. The First Amendment constrains a US president from restricting groups within the US from campaigning for abortion rights. Foreign policy gives the president more leeway to signal their views on the issue to their co-partisans in ways they simply wouldn't be able to do in the domestic realm.

The rule was introduced by Republican President Ronald Reagan to appeal to conservative evangelical voters in advance of his re-election campaign in 1984. Rescinding the Mexico City Rule has become an almost ritualistic aspect of the first week in office of a new Democratic president. In 1993, Bill Clinton overturned the order two days into office. In 2001, Republican George W. Bush restored the rule two days after his inauguration. In 2009, Democrat Barack Obama repealed the rule three days into office. In 2017, Republican Donald Trump reintroduced the Mexico City Rule in his first week in office. In January 2021, Joe Biden repealed the Mexico City Rule once again. The Mexico City Rule illustrates the greater room foreign policy provides to presidents to use the executive branch to send signals to their partisan constituencies. It is an executive order, meaning that it can be introduced and reversed by presidential action alone without reference to Congress.

The president can also use his powers as commander-in-chief to craft military policy according to the demands of domestic constituencies. In June 2016, the Obama Administration ended the ban on transgender military personnel, six years after President Obama had signed into law the repeal of the ban on homosexual soldiers. As a candidate, Donald Trump dismissed the inclusion of transgendered soldiers as 'politically correct'. Six months into office, evangelical groups urged the president to reimpose the ban. The Family Research Council, a conservative Christian group, had run adverts falsely likening the costs of a sex change surgery to a fighter jet. FOX News commentator, Tucker Carlson, whose programme the president was known to watch, questioned whether the diversion of resources to sex change surgeries and treatments was making America less safe on the battlefront. On 10 July 2017, Christian leaders visited the president in the Oval Office and laid hands on Trump in prayer. Reports connected to those who attended the meeting revealed that the leaders discussed the need for a ban on transgender troops (Protess et al, 2017). On 26 June 2017, Trump tweeted:

> After consultation with my Generals and military experts, please be advised that the United States Government will

not accept or allow transgender individuals to serve in any capacity in the US Military. Our military must be focused on decisive and overwhelming victory and cannot be burdened with the tremendous medical costs and disruption that transgender in the military would entail. Thank you.

The tweet appears to have come as a complete surprise to the president's military experts, in spite of the president's own protestations. It was made three weeks after Secretary of Defense Jim Mattis had announced a six-month review of opening the military to transgender Americans. Mattis had been on holiday at the time of the tweet, and the Pentagon was clearly caught by surprise. The Department of Defense spokesperson Jeff Davis simply stated, 'We refer all questions about the President's statements to the White House'. Yet already, the administrative state was clicking into gear to defend and implement the president's policy declaration. The following month, President Trump signed a memorandum instructing Secretary of Defense Mattis to implement the ban within six months. The ban was subjected to numerous court challenges (see, for example, *Jane Doe v Trump*, *Stone v Trump*, *Karnoski v Trump* and *Stockman v Trump*), but the Supreme Court eventually validated the policy.

In some areas of foreign policy, Congress has delegated some of its own powers to the executive branch. This has been clearest on trade policy, where Congress has granted wide discretion to presidents for imposing tariffs.[11] The Trade Expansion Act of 1962 and the Trade Act of 1974 saw Congress give presidents the power to impose tariffs without congressional approval whenever they deemed foreign imports to be national security threats or injurious to US industries. These powers were used with great vigour by Donald Trump who, somewhat implausibly, declared cars imported from Japan and the EU to be a national security threat (Shepardson, 2019). These powers enabled President Trump to deliver on his 'America First' promises to his supporters. Michigan, a car-manufacturing state, helped to ensure Donald Trump's victory over Hillary Clinton in 2016. Nevertheless, Trump's tough approach to trade ultimately proved insufficient to hold the state in his failed 2020 re-election bid.

Trump gave new meaning to the idea of the 'permanent campaign' (Doherty, 2012). He was the first president in US history to file his re-election paperwork with the Federal Elections Commission (FEC) on Inauguration Day. From the beginning of his four-year presidency, Trump used the powers of the executive branch to deliver on promises he had made to his supporters about reducing immigration. Trump's executive powers gave him ample ability to make substantial changes. In his first week as president, Trump issued Executive Order 13769 and other instructions that clarified to public officials what the president's priorities were should officials come into contact with illegal immigrants. Trump directed the Department of Homeland Security to suspend the US Refugee Admissions Program for 120 days, suspended the entry of Syrian refugees indefinitely, and suspended for 90 days traveller visas to the US from a handful of majority-Muslim states (Iraq, Iran, Libya, Somalia, Sudan and Yemen). Trump instructed the Department of Housing and Urban Development to curtail housing assistance to illegal immigrants. He instructed the US military to suspend non-citizen recruitment. In spring 2019, Trump used his tariff powers to force Mexico to reduce migrant flows into the US. Trump threatened Mexico with tariffs as high as 25 per cent if they did not take tougher action to prevent migration into the US border. Mexico conceded to Trump's demands, deploying the army on its side of the border and agreeing to house asylum applicants on their side of the border while the US processed their claims. These actions demonstrate the ability of the US president to act with relative autonomy in some areas of foreign policy, but with the intention of appealing to domestic policy communities.

The two presidencies

According to the presidential scholar William Howell (2013), all presidents spend their time trying to acquire, protect and expand their power. Power, as an abstract concept, is amorphous, fleeting and contingent. It simply refers to the ability to get others to do something you would like them to do. The power of the presidency rests on many factors. Chief among these, it seems, are the formal powers given over to the president in Article II in the US Constitution. These powers (in the plural) are in one sense concrete and fixed. They include the power to pardon, appoint officers of the executive and judicial branches, veto legislation, and so on. But the president also faces a variety of fixed structural constraints on his powers (Jones, 1994). A president can appoint members of the executive and judiciary, but they are subject to a confirmation vote in the US Senate. A president may wage war, but Congress must declare it. A president can veto bills passed by Congress, but Congress can overturn the president's veto with a super-majority.

The eminent political scientist Richard Neustadt concluded that based on its formal constitutional powers alone, the US presidency is weak. He wrote in 1990, reflecting on half a century of studying the presidency, 'Weakness is still what I see: weakness in the sense of a great gap between what is expected of a man (or someday woman) and assured capacity to carry through' (Neustadt, 1990: ix). Many other scholars agree that the demands of the presidency outstripped the president's formal powers specified in Article II of the US Constitution (James, 2005). Neustadt believed that a president could become powerful, however, if he could skilfully persuade other members of the 'Washington Community', such as Congress and the media, to support his policy priorities. Other scholars have noted that presidents frequently attempt to build support in Washington by going 'public' with their proposals and using their unique connection with the national electorate to 'bully' members of Congress to act (Kernell, 1986). Yet empirical studies show that the president's independent ability to 'move' public opinion is limited and that presidents soon learn the limits of their powers of persuasion (Edwards, 2003).

There is some reason to think that presidential weakness is not uniform, however. The power of the presidency can vary, according to policy area. For many, the clear divide is between foreign and domestic policies. The so-called 'two presidencies' thesis forwards the idea that US has one, relatively weak president when it comes to domestic policy and another, more powerful president when it comes to foreign affairs. The political scientist Robert Dahl identified this as early as his 1950 book *Congress and Foreign Policy* in which he stated that the US president 'has long enjoyed substantial discretion' in foreign policy. Logically, the president has a few key advantages in foreign affairs.

First, the president has a 'first mover advantage'. Because the president has the authority to deploy troops (as commander-in-chief) and engage in negotiations with other countries (as chief diplomat), the president gets to set the agenda in foreign affairs. This means that Congress must be *reactive* to the president's foreign policy initiatives rather than proactive. For example, the president has the constitutional power to negotiate treaties and trade agreements, but it is the responsibility of Congress to ratify them into law. This means that the president has a much stronger ability to influence the details of these agreements than Congress, which can only offer an up-or-down approval of them. A long-time opponent of the North American Free Trade Agreement (NAFTA), President Donald Trump set about replacing the trade deal that had been signed into law by President Bill Clinton in 1993 with a new one of his own. Trump negotiated a new deal with the two relevant partner countries (Canada and Mexico) known as the United States–Mexico–Canada Agreement (USMCA). The trade deal opened up new Canadian markets for US exporters, increased labour standards in Mexico, and secured stronger country of origins rules across the three countries. The agreement was then presented to Congress as a fait accompli. With little room to demand adjustments, Congress overwhelmingly passed the agreement into law in December 2019, by votes of 385 to 41 in the House of Representatives and 89 to 10 in the Senate.

Second, the president has substantial organizational advantages over Congress. The president can receive advice from the literally thousands of expert sources within the civilian and military wings of the executive branch. Congress can collect information too, but, unlike the president, Congress must invite or compel experts to give their testimony, which is a slower, more costly and more arduous process. Jeffrey Taliaferro and colleagues conclude that 'the executive received privileged information from state agencies', which places it in a position to be 'more aware of the national interest and dictates of the international system than are other domestic actors' (Taliaferro et al, 2009: 33).

Third, the president might be said to have more pressing electoral incentives to deal with foreign affairs than individual members of Congress. If there is a foreign policy crisis, citizens typically look first to the White House for leadership, whereas when there are domestic policy failures (for example, social security payments, health insurance access and gun control), citizens will often turn to their member of Congress for assistance. David Mayhew (1974) famously assessed that most behaviour from members of Congress can be rationally analysed if re-election is understood to be most members' primary and overriding goal. Building on Mayhew, Howell contended that 'As members of Congress care foremost about their re-election prospects, they tend to invest more of their resources into direct domestic policy benefits to their home districts and states for which they can claim clear credit come election time' (2013: 135). Foreign policy, in contrast, is a collective good at a national level, which is not easily divisible for 'credit-claiming' by individual members of Congress.

The 'two presidencies' thesis was originally put to empirical scrutiny by Aaron Wildavsky in a 1966 article 'The two presidencies'. Wildavsky (1966) studied the proportion of roll call votes made by members of Congress that corresponded to the president's stated preference. He found that Congress was much more likely to defer to the president's position on foreign policy matters (about 65 per cent of the time) compared to domestic policy matters (about 40 per cent of the time). Other commentators have found empirical support for the thesis (Canes-Wrone et al, 2008). David Lewis (1997) found that presidents were less likely to implore voters to pressure their member of

Congress on foreign policy matters than they were on domestic policy matters. This might suggest that the president needs less 'help' from voters to pressure their representatives on foreign policy issues because Congress is more likely to defer to what the president wants anyway. Bryan Marshall and Richard Pacelle (2005) found that the strength of the president's party in Congress affects the number of executive orders he issues on domestic policy but not on foreign policy. This might suggest that presidents are more hampered on domestic policy than on foreign policy when their party loses control of Congress. That is to say, presidents resort to passing more executive orders on domestic policy to get around needing congressional approval, but when it comes to foreign policy, presidents have less need for executive orders because Congress will support them in statute, whichever party is in control. William Howell (2003) has shown that Congress is less likely to amend or overturn foreign policy directives from the president compared to domestic ones.

Congress has repeatedly tried to impair, constrain and respond to the president's institutional advantages, yet their record of success is mixed. Congress passed the War Powers Resolution in 1973, overriding President Richard Nixon's veto. The Act was intended to respond to the president's first mover advantage by forbidding US troops being sent overseas for more than 60 days without Congressional approval. In spite of the Act's strong wording and the dramatic circumstances of its passage (over Nixon's veto), it is believed to have been violated multiple times. In 1999, Bill Clinton kept the US bombing campaign in Kosovo going a fortnight longer than allowed under the War Powers Act. He was sued by Republican Congressman Tom Campbell for breaking the law, but the federal court threw the case out, saying it was a political, not a judicial, question. In effect, the court deferred to the president. Jeff Yates and Andrew Whitford (1998) find that the Supreme Court is more likely to defer to the president on foreign policy matters than on domestic affairs. In 2011, Barack Obama engaged US forces in Libya, but he informed Congress that he would not seek their approval because he argued that US involvement was limited and not involved in an actual war. The House of Representatives voted to reproach Obama, but he, in effect, got away with ignoring the Act.

There are, however, several reasons to be sceptical of the 'two presidencies' thesis. First, some commentators believe that Wildavsky's argument was contingent on a particular moment in time (Fleisher et al, 2000; Schraufnagel and Shellman, 2001). Wildavsky used as his dataset Congressional roll call votes in the 1940s, 1950s and early 1960s. This was a period of bipartisan agreement on foreign affairs as a result of the particular exigencies of the early years of the Cold War. Foreign policy was simply less contentious during these decades, so it is no surprise Wildavsky found greater agreement in Congress on the president's foreign policy initiatives than his domestic policy ones. Wildavsky even admitted as much in a co-authored piece he wrote with Duane Oldfield in 1989 entitled 'Reconsidering the two presidencies'. Brandon Prins and Bryan Marshall (2001) purported to show empirically that bipartisanship over foreign affairs deceased from the mid-1970s.

Second, some commentators would argue that the 'two presidencies' thesis minimizes presidential success in domestic policy. While presidents might struggle to pass major pieces of legislation through Congress, they can exert tremendous power in the domestic sphere through the executive branch bureaucracy. Some scholars have developed the notion of the 'administrative presidency' to study presidential leadership within the executive branch. Richard Nathan (1975), a pioneer of this concept, asserted that the president extends his power through his control of staff and the executive's bureaucratic organization.

A third critique of the 'two presidencies' thesis is that it unduly separates 'foreign' and 'domestic' policy. It is difficult – and perhaps increasingly difficult – to speak of foreign policy having no domestic implications, and vice versa. In fact, it has long been the case that policies that look ostensibly like 'foreign policy' often have domestic roots. For example, Presidents Eisenhower and Kennedy repeatedly tried to stop the B-70 bomber programme, which would have built super-fast nuclear-equipped planes. The problem was that USSR surface-to-air missiles in the late 1950s made the B-70 obsolete. However, Congress continued to appropriate funds for the project long after Eisenhower and Kennedy had expressed their disapproval. The fact that 21 of the 38 members of the Armed Services Committee would have seen some part of the B-70 manufactured in their congressional districts might have had some role in keeping the bomber programme going (Kotz, 1988). Such local considerations have continued to hamper US presidents' efforts to constrain the US's nuclear arsenal. President Barack Obama was blocked by Congress from trying to reduce the number of nuclear warheads, due to members of Congress seeking to protect jobs and investment in their states and congressional districts (Milner and Tingley, 2015). The House Speaker Tip O'Neill famously said, 'all politics is local'. It seems even nuclear warfare had to contend with local politics, further blurring the lines between domestic and foreign policy.

4

The Legislative Branch

In the realm of foreign policy, the legislative branch is often regarded as playing second fiddle to the executive branch. The executive branch, after all, contains the vital federal Departments of Defense, Homeland Security and State. It is headed by the president, who is commander-in-chief. US diplomats and soldiers are all employed through the executive branch. What, then, remains for Congress when it comes to making and shaping US foreign policy?

Quite a lot as it turns out. The Constitution grants a range of formal powers to Congress that it (and it alone) can exercise in foreign affairs. Article I specifies that it is the duty of Congress to 'provide for the common defense', 'to regulate commerce with foreign nations', to define and punish what constitutes as piracy and illegal acts at sea, 'to declare war', to raise and support armies and navies, to set the rules that govern the military, to ratify treaties, to confirm ambassadorial nominations, and to confirm executive appointments. In addition to these specific foreign policy powers, Congress has other powers with foreign policy implications. In particular, Congress alone can raise and appropriate public funds. Congress sets the budgets and funding conditions for all of the federal executive branches, including the military and the diplomatic corps. Congress funds the presidency. Without Congress, presidents have no source of income to fund their initiatives. This chapter regards the power of the purse as a highly important source of legislative power when it comes to shaping the direction of US foreign policy.

Furthermore, Congress has a duty to provide oversight to the functioning of the federal executive branch. Congress contains numerous committees, and many of these are paired with agencies within the executive branch. These congressional committees spend their time scrutinizing the conduct of the executive branch actors and holding them to account. Finally, Congress has informal powers that it can use to make and shape foreign affairs. Members of Congress, like the president, are political actors. Congress can use its influence in American political debate to raise or lower the political costs of presidents' foreign policy choices. They can even cut deals by promising to support the president's foreign policy agenda in exchange for some domestic policy concessions.

The first section of this chapter situates congressional influence on foreign policy in historical and theoretical context. The next two sections analyse two of the most important formal powers that Congress has: the power to declare war and the power to raise and direct the use of public finances. These sections assess the effectiveness of Congress in using these two powers to shape the course of US foreign policy. The fourth section discusses the role of Congress in scrutinizing the executive branch. The fifth section looks at the informal power Congress has to shape foreign affairs: its political role. While it is useful to examine the official, legal powers Congress has over foreign policy, formal powers alone are not enough to understand the full extent of the influence of Congress on foreign policy. Congress as a partisan and political actor is perhaps where the institution has often been most effective at shaping the direction of US foreign policy, but it is the side of the coin that is sometimes neglected in the academic literature.

Congressional influence on foreign policy in context

A number of commentators have argued that during and after the Second World War, the US president assumed a 'pre-eminence' in foreign affairs (Rockman, 1994). The post-Second World War decades were a period of broad bipartisan consensus on foreign affairs, driven by the imperatives of the Cold War. In 1947, President Harry Truman declared a commitment to contain the spread of communism throughout the world and that the US would offer aid and support to any nation that was engaged in a struggle to protect a liberal democratic constitution from a communist revolution. The **Truman Doctrine** of **containment**, as it became known, placed the US in a position of global leadership where the US was expected to be responsible for the maintenance of the Western liberal, capitalist, democratic global order.

Support for the Truman Doctrine was wide-ranging and was shared across political party. In the 1950s, Richard Nixon, as a Republican member of Congress, and then Dwight Eisenhower's vice president, was as equally supportive of the principle of communist containment as Massachusetts Democratic Senator John F. Kennedy. In the 1960 election, when Kennedy and Nixon faced off against each other, there was little disagreement between the two candidates over the role of the US in preserving this capitalist democratic order. The 1960 Republican party platform concluded with the line, 'We advocate an immovable resistance against every Communist aggression. We argue for a military might commensurate with our universal tasks.'[1] The Democratic platform made a similar commitment, 'we will use all the power, resources, and energy at our command to resist the further encroachment of Communism on freedom.'[2]

This is not to say that there was total agreement in US politics at this time over the desirability of the Truman Doctrine. Senator Robert Taft, who nearly won the Republican nomination for president in 1952, was a staunch critic. But in the mainstream of American public opinion and among elite policy actors, there was a broadly shared commitment in favour of containment and US global leadership, supported by impenetrable US military might and economic prosperity. In this context, Congress was largely compliant towards the requests of the executive when it came to military affairs. This was not because Congress believed that it had no role in foreign policy. It was simply the case that most members of Congress tended to share the same foreign policy commitments as the president, whether that was Truman, Eisenhower or Kennedy.

Many commentators point to the 1960s and 1970s as the decades when this consensus began to fray. The war in Vietnam shattered many Americans' sense that US military might was unchallengeable and undefeatable. Members of Congress grew increasingly weary of presidential commitments to invest further troops in South East Asia, especially as the death tolls began to mount and members of Congress had to start attending more and more funerals of their constituents who had died in the war. Furthermore, the shambles of the Vietnam War embarrassed Congress because it was Congress that had given the Johnson Administration a blank cheque to intervene militarily in its 1964 Gulf of Tonkin Resolution.

At this time, too, presidential administrations took actions that seriously diminished public confidence in their integrity. A 'credibility gap' had grown between President Johnson and the American public over the conduct of the Vietnam War. The Johnson Administration continually claimed that the war was winnable – that victory was just around the corner – while the US military death toll rose into the tens of thousands. In January 1968, an aggressive military push by the North Vietnamese into South Vietnam, called the 'Tet Offensive', led to the deaths and injuries of more Americans than any other part of the war. Within a week, 543 US soldiers were killed and more than 2,500 were injured. The Tet Offensive created a crisis for the Johnson Administration because it left the public (and Congress) believing that the war was unwinnable.

This lack of confidence in the president was intensified in the years to come by the excesses of the Nixon Administration, particularly by the Watergate scandal. In this context, Congress tried to reclaim authority. In response to the scandals of the 1970s, public appetite for legislative scrutiny strengthened. The members of Congress elected in the wake of Watergate in 1974 and 1976, known as the 'Watergate babies', carried a reformist zeal that was far less deferential to the executive branch than in the past (Andelic, 2019). For example, revelations of abuse by the intelligence agencies – such as covert operations, political assassinations, spying on political activists and eavesdropping by the National Security Council – provoked congressional action. A special committee of the US Senate (the Church Committee) and a select committee of the US House of Representatives (the Pike Committee) conducted high-profile enquiries, which led to the permanent establishment of the Select Committee on Intelligence in the US Senate. Loch Johnson calls 1975 an '*annus mirabilis*' for legislative accountability over the executive branch (Johnson, 2008: 199). Others have called it the 'Year of Intelligence' (*The New York Times*, 1975). The following year, Washington outsider and political reformer Jimmy Carter was elected to the presidency. Carter signed into law a raft of significant pieces of oversight legislation. The most noteworthy of these were the Inspector General Act, the Civil Service Reform Act and the Ethics in Government Act. These Acts pertained to executive oversight, ethics and good government rather than foreign policy directly, but they were indicative of a turn in congressional posture when the legislature sought to assert itself over the president much more strongly.

Scholars who hold the view that the post-Vietnam Congress retook the political initiative on foreign affairs are sometimes known as 'the resurgence school' (Melanson, 1996). However, other commentators have critiqued the resurgence school account. They argue that while members of Congress became rhetorically more hostile towards presidential actions overseas after Vietnam, in practice, Congress remained pretty compliant. They may have spoken with a sharper tongue, but they continued to swallow the president's foreign policy initiatives. For example, there has almost never been a war that Congress has stopped. Congress acquiesced to Ronald Reagan's invasion of Grenada, George H.W. Bush's invasion of Panama, Bill

Clinton's bombings in the Balkans and George W. Bush's wars in Afghanistan and Iraq. Commentators who doubt that Congress has become more assertive form 'the acquiescence school' (Hinckley, 1994; Hendrickson, 2015).

James Scott and Ralph Carter (2002) have proposed a way to resolve these two conflicting views by separating out the content and volume of congressional activity (that is, what it does *versus* how much it does). In their article 'Acting on the Hill', they argue that the *level* of formal congressional activity in foreign affairs has declined since the Second World War. Congress is passing fewer bills and issuing fewer declarations about foreign policy now than they were before the Vietnam War. However, the *content* of Congress's action has become more assertive. Although Congress is doing less, when it does take action on foreign policy matters, it does so in a way that is much more antagonistic towards the president than before the Vietnam period.

Scott and Carter believe that there are four types of actions Congress can take on foreign affairs: compliance; resistance/modification; rejection; and independence/entrepreneurship. **Compliance** refers to when Congress accedes to a president's request with little protest. Examples include the Gulf of Tonkin Resolution in 1964 and the Authorization for the Use of Force Against Terrorism in 2001. In both of these instances, Congress decided to give broad approval for the use of force overseas, in spite of a relatively short period of time to review the evidence and consider the implications fully. In both instances, a crisis (or perceived crisis) drove Congress to act hastily and comply with the president's requests.

Resistance/modification refers to when Congress broadly accepts what the president wants but forces the president to compromise, modifying his proposals. For example, in the 1990s, President Bill Clinton asked Congress to approve $18 billion to fund the International Monetary Fund (IMF), but the Republican majority in Congress forced Clinton to request structural changes to the IMF before they agreed to appropriate the money. During the Obama presidency, the president's military generals advised Obama to support a 'surge' of US troops into Afghanistan to quell spiralling violence. Congress, however, contained a large number of sceptics of the wisdom of sending more troops into Afghanistan, not least from members of his own party. To placate their criticism, Obama announced a surge of troops in Afghanistan, but also announced that he would be withdrawing them after 18 months.

Rejection refers to when Congress fails to approve the president's request. There are many examples of this, such as the Senate's rejection of the Comprehensive Test Ban Treaty in 1999, Congress blocking President Obama's attempt to close Guantanamo Bay prison in 2009, and Congress's refusal to bring the Trans-Pacific Partnership (TPP) to a vote in 2016, effectively scuttling the US's participation in the TPP.

Finally, independence/entrepreneurship relates to when Congress acts on foreign policy without the president's lead and/or in defiance of the president's preferences. On these occasions, Congress is effectively crafting its own foreign policy. Sometimes these acts of policy entrepreneurship are of relatively low salience, such as when Congress insists on funding defence projects that the president hasn't requested because they support jobs in their districts. Others, however, can be acts of major consequence, such as Congress's vote to override Ronald Reagan's veto in 1986 and place sanctions on apartheid South Africa. Congress's 1995 vote to move the US Embassy from Tel Aviv to Jerusalem caused irritation for Presidents Clinton, Bush and Obama, who all 'delayed' the implementation of this instruction due to worries about its impact on the peace process. House Republicans' invitation of Israeli Prime Minister Binyamin Netanyahu to speak to a joint session of Congress in 2015 was a clear repudiation of Barack Obama's approach to Israel and an embarrassment to the Obama Administration, which refused to give its blessing to Netanyahu's visit.

Based on the prevalence of these different types of actions, Scott and Carter (2002) develop a typology for how we should think about Congresses at different points in time:

- Supportive (high activity, low assertiveness)
- Competitive (high activity, high assertiveness)
- Disengaged (low activity, low assertiveness)
- Strategic (low activity, high assertiveness).

Congress's disposition towards the president varies according to circumstance. When the stakes are low, such as during peacetime and periods of global stability, Congress is more likely to take an assertive role. But when the stakes are high, such as in the wake of an immediate external threat or period of global instability, Congress is more likely to defer to the president. For example, in the 1990s, a period of high global stability and economic prosperity, Congress continually blocked payment of the US's membership dues to the UN. However, after the September 11 terrorist attacks, Congress became extremely supportive of the president. Not only did Congress grant broad authority to the president to intervene militarily against terrorists anywhere in the world, but it also agreed to engage with the international world in a more constructive posture than before. For example, Congress agreed with President Bush's request to pay the US's long backdated UN dues and agreed to lift sanctions on the military regime in Pakistan, both 'unthinkable' before 9/11.

Additionally, the measurable success of the president's foreign policy initiatives matter. When the president is doing well, Congress is less likely to get involved than when his policies seem to be going awry. Hendrickson (2015) contends that party leaders do their best to avoid tying their party and Congress to potentially unpopular military incursions, especially when the public is reticent about troop deployment abroad. This is one of the challenges Barack Obama faced when considering whether or not to intervene in Syria, for example.

Power to declare war

Having discussed the historical and theoretical context of Congress and foreign policy, we must now look at the formal institutional powers of the legislative branch. In particular, focus should be given to the power of Congress to declare war and to control spending. On the first measure, the power to declare war, Congress at first glance seems to have been remarkably neglectful. Congress has not declared war on another country since 1942. People often cite this fact as evidence of congressional weakness. However, it would be wrong to think that Congress has not given its blessing to any US military interventions since the Second World War. Congress has provided 'authorization' on at least six occasions since 1957. An authorization lacks the formal status of a declaration of war, but it is in effect doing the same thing. Both declarations of war and authorizations for the use of force send American troops abroad to fight in dangerous conflicts.

The first of these authorizations in the post-Second World War period was Congress's Joint Resolution to Promote Stability in the Middle East. The resolution stated, 'if the President determines the necessity thereof, the United States is prepared to use armed forces to assist any such nation or group of such nations requesting assistance against armed aggression from any country controlled by international communism'.[3] President Eisenhower used this resolution the following year to send over 8,000 US troops to Lebanon, on the request of the Lebanese President Camille Chamoun, to prevent a pro-communist pan-Arabist takeover in the country.

Perhaps the most famous (or infamous) of these authorizations was the Gulf of Tonkin Resolution. The resolution was passed in 1964 after US intelligence claimed that a US warship, the USS *Maddox*, had been fired upon in the Gulf of Tonkin between China and North Vietnam. With only nine hours of debate, Congress quickly voted through a resolution that gave the president broad powers in South East Asia. The Gulf of Tonkin Resolution stated, 'the United States is, therefore, prepared, as the President determines, to take all necessary steps, including the use of armed force, to assist any member or protocol state of the Southeast Asia Collective Defense Treaty requesting assistance in defense of its freedom'.[4] Congress passed the Gulf of Tonkin Resolution with huge majorities. In the House of Representatives, not a single member voted against it. In the Senate, only two senators, both Democrats, voted against. One of the senators who voted against, Democrat Senator Wayne Morse, only did so because he believed that the authorization needed to take the form of a formal declaration of war. The Gulf of Tonkin authorization became the legal basis on which the war in Vietnam was fought. A report by the National Security Agency in 2005 concluded that in fact there had been no aggression towards USS *Maddox* in the Gulf of Tonkin on the night in question, and that it is possible that the USS *Maddox* confused bad weather for an enemy attack. President Lyndon Johnson privately conceded that the Vietcong may not have attacked the USS *Maddox*, remarking, 'For all I know, our Navy was shooting at whales out there' (Goulden, 1969: 160).

Another authorization worth highlighting because of its enduring geopolitical consequences is the 2001 Authorization for Use of Military Force. This was passed three days after the September 11, 2001 attacks in New York, Pennsylvania and Virginia. The resolution provided extremely broad authority: 'That the President is authorized to use all necessary and appropriate force against those nations, organizations, or persons he determines planned, authorized, committed, or aided the terrorist attacks that occurred on September 11, 2001, or harbored such organizations or persons.'[5] Congress passed this resolution with an overwhelming majority. It did not receive a single vote against in the Senate, and only one member of the House of Representatives voted against it. The one opponent, Barbara Lee of California, presciently warned that the authorization would be another Gulf of Tonkin Resolution. In many ways, this was an understatement. Its main authorization was to permit the US invasion of Afghanistan to remove the Taliban regime that had provided shelter to the al-Qaeda organization. However, the authorization has been interpreted broadly to facilitate US military incursions in counter-terrorism activities in Libya, Syria, Yemen, Somalia and Iraq since the emergence of ISIS after the Arab Spring.

While Congress has not passed a piece of legislation that is formally phrased as a 'declaration of war', these authorizations amount to something similar. The wisdom of these authorizations may be questioned, but it is an exaggeration to say that Congress has played no role in sending US troops abroad since the Second World War.

As discussed in the previous chapter, however, the US president enjoys a 'first mover' advantage in foreign affairs. Because the president is commander-in-chief of the armed forces, he is empowered to direct US troops according to his instructions. This includes his ability to deploy troops overseas. While the president should constitutionally request congressional authorization for the use of force, once troops are in a conflict situation, it becomes more difficult for Congress to chastise the president and to ask for the troops to be returned home.

Congress has, however, attempted to limit the president's ability to sends troops overseas without pre-authorization from Congress. The most significant legislative constraint is the War Powers Act of 1973. President Richard Nixon vetoed the Act but Congress overpowered the president's veto with a two-thirds majority. The War Powers Act provides a statutory guide to when and how presidents can send troops into war and for how long. The Act says that a president can send troops into war only under three conditions: a formal declaration of war; an authorization for the use of force; or 'a national emergency created by an attack upon the United States, its territories, or its armed forces'.[6] The War Powers Act clarifies that if the president follows the third path, 'in every possible instance [he] shall consult with Congress' before sending forces into hostilities. The term 'consultation' has ironically empowered the president. 'Consultation' is different than specifying that the president needs to *ask* Congress's permission before sending armed forces into hostilities. 'Consult' in practice has transformed into 'inform' after the decision was already taken.

Let us consider the example of President Ronald Reagan's invasion of Grenada. In October 1983, the prime minister of Grenada, Maurice Bishop, was kidnapped and murdered. Bishop was a socialist, but he chose to keep Grenada 'non-aligned' in the Cold War struggle between the US and the USSR. Bishop was replaced by a military dictatorship through the People's Revolutionary Army (PRA). The PRA were staunchly pro-Soviet and invited Cuban engineers and military personnel to Grenada to build its defence capabilities. Fearing Grenada could become another Soviet outpost in the Caribbean, Reagan reacted by sending US troops to invade Grenada, partly under the pretence that American students at a medical university were endangered. The day before the invasion President Reagan invited congressional leaders to the White House to 'inform' them that the invasion was going to take place. Reagan officials argued that this was consistent with the 'consultation' language of the War Powers Resolution. Others have called it an 'egregious violation of the War Powers Resolution' (Hendrickson, 2015: 92).

One of the problems with this criticism is how realistic is it to expect the president to 'ask for permission' before each military engagement. Sometimes military operations demand speed and secrecy to be effective. How does the president meet those goals while also satisfying his War Powers Resolution requirements to 'consult' with Congress? The War Powers Act still gives the president considerable leeway to use his first mover advantage. After US troops enter a warzone, Congress has an incentive to be compliant with the president's mission. They want to be seen as loyal to the mission and US troops. This is sometimes called the 'rally around the flag' phenomenon (Phillips, 2006: 388). The example of the powerful Georgia Democrat Senator Richard Russell captures this well. Russell had been a long-standing opponent of US military build-up in Vietnam. He had expressed his opposition as early as 1954. Yet, by 1965, Russell had abandoned his opposition to the war. He wrote in a letter to his constituent, 'Every protest will cause the Communists to believe they can win if they hold on a little longer.... We are there now, and the time for debate has passed. Our flag is committed, and – more importantly – American boys are under fire' (quoted in Herring, 1987: 185). President Johnson had sufficiently raised the stakes such that opposition to the president's foreign policy was not a simple question of policy disagreement. Disagreement was portrayed as a danger to American lives.

Members of Congress might protest the president's actions abroad, but the president usually evades sanction. Presidents have simply ignored Congress altogether and gotten away with it. This was the case with the US military involvement in Libya in 2011. As mentioned in the previous chapter, President Obama did not bother asking Congress for permission to use US forces in Libya. In fact, Obama wrote a letter to Congress explaining to them why he didn't need to ask for their approval. The House of Representatives voted *against* giving Obama authorization to use force (123 votes in favour, 295 votes against), but he did so anyway. Obama has since described the US intervention in Libya (and the failure to have a plan to secure the country after the invasion) as the 'worst mistake' of his presidency.

Power of the purse

Senator Robert Byrd described the power of the purse as 'the greatest power in our constitutional system' (Schmitt, 1995). As discussed in Chapter 3, the Department of Defense, the US military and the intelligence services are all housed within the executive branch. However, they all depend for their funding on the legislative branch. Only Congress can raise and appropriate public funds. Because presidents cannot make durable policy decisions without sustained funding, they must always turn to Congress for fiscal support eventually. For this reason, Helen Milner and Dustin Tingley describe Congress as a 'long-term constraint' on the president (2015: xii).

In one sense, the power of the purse can be highly effective. If Congress can shut off the taps from which financial resources flow, it makes continued military efforts difficult, hazardous and unfeasible. One of the most visible examples of Congress asserting its authority was in the later stages of the Vietnam War. In 1970, Congress passed the Special Foreign Assistance Act, which provided funding for the continuation of the war in South East Asia. Congress attached to the bill a line that prohibited defence appropriations from being used in Cambodia. The line read, 'none of the funds authorized ... may be used to finance the introduction of United States ground combat troops into Cambodia, or to provide United States advisers to or for Cambodian military forces in Cambodia'.[7] In effect, Congress was using its power of the purse to prevent the Nixon Administration from continuing military interventions in Cambodia. It should be noted that the precise language of the bill was written after extensive negotiation between congressional leaders and the Nixon White House. However, this bill was still extremely significant, because it is doubtful whether Nixon would have withdrawn from Cambodia if Congress had not forced his hand.

Relatively soon afterwards, Congress used its appropriations powers to limit the US role in South East Asia further. After the Paris Peace Accords in 1973, Congress refused to appropriate any further funds to support combat missions in Vietnam. This ended up tying President Gerald Ford's hands quite considerably as North Vietnam proceeded to invade South Vietnam in 1975. Ford was unable to respond militarily to counter the invasion of Saigon or even to send armed troops to protect US forces. The result was a panicked evacuation, with thousands of US Embassy staff and Vietnamese who had worked for the US government hastily evacuated in helicopters. Henry Kissinger, who served as secretary of state for Nixon and Ford, never forgave

Congress for this. In his 2003 book *Ending the Vietnam War* Kissinger accused Congress of effectively losing South Vietnam to communism due to their meddling. The 1973 Case-Church amendment cut off all funds for military operations in Indochina, which meant in Kissinger's eyes 'that Congress would, in effect, cut off aid to a beleaguered ally'. When Saigon was invaded, 'Congress exhibited no urgency about responding to Ford's request' for support, which, according to Kissinger, resulted in 'strangling America's allies' in South Vietnam (Kissinger, 2003: 544, 511).

While potent, the power of the purse is an extremely blunt instrument. The political costs of using this power can be high. Members of Congress who try to cut off funding to the military open themselves up to the accusation of not supporting the troops and putting American servicemen and servicewomen in harm's way. Many commentators have focused on the role of Congress in *declaring* war. Fewer scholars have looked at the role of Congress after war is underway. In some cases this is because commentators, such as James Meernik (1994), regard Congress as largely irrelevant. Meernik writes that the president alone 'exercises supreme control over the nation's military actions' (1994: 122–3). However, as we have seen, when it comes to Congress's power of the purse, Congress can have influence on the endurance of a military operation and can bring intervention to a speedy, if inelegant, end.

Congressional oversight

One of the hallmarks of the American legislative system is its tradition of strong, autonomous, specialist committees. In the US agencies that fall under the federal executive are subject to strict oversight from the federal legislature. Some presidents, most notably George W. Bush, have attempted to overturn this well-established overlapping relationship of accountability through the promotion of the idea of a 'unitary executive', but Bush's argument that the federal executive departments could act without regard to Congress has found little support among constitutional scholars (Waterman, 2009). Article I of the US Constitution provides Congress with numerous justifications for monitoring the federal executive, most obviously over the funding of executive agencies and the confirmation process of leadership positions.

Both the House and Senate have their own committees that overlap. When it comes to military affairs, the Department of Defense is scrutinized by the House and Senate Armed Services Committees.

When it comes to foreign affairs, the State Department is scrutinized by the House Committee on Foreign Affairs and the Senate Foreign Relations Committee. These committees also have subcommittees within them that specialize further on certain subject matters. For example, the Foreign Relations Committee has a subcommittee on European Affairs, another on African and Middle Eastern Affairs, and so on. These committees scrutinize their respective department. They review its performance, address any shortcomings and, perhaps most importantly of all, determine whether the department is spending taxpayers' money well. Committees have substantial input on the budget process for the department they monitor.

Committees in the US Congress are defined by their small size, independent budgets, permanent support staff, subject specialism and power to investigate and collect evidence. Many observers argue that committees are where members of Congress can really get stuck in and develop a policy specialism. The quality of debate is theoretically higher because committee members are drawn to join a committee by virtue of their interest in the subject area (for example, environment, agriculture, healthcare, and so on). Members work together, sometimes over many years, which can create a kind of committee solidarity and comradery.

In her book *Watchdogs on the Hill*, Linda Fowler (2015) argues that the Senate Armed Services Committee and the Senate Foreign Relations Committee have been particularly bad at exercising oversight. She argues that this is in part because the committees have a desire to protect the military's reputation and to promote the image of unity. Senators are concerned that disagreement at home might damage the US's image abroad. Fowler argues that senators form a committee solidarity, which means that they err towards consensus, even at the expense of proper scrutiny. She thinks this is particularly true when Republicans occupy the White House, whom Fowler believes have a higher reputation of competence in foreign affairs. In her book, Fowler argues that such preferences led to the Armed Services Committee failing to scrutinize serious failings at the Walter Reed Army Hospital in Washington, DC in 2007. It took newspapers and a media frenzy ('sounding the fire alarm') for senators to act in response to lurid allegations of appalling conditions in which former servicemen and servicewomen were housed.

Oversight is intended to ensure executive branch accountability, but 'accountability' is an exceedingly ambiguous concept. There are numerous mechanisms for accountability: reporting requirements, professional codes of ethics, oaths of office, merit-based hiring and promotion, responsiveness to political principals through partisan attachment, performance targets, performance budgeting, elections, and more. However, some of these mechanisms, such as elections and merit-based hiring, are not inherently compatible. This suggests that the practical expression of 'accountability' is contingent on the contextual priorities of a particular system.

Theoretically, there are two ways that members of Congress exercise oversight. Oversight can be prospective (that is, monitoring to make sure everything is chugging along smoothly) or retrospective (that is, reactive to when something goes wrong). Matthew McCubbins and Thomas Schwartz, in a 1984 article 'Congressional oversight overlooked', proposed two ways of thinking about congressional oversight. They called the prospective oversight approach the 'police patrol' model and the retrospective approach the 'fire alarm model'. McCubbins and Schwartz argued that members of Congress prefer 'fire alarms' to 'police patrols' because they take less of members of Congress's time, and members of Congress gain more visibility for 'putting out fires' than 'sniffing out smoke' (McCubbins and Schwartz, 1987: 429). By adopting a decentralized, 'fire alarm' model of bureaucratic oversight, members of Congress also tend to rely on constituents and relevant interest groups to monitor the federal bureaucracy on their behalf. Accordingly, constituents are expected to notify their representative if there is a performance failure within a federal executive agency. This gives members an electoral incentive to intervene directly within the bureaucracy to adjust agency operation to be more reflective of the electorate's preferences.

This preference for fire alarms perhaps makes sense when it comes to making sure that veterans are getting access to free healthcare, that students are receiving their Pell grant on time,[8] or that a federal infrastructure project is completed on time. But it can be a bit more awkward when it comes to foreign affairs. For example, when a scandal arises about the US military, it not only makes the US government look bad, but it can potentially damage troop morale overseas or become a propaganda tool by foreign actors. Similarly, it is one thing when a constituent writes to their member of Congress sounding the fire alarm; it is another thing when the person or entity sounding the alarm is a foreign citizen or foreign government.

Political influence

Beyond its formal powers, Congress can influence the course of US foreign policy through informal means. Congress is a political body, not simply a legal one. In order for presidents to secure Congress's legal (formal) support, there must be some level of political agreement. Even when Congress cannot stop a president's actions in the foreign policy space in the immediate term, it can cause a president to regret his actions and make his life difficult through political critique and contestation. Congress can shape the political context in which a president operates. At the very least, this informal influence means that Congress remains relevant in foreign policy.

In *After the Rubicon*, Douglas Kriner (2010) argues that presidents are constantly anticipating congressional reactions to their foreign policy. Members of Congress can raise or lower the costs of continuing to wage war in a number of ways. Congress can lower the political costs for a president by tying its institutional prestige to a president's military or foreign decisions. But when Congress is opposed to or critical of presidential actions abroad, it can make its disagreement known – not just by formal sanction, but also by influencing the political dynamics. Members of Congress can criticize the president publicly. They can even campaign against the president.

Members can also express their dissatisfaction with the president's foreign policy by undermining his domestic policy agenda. The term that is sometimes used is 'intermestic' policy, which is a portmanteau for 'international and domestic' policy. It acknowledges how interlinked these two areas of policy can be. Several presidents have found that the domestic policies and programmes that they wanted to get passed fail after Congress becomes uncooperative in response to an unpopular war. Lyndon Johnson's presidency was ultimately undone by the Vietnam War. His Civil Rights Bill of 1966 failed to pass Congress in part because of the growing unpopularity of the war. He failed to implement the recommendations of the Kerner Commission Report on Civil Disorders in 1968 because of congressional unhappiness with the Vietnam War. Johnson ultimately decided not to run for re-election in 1968 because of the mounting unpopularity of the war.

George W. Bush faced a similar problem in the mid-2000s as the Iraq War mounted in unpopularity. In his second term, Bush had two major domestic policy initiatives: privatizing social security and granting a path to legal status for illegal immigrants. Both failed, in part, because the Iraq War had ruined Bush's credibility and his popularity in Congress. Indeed, Bush lost control of both houses of Congress in 2006 on the back of the unpopular Iraq War.

Therefore, while Congress might not be very good at stopping a president from going to war, it can still be quite effective at shaping the duration, scale and scope of military intervention by forcing the president to anticipate how much Congress would tolerate politically.

For example, President George H.W. Bush concluded that the costs of overthrowing Saddam Hussein were too high – not only for the military, but also in terms of whether Congress and the public would support a drawn-out invasion and occupation of the country. He therefore decided to limit his mission in 1991 to driving Iraqi troops from Kuwait. Similarly, archival sources reveal that while President Reagan was advised by the Department of Defense to maintain troops in Grenada after the successful overthrow of the PRA, Reagan decided not do so because he was aware that congressional support for a lengthier occupation was unlikely. If Reagan had worked harder to win congressional buy-in at the start of the invasion, he may have found a more pliant Congress to support a sustained US presence in the later stages. The Grenada case shows the long-term costs that presidents incur from disrespecting congressional authority.

Congress can even constrain presidential action that seemingly carries public support. The Battle of Mogadishu in October 1993 is remembered for the shooting down of two US Black Hawk helicopters, memorialized in the film *Black Hawk Down*. After this incident and the humiliation of the killed soldiers being dragged through the streets of Mogadishu, President Bill Clinton withdrew US troops from the mission in Somalia. What is often forgotten is that the US public actually wanted retaliation, not withdrawal. It was Congress that pressured Clinton to withdraw from Somalia, pressure that had begun even before the Black Hawk Down tragedy. As a consequence of this fiasco, Congress placed strict limitations on the scope of the US military effort in Rwanda during the genocide in the country the following year. Congress limited President Clinton to use the military only to support US citizens in the country, leaving the internecine warfare to continue. As many as one million people died in the bloodshed.

Conclusion

Commentators from 'the acquiescence school' of congressional scholarship lament what they perceive to be Congress's weakness in the face of executive power in foreign affairs. I think we should question, however, whether a more assertive Congress necessarily means a more influential Congress. Simply looking at the absence of formal congressional action to constrain presidents is insufficient to drawing the conclusion that Congress is 'powerless' when it comes to military intervention. Congress can change the political calculus for incumbent presidents, and presidents who ignore Congress can sustain long-term damage.

Yet this relationship is ultimately reciprocal. If Congress acts too competitively towards a president's foreign policy agenda, then they may drive a president to act unilaterally anyway. There is a potential 'backlash' effect whereby presidents become fatigued by their battles with Congress on foreign affairs and decide not to deal with them at all, thus further marginalizing an assertive Congress. For example, Barack Obama expended enormous time and energy on the New Strategic Arms Reduction Treaty (START) with Russia in the first two years of his presidency. While the Senate finally ratified the treaty 71–26, it took Obama until the 'lame duck session' of the 2010 Congress (December 2010) to ratify a treaty he had agreed with Russia more than a year earlier. This experience burned Obama, and it meant that when it came to the Comprehensive Nuclear Test Ban Treaty, Obama embraced the Treaty but did not bother asking the Senate to ratify it. By being excessively contentious with the first Treaty, Congress ensured that it was sidelined by Obama the second time around.

The relationship between the legislative and executive branches is complicated, fluid and often abstruse. Yet, while both branches can exert dramatic displays of foreign policy autonomy from time to time, ultimately neither can operate without the consent of the other branch for too long. Congress's formal powers can, on the face of it, seem sometimes neglected. Yet, as a political body, there is no doubt that Congress can make presidents' lives a misery. A foreign policy misstep can endanger not only a long-term military or diplomatic mission, but also a president's domestic agenda.

Congress is also where the American public are most visibly represented in the federal government. The direct relationship between members of Congress and their constituents means that members see themselves as having an important role in being the voice of the public in the face of the sometimes stuffy foreign policy and military establishment based in the DC beltway. Congress also has an educative function. Its oversight informs the public, spurs debate and increases scrutiny of the administration's conduct of foreign relations. But is it right to think that the American public want this role? Americans are notoriously unknowledgeable about the rest of the world. Is the American public apathetic about foreign affairs? This will be the subject of the next chapter, as we turn to look at public opinion.

PART III

The Politicians and Publics of US Foreign Policy

5

Public Opinion, the Media
and Partisanship

For decades, academics, politicians and media commentators have debated the role of public opinion in US foreign policy (Johnstone and Laville, 2010). One dimension of this debate has been normative. The very principle of public influence in foreign policy has been questioned. *Should* the average citizen be able to influence foreign policy outcomes given the stakes and complexity involved? Those who think so emphasize the benign effects of an engaged public in pushing policymakers to make the 'right' decisions and sanctioning them at the ballot box when they get it wrong. The theory of democratic peace is partly premised on the notion that voters in democracies constrain their leaders from pursuing reckless militarism. On the other side, for many years commentators have warned that the American public does not know very much about foreign affairs. According to this perspective, foreign policy requires specialist knowledge, which ordinary voters lack. Regrettably, the ignorant public pressures politicians to make simplistic, moralistic and ill-judged decisions to satisfy transient public moods and the public's hungering for 'quick results', even when these decisions do not serve objective US interests (Morgenthau, 1973 [1948]: 135, 146–8).

There is also an empirical debate over the extent to which the public influences foreign policy. There are daunting methodological challenges to measuring the causal effect of public opinion on any policy outcomes, let alone on those in the foreign policy realm. Yet, the fact that politicians seem to *perceive* that public opinion matters can lead us at the very least to rule out the view that public opinion is *irrelevant* to foreign policy. Politicians ignore the public mood at their peril. Protests against the war in Vietnam compelled President Lyndon Johnson to withdraw his campaign for re-election in 1968, in spite of having been elected four years earlier with an astonishing 61 per cent of the vote. His Democratic predecessor Harry Truman faced a similar fate in 1952 when the war in Korea was unresolved. In 1976, Gerald Ford's seeming ignorance about Soviet domination in Poland may have cost him the presidency. The unpopular war in Iraq arguably handed the Democrats joint control of Congress in 2006 and contributed to anti-war Senator Barack Obama's upset against the pro-war Senator Hillary Clinton in the 2008 Democratic nomination contest. Public fatigue with the wars in Afghanistan and Iraq may have indirectly played a role in the rise of Donald Trump (Kriner and Shen, 2020).

This chapter engages with these debates but also considers the process by which Americans gather information about foreign affairs. Parties and the media, this chapter argues, play significant roles. Not only are parties and the media conduits of information, but these organizations also use their influence to mobilize the public. Over a century ago, President William McKinley, who expanded the US's vast overseas imperial territories, was known to be so concerned about media coverage during the Spanish–American War that he read as many as 18 different newspapers a day (Smith, 2010). In the contemporary era, this preoccupation with the media has only intensified. Donald Trump, in many ways a creation of the media, famously watched Fox News most days as president, and would sometimes 'live tweet' his commentary. It is important to understand the partisan and ideological filters through which voters interpret information about foreign events. Before measuring the extent to which voters influence foreign policy, we must understand their underlying motivations for wanting to influence foreign policy in the first place.

To do this, the chapter is divided into four sections, with each answering a different question. First, the chapter asks, 'What do Americans think about foreign policy?' This section looks at both the content of Americans' thoughts about foreign policy as well as their level of interest (and apathy). The second section interrogates the question, 'To what extent do Americans agree with each other on foreign policy?' In this section, we explore how partisanship and ideology influence voters' assumptions about America's role in the world. Third, the chapter asks, 'How do Americans gather information about foreign policy?' This section uncovers the sources from which Americans learn about the wider world and the US's role in it. The fourth section looks at how Americans try to convey these thoughts to their elected officials. It explores the question, 'How do ordinary Americans mobilize to change foreign policy?' It looks at the extent to which Americans influence foreign policy. When Americans express a view about their country's role in the world, how well do policymakers listen? The chapter concludes that the American public (in general) does not have a sustained interest in foreign affairs, but public opinion sets the background conditions for policymakers. When policymakers deviate from these background conditions, they are liable to face electoral sanction.

Public knowledge

It is an unflattering cliché, widely repeated outside the US, that Americans know relatively little about the rest of the world. This impression is partly based on the observation that Americans are less likely to spend time outside their own country than people from other countries, especially Europeans – 83 per cent of people in England and Wales have a passport (ONS, 2013) compared to just 46 per cent of American citizens.[1] This figure is high by historical US standards. When the US invaded Afghanistan in 2003, just 21 per cent of Americans had a passport. When the Berlin Wall came down in 1989, only 3 per cent of Americans had passports to travel to the newly unified Germany (*The Telegraph*, 2018). According to YouGov, 48 per cent of Americans have never travelled abroad compared to only 8 per cent of people in the UK. Part of this difference is explained by geography and some of it by American political economy. For example, Americans have no federal right to paid holiday leave, whereas British workers have the right to 28 days paid holiday. But it is also about worldview. In the same YouGov survey, respondents were asked if money were not a problem, would they choose to go on holiday at home or abroad? A total of 43 per cent of Americans said they would go on holiday in the US compared to 19 per cent of British who said they would go on holiday in Britain (Moore and Dahlgreen, 2014).

Various studies reveal relatively low levels of knowledge about foreign politics among the American public compared to citizens of peer democracies. James Curran and colleagues published a study in 2009 in the *European Journal of Communication* that surveyed American, British and Danish respondents about foreign affairs. Respondents were asked a set of basic questions about international politics. For example, 'Who is president of France?' 'What is the Kyoto Agreement about?' They found that Americans scored much lower than residents of the two comparator countries, even on questions with direct relevance to the US, such as 'Where are the Taliban from?' (Curran et al, 2009).

The pattern has held in more recent studies. A 2019 survey conducted by Gallup on behalf of the Council on Foreign Relations

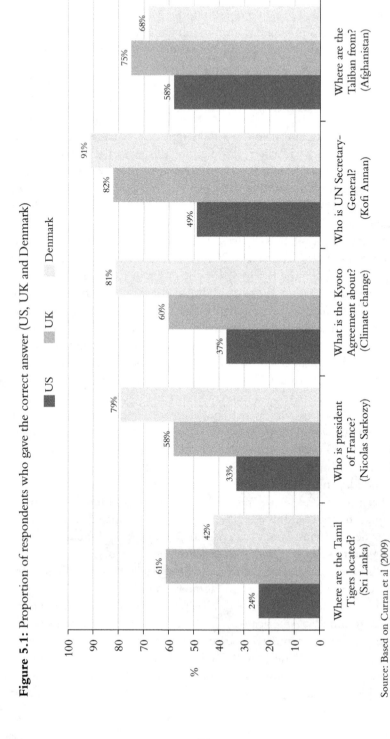

Figure 5.1: Proportion of respondents who gave the correct answer (US, UK and Denmark)

Source: Based on Curran et al (2009)

and National Geographic found alarmingly high levels of ignorance among the American public about basic details of foreign affairs. Less than half of respondents (47 per cent) could correctly identify Afghanistan as the country that harboured al-Qaeda in advance of the September 11, 2001 attacks, in spite of the fact that the US had been at war in Afghanistan for nearly two decades by the time of the poll.

These data lead to dispiriting conclusions about the American public: untravelled, unworldly and unknowledgeable. It has been said that when politicians debate foreign policy issues in front of the American public they 'waltz before a blind audience' (Aldrich et al, 1989). Over the decades, many commentators have simply concluded that Americans are apathetic about foreign affairs. When First Lady Melania Trump wore a jacket emblazoned with the words, 'I really don't care. Do U [sic]?', she could have been offering an analysis of general US attitudes towards foreign policy. Philip Converse (1964), a leading scholar of public opinion during the Cold War, argued that the American public's views on foreign policy were unstructured and incoherent. John Dewey, the early 20th-century commentator, wrote that Americans were liable to act from 'crudely intelligized emotion and from habit rather than rational consideration' (1954 [1927]: 334). Dewey argued that it would take a 'new race of human beings' to be an 'omnicompetent individual' who could know about the relevant aspects of foreign policy (1954 [1927]: 158).

Some commentators are quite nonplussed about this ignorance. An apathetic public means that foreign policy is left to those 'in the know'. Because most of the public don't know or don't care about foreign policy, it means that the sort of people who do set the course of US foreign policy are those who are informed about geography, diplomacy, history and other matters of world affairs. This group of Americans who take an active interest in foreign affairs is sometimes called the 'attentive public' (Melanson, 2000: 36). Figures vary for the proportion of Americans who constitute the 'attentive public', but some scholars think that about 10 per cent of the public have a sustained interest in US foreign policy, while the remainder of the US population is disengaged, except during periods of acute foreign policy crisis or war (Almond, 1962 [1950]; Small, 1991).

Another viewpoint along these lines is that while Americans as a whole are apathetic about foreign affairs, there are subsections of the population who are motivated by and knowledgeable about specific issues, perhaps because they affect them directly (for example, Jews on Israel, manufacturer workers' unions on trade, Irish Americans on peace in Northern Ireland, and so on). As Robert Lieberman contends, 'even relatively small groups can exercise considerable influence if they are strongly connected to a particular issue and the rest of the public largely indifferent' (2009: 140). These are sometimes called 'issue publics'. Most Americans stay out of foreign policy debates in general, but from time to time, subgroups of Americans may get involved when their 'special subject' comes up. These issue publics will be discussed in detail in Chapters 6 and 7.

Other commentators look at the same data and are much less complacent. They agree that Americans are ignorant about foreign policy, but they are concerned that poorly informed Americans seek to influence US foreign policy anyway. The public, in its hubris, might simply get things 'wrong' and push their elected leaders to pursue policies that actively harm the US and its interests because they don't really understand the issues. There is some evidence that the public is dangerously uninformed on basic matters of foreign affairs. Richard Sobel (1989) found that in the year in which Congress approved $24 million to support the right-wing Contra rebels against the socialist Sandinista government in Nicaragua (1984), more Americans thought that the US government was supporting the socialist government than the right-wing rebels.

Because of these risks, some American commentators have argued from a normative position that the American public *should* stay out of foreign policy. They fear that the American public is boorish and overreactive. An early proponent of this view was the American journalist Walter Lippmann who argued, 'The unhappy truth is that the prevailing public opinion has been destructively wrong at critical junctures. The people have impressed a critical veto upon the judgements of informed and responsible officials.' The public were, in Lippmann's estimation, 'too pacifist in peace and too bellicose in war' (Lippmann, 1955: 20).

There are, however, defenders of the ordinary American citizen and their role in shaping US foreign policy. These commentators accept that ordinary Americans may not be fully conversant with all details of foreign policy. However, the relative lack of interest does not mean that the public are irrational or incoherent when they do think about foreign policy. Studies have shown that American voters have structured sets of opinions about foreign policy and America's place in the world (Hurwitz and Peffley, 1987). A paucity of information does not necessarily impede consistency. James McCormick (2011) argues that Americans are 'cognitive misers' who seek information shortcuts to arrive at political judgements. A lack of detailed knowledge can actually help Americans be consistent. People maintain relatively core beliefs without having to contend with challenging information that might muddy the waters.

Partisanship and ideology

We have not yet considered the degree to which Americans agree among themselves on foreign affairs. Foreign policy has played an important role in structuring party competition in the US. These differences are real, but sometimes overstated. Given that the US is believed to be so highly polarized between Republicans and Democrats, conservatives and liberals, we might expect to see those sharp divisions over domestic policies carry over into foreign affairs. On certain matters, they clearly do, but on the fundamentals, divisions are not quite as sharp as we might expect.

The first American party system was structured around debates over the role of the US in the international system. This is not an unusual phenomenon for newly independent states. The politics of postcolonial states in the mid-20th century was, to a large degree, dominated around the extent to which the newly independent country would remain aligned to the former imperial power (Schwartz, 2009). A key axis of politics in post-Soviet Eastern Europe remains, even today, the extent to which a country will be aligned to Russia. In the late 18th- and early 19th-century US, the question was the extent to which the US should be aligned with the UK. The Federalist Party supported close trade links. They were enthusiastic supporters of the Treaty of Amity between the two countries, negotiated by John Jay in 1795, sometimes known as the 'Jay Treaty'. In contrast, the 'Old Republicans' (who later, confusingly, became the Democratic Party) were suspicious of trade and too much commercial activity. Their electoral base was (the more numerous) set of subsistence farmers in the country (Shefter, 2002).

Foreign policy can, to some extent, explain the unusual alliances that held together the broad party coalitions of the 19th and early 20th centuries (Hofstadter, 1960). Martin Shefter (2002: 116–17) describes the US's relationship with British economic hegemony as 'the central cleavage' of the American party systems of the 19th century. In the 19th century, the Democratic Party was a coalition of the rural South and the urban North. Republicans, uncharitably, called the Democrats the party of 'Rum, Romanism, and rebellion' to describe its electoral coalition consisting of the anti-temperance, immigrant Catholics of the urban North and the Confederate-sympathizing whites of the rural South (Summers, 2003). The partisan politics of trade goes some way to explaining this odd coupling. In the 19th century, Britain purchased nearly half of the world's cotton for its textile mills. The chief exporter of cotton was the US South, which itself was dependent on urban financiers, based in New York and other major cities, for credit and for organizing shipments to the UK. New York facilitated the export of southern cotton and the import of British manufactured goods, many of which were purchased by the southern US cotton aristocracy. The Democratic Party coalition was dependent on a British hegemonic world order that presupposed free trade, as Shefter (2002) has convincingly argued.

Manufacturers in the North, however, tended to be opposed to free trade because they were unable to compete with British manufactured goods, either internationally or on the domestic market (Pletcher, 1998: 34–41; Jeffreys-Jones, 2010: 61). The Whig Party (which, in the mid-1850s became the 'new' Republican Party), instead, supported high tariffs on European goods, which gave American manufacturers a competitive edge in the domestic market. On top of this, the Whigs/ Republicans sought to strengthen and integrate the US domestic market by using the revenues from tariffs to fund infrastructure projects, which facilitated domestic commerce and manufacturing, such as canal and railway construction. They also saw an important role for an active federal government that could apply national, common standards across the 'single market' of the US (Montgomery, 1967). This system was known as the 'American system'.

The long-term strategy of Republican lawmakers, however, was not indefinite autarky. They sought to create an industrial working class with the skills and discipline to compete directly with British manufacturers. Their cultural programme – prohibition and widespread public education – was supportive of this end. As US manufacturing capabilities increased, US politicians of all parties increasingly turned away from tariffs and supported the export of US goods on the open market. For most of the 20th century, there was (broadly speaking) a bipartisan consensus on free trade. In this context, bipartisan majorities in Congress supported giving presidents broad discretion over the negotiation (for example, the Reciprocal Trade Agreement Act of 1934) and imposition (for example, the Trade Expansion Act of 1962 and the Trade Act of 1974) of tariffs. It was assumed that presidents of both parties would use their new tariff powers sparingly and with a bias towards free trade where practicable. A sign of this bipartisan harmony, the Trade Act of 1974 was passed by a Democratic Congress, but gave powers over tariffs to a Republican president, Gerald Ford.

In 1985, President Ronald Reagan signed the first bilateral free trade agreement – between the US and Israel – which passed the Senate and House with not a single vote of opposition. Perhaps the most famous (or infamous) free trade agreement was the North American Free Trade Agreement (NAFTA), signed by President Bill Clinton (although negotiations had begun by President George H.W. Bush). NAFTA opened up US, Mexican and Canadian markets to each other with minimal barriers. While many economists agree that NAFTA has boosted productivity, exchange and wealth among the three countries, there are concerns that it has decimated key US industries and generated higher levels of inequality. Unions hated NAFTA because companies could threaten workers that if they did not accept lower pay, worse conditions, and so forth, then the factory in, say, Indiana would close and be reopened in, say, Tijuana, Mexico, with no penalty for the business. NAFTA-style agreements facilitate higher volumes of trade, but contain no measures to ensure that increased trade flows will be reciprocal or that the gains are widely shared. Many of the provisions actively hinder or deter social policies. This issue was a central concern in the 1992 election. It propelled a previously unelected billionaire candidate named Ross Perot to national attention. On the anti-trade wave, Perot secured 19 per cent of the popular vote, more than any recent third-party candidate.

Under President George W. Bush, the US signed more free trade agreements than ever before, including a multilateral trade deal with Central American countries (CAFTA) and bilateral trade deals with countries such as Bahrain, Morocco, Chile, Singapore, Australia, Oman and Peru. Some of the deals were controversial, especially CATFA, which only passed the House by two votes (217–215). However, the issue did not truly break into public consciousness in the way in which NAFTA had done.

The consensus over free trade has faced renewed challenge in recent times, with the candidacies of trade sceptics Donald Trump (on the right) and Bernie Sanders (on the left) reviving old arguments about the threat of international competition to US workers. Edward Mansfield and colleagues (2019) found that Americans overall, and especially those in import-vulnerable jobs, became much less supportive of trade during the Great Recession of 2007–09. This support became apparent in the 2016 election.

By the time that Trump took office, only 20 per cent of Republicans thought that NAFTA was 'good' for the US compared to about 70 per cent of Democrats. A decade earlier there had been no clear partisan divide (Jacobs and Milkis, 2020). The 2018 Cooperative Congressional

Election Study found that 85 per cent of Republicans supported tariffs on Chinese goods compared to 28 per cent of Democrats. Donald Trump used his powers in the Trade Expansion Act and the Trade Act to apply tariffs vigorously on a range of products from US adversaries and allies alike. These partisan differences were real, but they spoke mostly to the extent to which Trump had polarized views on specific trading arrangements. Voters' assessments of Trump became a prism through which to evaluate the policy measures proposed by the president.[2]

The 2016 election caused foreign policy elites to wake up to the reality that trade deals have been perceived by many US voters as bad for American labour, even if they are good for American capital. Increased economic vulnerability as a result of the recession has made Americans less supportive of trade deals, which, while opening up new markets, also expose US workers to more competition. In this way, the 2016 election potentially marked a turn away from the movement towards freer trade that defined the 20th century, and revisited and revived some of the old debates about trade, tariffs and competitions that defined US party politics in the 19th century.

Yet before long, members of Congress showed that an underlying commitment to free trade remains at the heart of both modern parties. Donald Trump's renegotiation of NAFTA, the US–Mexico–Canada Agreement (USMCA), was passed with wide bipartisan majorities in 2019. As Table 5.1 shows, 193 House Democrats voted for Trump's trade bill on 19 December 2019, just one day after nearly all House Democrats had voted to impeach the president.[3] A broad consensus exists for free trade in principle, even if support for specific tariffs varied, according to Trump's perceptions. Republicans, on the whole, had not become overnight converts to the old 'American system' of their 19th-century party forefathers.

Broad bipartisanship can be detected across a variety of foreign policy areas, such as US military intervention. When asked about specific scenarios for war, there are some partisan differences, but

Table 5.1: Congressional support for the US-Mexico-Canada Agreement (USMCA), 2019–20

	House (19 Dec 2019)		Senate (16 Jan 2020)	
	Yes	No	Yes	No
Democrat	193	39	38	9
Republican	192	2	51	1
Total	385	41	89	10

Source: US Congress (2019–20)

Table 5.2: Would you support sending US troops abroad if ...

	Democrats (%)	Republicans (%)	Difference (%)
China invaded Taiwan	25.9	35.1	+9.2
North Korea invaded South Korea	39.5	50.6	+11.1
Israel was invaded by neighbours	43.8	63.7	+19.9

Source: Based on Smeltz et al (2012)

the gaps are not enormous. Table 5.2 shows that the Republicans are somewhat more hawkish than the Democrats.

When it comes to sending US troops abroad to support broader foreign policy goals (for example, stopping genocide, supporting a humanitarian cause), we find quite a lot of common ground between Republicans and Democrats. Clear majorities in both parties would support sending US troops to ensure US access to oil, to deal with humanitarian crises and to stop genocide (see Table 5.3). In fact, on the last two, the Democrats are slightly more hawkish than the Republicans.

When we look at ideology and beliefs about the US's role in the world, we find almost no difference between people who identify as liberal and those who identify as conservative – 67.0 per cent of liberals think that the US should take an active role in foreign affairs and 66.9 per cent of conservatives agree. They are statistically indistinguishable. The same is true when we look at responses to the question 'Is the US playing the role of the world policeman more than it should be?' – 76.8 per cent of liberals say 'yes', as do 75.2 per cent of conservatives – another statistically indistinguishable amount.[4]

James McCormick argues that differences among the public about US foreign policy are 'modest – with more consensus than dissensus being the norm' (2011: 143). On the basics about the US's role in the world, there is widespread agreement. Large majorities of both Democrats and Republicans view the US as the greatest, or one of the greatest, countries in the world (see Figure 5.2). They see the US as

Table 5.3: Would you support sending US troops abroad to ...

	Democrats (%)	Republicans (%)	Difference (%)
Ensure US access to oil	51.9	58.7	+6.8
Deal with humanitarian crises	70.7	64.0	−6.7
Stop genocide	77.7	71.1	−6.6

Source: Based on Smeltz et al (2012)

Table 5.4: Ideology and the US's role in the world (% agreeing)

Question	Liberal (%)	Moderate (%)	Conservative (%)	Liberal/ Conservative difference (%)
Will it be best for the future of the country if we take an active part in world affairs?	67.0	51.8	66.9	0.1
Is the US playing the role of the world policeman more than it should be?	76.8	83.0	75.2	1.6

Source: Based on Smeltz et al (2012)

having an important leadership role to play. They are not fully signed up to the idea that the US should operate as a neocolonial superpower, but they do not want their country to shirk from the world stage altogether. That is not to say there are no partisan differences on these fundamental claims about the US's role in the world. Republicans are more likely to see their country as the greatest in the world. Young voters are the least likely to do so. But by and large there is more that unites Americans on these core questions than that which divides them.

Issues that are abstract and low salience tend to be less polarized (Graham, 1994). It is in the detail where the partisan divides emerge.

Figure 5.2: Is America the greatest country/one of the greatest countries in the world, or are there better countries? (By party and year of birth)

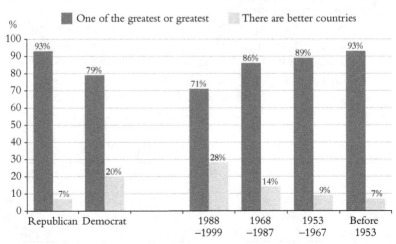

Source: Based on Smeltz et al (2012)

Miroslav Nincic summarizes, 'American foreign policy reflects domestic politics.... Except when external threats are stark and immediate (a rare occurrence), much about how the United States deals with the international community flows from partisan politics and electoral calculations' (2012: 153). This suggests that party leadership is crucial to providing voters with cues, or signals, about what to think on the particulars of foreign policy, especially on matters that may not have a direct relevance to the electorate (Levendusky, 2009).

The media

If we return to the commentators who worry that the American public is moody, superficial and unstable, they would argue that the American public can be easily led on foreign policy matters by politicians and demagogues because the public don't have sufficient information on which to base informed decisions. Gabriel Almond, in his classic book *The American People and Foreign Policy* (1950), worried that the American public was liable to be swayed by prejudice, incomplete information and charismatic leaders. Some commentators believe that Americans have tended to defer to the president's judgement more often than not. If the president says something is a matter of national security concern, then many Americans assume that the president must be right. For example, a majority of Americans told opinion pollsters in 1965 that they opposed American bombings of Hanoi, but once President Lyndon Johnson declared that they were necessary, 85 per cent of Americans supported the bombings.

Moreover, politicians might be able to manipulate an unknowledgeable public not only to win support for their own policy initiatives abroad, but also to bolster themselves. George H.W. Bush found that each time he sent American troops abroad, his approval rating shot up. When he sent troops into Panama, his approval rating went up to 80 per cent in January 1990. When he sent troops into Kuwait in early 1991, his approval rating shot up 90 per cent. The 1997 film *Wag the Dog* captured this cynicism. It's a story about an American president who is caught having an affair with a member of staff. In order to boost his approval ratings before a presidential election, his advisers suggest invading a foreign country. Rather than send troops into harm's way, the president invites a Hollywood director to produce dramatic war images in a film studio. The footage is then sent onto network and cable news networks, with the public thinking there is a war going on in a remote part of Albania. Thus, the president enjoys all of the benefits of the 'rally behind the flag' effect without exacting real costs to human lives. The film was seen as somewhat prophetic. It was released in December 1997, one month before the Monica Lewinsky sex scandal became public. As the scandal intensified in the months to follow, President Clinton ordered bombing campaigns in Sudan, Iraq and Kosovo.

While fiction, *Wag the Dog* underlines the critical role of the media as an intermediary in providing the public with information about the outside world. This is especially true for events that happen abroad and do not affect Americans directly in their day-to-day lives. As political scientists Benjamin Page and Robert Shapiro (1992: 321) have written, 'Many events – especially distant happenings in foreign affairs – do not directly and immediately affect ordinary citizens.' The events do not 'speak for themselves' as it were. They have to be reported and also *interpreted*. The media, then, plays a role both in the conveyance and interpretation of political information.

Many people have written about the idea of 'fake news', suggesting that it is a new and worrying phenomenon in Western politics (Albright, 2017; Farkas and Schou, 2019). Yet this is not a new idea. Walter Lippmann wrote several books in the 1920s and 1930s in which he worried about fake news. In his 1920 book *Liberty and the News*, Lippmann argued that left-leaning Western journalists had projected their aspirations about the Russian Revolution into their reporting. They interpreted the facts of the Revolution through an excessively rosy frame, often ignoring 'inconvenient' truths to their reporting. This meant, in turn, that the US public did not have adequate knowledge to interpret the events that were unfolding in Russia.

Two years later, Lippmann published his most famous book, *Public Opinion*, whose bland title masks its explosive contents. Lippmann argued that the public did not know what it didn't know. People's knowledge was extremely dependent on what was reported to them, but Lippmann was frustrated that people rarely shared common facts. This could lead perfectly intelligent people to make drastically different decisions. In the book, Lippmann writes about a remote island populated by the British, French and Germans. It takes a year for outside information to reach the island. The First World War breaks out and the British and French become sworn enemies of the Germans – except the British and the French on the island don't know it. For 12 months, the three groups cooperate peacefully until they find out that they are each other's enemies and start shooting each other.

It is a rather silly example, but Lippmann points out that all of humanity has acted based on 'knowledge' that we now know to be 'fake'. For example, people in the past used to make decisions on the basis that the world was flat. We now know this to be 'fake' knowledge, but at the time, given what we thought was our knowledge, we made perfectly rational calculations. Lippmann himself was a writer for many American newspapers. On his retirement in 1967, his newspaper column was read weekly by millions of Americans. He believed it was important for the public to become informed by expert sources, which evidently included his own newspaper columns.

Lippmann took a disparaging view of low-grade news sources, yet since his death, television and social media have increasingly mixed news and entertainment. While many observers have raised the alarm about the propensity of the public to draw from non-elite news sources, a few scholars have argued that entertainment news provides a vital public service function (Chaffee and Kanihan, 1997). Matthew Baum (2002) argues that many normally politically inattentive Americans are exposed to high-profile foreign policy events as an incidental by-product of watching entertainment on American television. 'Soft media', as Baum defines it, includes late night talk shows, comedy programmes, daytime television talk shows, weekly news programmes and entertainment news. While many of the consumers of these media watch them to be entertained (not to be informed), Baum found that many Americans gain most of their information about current affairs from these programmes.

Baum contends that soft news tends to use 'cheap' framing techniques: us versus them, 'human impact' stories, morality tales (for example, of injustice). Foreign policy crises are particularly apt for this kind of framing. They are attention-grabbing, easy to package, apt for a soap opera, and an often visually made-for-television format. An example of such framing took place during the US's involvement in the 1995 NATO bombing of Bosnia under President Bill Clinton. Most of the mainstream news media was focused on military tactics, the role of NATO, international diplomacy, nation-building, ethnic cleansing, and so on. Soft news focused on the story of a brave US Air Force pilot named Scott O'Grady who was shot down and survived for five days eating grass and insects before being rescued. One reaction might be to look at this example and lament how vapid many Americans' news sources are. However, were it not for these sources, many members of the public might not receive any information about world affairs at all.

Mobilizing public opinion

One of the problems that lawmakers face is actually finding out what the public wants. President William McKinley tested public opinion through a relatively inventive method. After US victory in the Spanish–American War of 1898, the former Spanish territories of Puerto Rico and Guam became US colonial possessions, the US purchased the Philippines for $20 million, and the government placed Cuba under US military rule (Immerwahr, 2019: 72–3). Having seized Spain's empire, the McKinley Administration was uncertain about what it should do with the territories: sell them on, return them to Spain, control them from the US or grant the local populations self-determination? To gauge US public opinion (not the opinion of the people living in these territories, it should be pointed out), McKinley went on a tour of the US delivering different versions of a speech about the post-Spanish–American War settlement. One speech called for keeping the US's new colonial possessions; one did not. McKinley instructed his aides to measure the enthusiasm of the crowd according to the speech's content. They found that McKinley's more ardently imperialist speeches tended to receive a more enthusiastic reception (May, 1961: 252–62).

In more recent times, the science of opinion polling has provided presidents and other policymakers with a relatively speedy and accurate method of measuring public opinion. But polls can sometimes be problematic. Political scientists have found that the wording of a survey question can produce quite dramatically different results. In the 1980s, for example, support for the Contras in Nicaragua was higher in polls that clarified that the Contras were fighting 'communism'. During Vietnam, polls that made reference to the 'costs of the war' or the 'increase in the killings of US troops' tended to produce results that were less supportive of military engagement.

Another way in which the American public let their opinions be known on foreign policy is through elections (Divine, 1974; Armacost, 2015; Preston, 2015; Johnstone and Priest, 2017b). The extent to which elections can be used to measure public influence on policy has been widely debated. There has long been recognition in the academic scholarship that war deaths impose an electoral cost (Cotton, 1986; Hibbs, 2000; Gartner et al, 2004; Grose and Oppenheimer, 2007; Karol and Miguel, 2007; Gartner and Segura, 2008). War deaths are not evenly distributed across the US (Kriner and Shen, 2016; Schafer, 2017). This fact allows political scientists to manipulate data to isolate the causal effect of war deaths on political behaviour. Douglas Kriner and Francis Shen (2020) argue that in the 2016 election, Democrat Hillary Clinton faced an electoral 'cost' for her support for the Iraq and Afghanistan Wars. They found that there was a statistically meaningful correlation between the war casualty rates at both state and local levels and support for Donald Trump. Specifically, they found that a two-standard deviation increase in the war death rate in a state produced an estimated 2.6 per cent increase in electoral support for Donald Trump (2020: 250). This effect was enough to tip Pennsylvania, Wisconsin and Michigan from the Democratic to Republican columns, handing Trump his electoral college majority.

Because the House of Representatives and one-third of the Senate are elected every two years, Americans have ample opportunity to show through their votes what they think about foreign affairs. One of the problems with this approach, however, is that elections contain 'a bundle of issues', as Kenneth Arrow (1963 [1951]) wrote in his classic *Social Choice and Individual Values*. There is a whole set of policies on the table, not just foreign policy issues. It is questionable, therefore, whether a vote for a particular *candidate* is a good sign for what Americans think about a particular *issue*, particularly if that issue is of lower salience (that is, importance) to American voters than certain domestic policy concerns.

Some commentators doubt that foreign policy is the prevailing concern in most US elections. Indeed, in most elections, about 1 in 10 voters cite foreign policy as their top concern: 13 per cent in 2016, 15 per cent in 2008 and 10 per cent in 2000.[5] The 2020 exit poll didn't even include a foreign policy option, so low had the salience of foreign affairs been in the campaign.[6] There are exceptions. Foreign affairs were predominant, if not dominant, issues in the presidential elections of 1968, 1980 and 2004 (Preston, 2015). They were also overwhelmingly important in the congressional midterm elections of 2002 and 2006. Even other elections, which were not necessarily centrally focused on foreign policy, also contained important debates over foreign policy that bled into general concerns about a leader's competence or strength. For example, John F. Kennedy's hammering of the Eisenhower Administration over the 'missile gap' with the USSR in the 1960 presidential election undoubtedly had an effect on people's perceptions of Richard Nixon's competence or strength, given that Nixon was Eisenhower's vice president. Once president, Richard Nixon interpreted his party's loss in the 1970 midterm elections as a sign that he needed to shift more vigorously to foreign policy leadership (Sandbrook, 2008).

A tired cliché of American politics is that economic concerns trump all other considerations. The line attributed to Bill Clinton's chief strategist James Carville when Clinton ran for president in 1992 was 'it's the economy, stupid'. This observation was itself an allusion to the fact that although George H.W. Bush was highly rated for his military interventions in Panama and Kuwait, Clinton would ultimately triumph because voters cared more about the economy. Clinton's victory against Bush was taken as vindication of this domestically oriented strategy. While Carville may have been right in 1992, we should not discount the importance of foreign policy in US elections entirely.[7]

Foreign policy can serve as a key valence issue by which to evaluate candidates in an election (Preston, 2015). Perceived foreign policy weakness can be devastating to a presidential candidate. In the 1980 presidential election, Ronald Reagan claimed that Jimmy Carter's foreign policy was 'bordering on appeasement', which fed into concerns that Carter was not a strong leader. In the 2004 presidential election, Senator John Kerry was trusted more on the economy than incumbent President George W. Bush – 49 per cent of voters trusted Kerry compared to 43 per cent who trusted Bush (Nincic, 2012). But opinion polls showed that just as many people were concerned about Iraq as they were about the economy, an unusually high salience for a foreign policy issue. The lingering memory of the 9/11 attacks, coupled with America's involvement in wars in Afghanistan and Iraq, was successfully deployed by the Bush campaign to portray the president as a patriotic and heroic leader. Analysts of the campaign have concluded that Bush, Cheney and their surrogates practised exceptionally disciplined message control, focusing on Bush's role in fighting the war on terror and linking Iraq to this larger struggle (Magleby et al, 2007).

At the time, the public mood towards the Iraq War was turning, but there was a broad sense that what the war needed to be brought to a successful end was strong leadership. Former President Bill Clinton mused at the time, 'When people are insecure, they'd rather have somebody who is strong and wrong than someone who's weak and right' (quoted in Smith, 2011). The Bush campaign's overarching narrative centred on the need for Americans to vote for strong leadership to keep their country safe. Kevin Phillips is right to observe the important influence of 'the rally-round effect after September 11, 2001' on the outcome of the 2004 election (2006: 388). In the summer of 2004, Bush and his surrogates viciously attacked Kerry for his apparent weakness on the Iraq issue, and on military affairs more generally. In spite of Kerry being a decorated Vietnam War veteran and Bush having avoided being sent to Vietnam, Bush was able to portray Kerry as someone who didn't support American troops. Attack advertisements by so-called Swift Boat Veterans for Truth challenged Kerry's wartime heroism and patriotism. Public confidence in Kerry as a future commander-in-chief plummeted, and Bush was trusted on Iraq 51 per cent to Kerry's 39 per cent. Only 33 per cent of Americans thought that Kerry would do a better job fighting terrorism compared to 60 per cent who sided with Bush (Preston, 2015). The fact that Kerry only lost the popular vote by 2 percentage points (and came even closer to winning the electoral college) shows that some of the people who thought Bush would do a better job fighting terrorism still voted for Kerry anyway. But perhaps Carville's phrase needs revisiting: 'It's mostly the economy, stupid, but foreign policy weakness can play a decisive role in a close election.'

Sometimes the Iraq War is raised as an example of the impotence of public opinion in constraining foreign policy elites. A common view is that the Bush Administration pushed forward with the invasion, in spite of widespread public scepticism. Yet support for the war was very high: 71 per cent by the time the invasion began (Oliphant, 2018). This support is sometimes portrayed as a misapprehension, due to the deceitful chicanery of the Bush Administration. No doubt, the Bush Administration's case for war was built on faulty, flawed and simply incorrect information that was shared with the public with alarming recklessness (Woodward, 2004). Yet it is questionable as to whether this public relations effort was even needed in the first place. Regime change in Iraq had been a popular view in the US since the end of the first war in Iraq in 1991. Between 1991 and 2003, every public poll on the matter found majority support for removing Saddam Hussein from power (Lucas, 2010). Much like the Watergate break-in was not necessary for Nixon to win re-election against George McGovern in 1972, the Bush Administration's overinflated case for invasion does not appear to have been necessary to build public support for invasion. It was only once the war dragged on much longer than people expected that the US public turned against it. Only 21 per cent of Americans in April 2003 thought that US troops would be in Iraq for longer than two years (Lucas, 2010). In the 2006 election, this issue came back to bite Bush, as public confidence flowed away from Bush – 83 per cent of Americans in the 2006 congressional midterms cited Iraq as a 'very important' or the 'most important' issue. Bush suffered huge defeats in both chambers of Congress, seeing Democrats regain full control of Congress for the first time since the 1992 elections.

The early 21st-century political struggles over the war in Iraq were admittedly unusual in the high levels of public interest in this foreign policy concern. As demonstrated earlier, most of the time foreign policy is a low-salience matter. Although Americans only intermittently convey their positions to policymakers directly, they do subtly shape the entire context of US foreign policymaking. The public, as Bernard Cohen wrote in *The Political Process and Foreign Policy* (1957), generates a 'climate of opinion' that structures the way in which political actors made decisions about foreign affairs. The climate of opinion set out the broad outlines of what was 'acceptable' policy, without necessarily dictating the day-to-day choices of decision-makers. The public, therefore, acts as a broad constraint on the range of possibilities available to foreign policymakers (see Sobel, 2001). As Thomas Risse-Kappen writes, 'in most cases mass public opinion set broad and unspecified limits to the foreign policy choices [and] defined the range of options available for implementing policy goals' (1991: 510).

One way in which the 'climate of opinion' thesis seems to have some validity is when we consider the **searing effect** of disastrous military interventions. The 'searing effect' refers to when American public support for military intervention runs hot, but perhaps too hot, as the campaign fails, leaving the American public burned from the experience and unlikely to agitate for similar military adventures. An example of the searing effect is the **Vietnam Syndrome**. Americans were so burned from the experience of the failed war in South East Asia that they wanted to resist sending American troops anywhere else in the world. As discussed in the previous chapter, President Gerald Ford found that the public (and by extension, Congress) were so fatigued by the war, that there was no public support to send troops into South Vietnam in 1975 to protect the country and US interests from invasion by North Vietnam. Ford similarly found that the public had no interest in supporting a war in Angola to support the National Liberation Front of Angola against the pro-Soviet Popular Movement for the Liberation of Angola (Johnson, 2006: 221–3).

A 1974 poll found that Americans had lost willingness to support their allies in the face of military attack. Only 27 per cent said they'd support sending US troops to Israel to protect it from invasion; only 39 per cent said they'd support sending US troops to Western Europe in the case of an attack; only 37 per cent said they'd support even economic assistance to allies who were attacked. The one exception was Canada – 77 per cent of Americans said they would support sending troops into Canada if it was attacked. In the 1980 election, however, Ronald Reagan sought to cure the American public from its Vietnam Syndrome. Reagan told the Veterans of Foreign Wars, 'For too long, we have lived with the "Vietnam Syndrome".... It is time we recognized that ours was, in truth, a noble cause.... There is a lesson for all of us in Vietnam. If we are forced to fight, we must have the means and the determination to prevail or we will not have what it takes to secure the peace.'[8] Reagan sought to heal the searing effects of the war by explaining to Americans that the effort had been a noble and good one. The problem, as Reagan saw it, was not too much militarism, but too little of it.

While Reagan may have been relatively successful (as was his successor George H.W. Bush) in ending the Vietnam Syndrome, the US later experienced an **Iraq syndrome** (Mueller, 2005). After a decade of failed wars in the Middle East, the Obama Administration recognized the public's distaste for large-scale military interventions, turning to 'light-touch' (from the US perspective) drone warfare (Hall Kindervater, 2017). Obama's Secretary of Defense Robert Gates said in a speech at West Point in 2011 that 'any future defense secretary who advises the president to again send a big American land army into Asia or into the Middle East or Africa should have his head examined'.

The consequences were felt later in the Obama Administration, when the public failed to show enthusiasm for US incursions in Libya and Syria. Only 12 per cent of Americans in one YouGov poll said that they favoured military troops in Libya. As a result, the US adopted a 'lead from behind' approach in Libya, as there simply wasn't the public support for a sustained effort. Similarly, the Obama Administration was extremely reluctant to put troops into Syria, even after Barack Obama declared that Bashar al-Assad's use of chemical weapons represented a 'red line'. Secretary of State John Kerry ludicrously tried to assure the American public that if there were going to be bombings in Syria, they would be 'unbelievably small'. In recent years, neither President Donald Trump nor President Joe Biden have actively promoted the idea of a US invasion and occupation of another country. It feels that American public opinion is on a loop. Successful ventures with low casualties (such as the first Gulf war or the early, misleading stages of the Afghan war) encourage public support for future military intervention. Failed wars such as Korea, Vietnam and Iraq make the public more sceptical.

Finally, we must understand how US policymaking structures distort public influence. Jacobs and Page (2005) argue that there is a pattern of 'non-influence' of the public in directing policy outcomes. We've already entertained the hypotheses that the public do not care or cannot express their views through elections. These claims appear to be overstated. But if there is a general pattern of non-influence, it may not be due to public apathy or inattention, but to the very structures of the US Constitution that impair the public from exercising control on outcomes as directly as they might otherwise like.

One of the most obviously undemocratic features of the US Constitution is the Senate (Johnson, 2020b). The power of the Senate in foreign affairs gives disproportionate weight to citizens from underpopulated states at the expense of states with large cities. Because each state receives two senators, regardless of population, the US Senate is, in effect, full of rotten boroughs. The 600,000 residents of Wyoming have the same number of representatives as the 40 million residents of California. This 'apportionment' scheme has, in the last 50 years, consistently given Republican administrations a structural edge over policy matters while making it more difficult for Democratic administrations to pass their favoured policies. Walter Russell Mead (2012) argues that Senate malapportionment empowers populist elements in US foreign policy disproportionately because it severely underrepresents the urban communities that are least likely to contain supporters of populist causes. In practice, the Senate gives extra weight to the views of people who are sceptical of agreements like the Kyoto Protocol on climate change, NAFTA and membership of the WTO, US membership in the International Criminal Court, and paying the US's share of UN membership fees. We should also take seriously how the US's political institutions distort public opinion, causing a disjuncture between the public and policy outcomes that has little to do with the public's level of interest and more to do with the underlying undemocratic structures of the US constitutional order.

Some might say that citizen non-influence is the way the system is meant to work. The Constitution places foreign policy matters at a distance from the public. It placed the right to 'originate' money bills (that is, taxes and spending) with the House of Representatives, but various foreign policy matters (for example, treaty ratification, confirmation of ambassadorial nominations and confirmation of presidential nominations for diplomatic and civilian military positions) were left exclusively to the Senate. Unlike now, the major distinguishing factor between the House and the Senate was that the Senate was unelected. Senators were appointed by their state legislature, a phenomenon that continued until the ratification of the Seventeenth Amendment in 1913. This put the legislature's influence over certain policy matters at a distance from public opinion. The 'wisdom' of the Founders, some might say, was to keep foreign policy at arm's length from the public.

We should question whether it really *matters* what the original authors of the Constitution thought or wanted. Milner and Tingley write, 'Simple appeals to the Constitution do not render a complete understanding of who controls US foreign policy' (2015: 74). In a similar vein, neither do appeals to the Constitution as some kind of timeless, prescriptive framework. The Constitution was authored well before the revolutions of mass democracy throughout the world. There is little reason why the Founders' apprehensions about mass publics should normatively be shared today. Indeed, there is much to revile about the Founders' attitudes on a range of topics.

Conclusion

Establishing the causal influence of the public on any particular policy outcome is a difficult task. These methodological challenges are even more complicated when it comes to measuring foreign policy impact. The public can support higher taxes on the rich, and it is straightforward enough to determine whether these calls are heard, but it is more difficult when it comes to abstract foreign policy goals such as 'security' and 'democracy promotion'.

Although the American people are not irrational when it comes to foreign policy, they are sometimes inattentive to matters beyond America's shores. It takes a foreign policy crisis to awaken the broad majority of American electors. Republican Senator Arthur Vandenberg told President Harry Truman that he ought to 'scare the hell out of the country' in order to get them to take note of the communist threat (Dione, 2003). The Pearl Harbor attack in 1941 and the attacks of September 11, 2001 were dramatic moments where Americans were scared, and public opinion mobilized behind military intervention. But sometimes intervention can go dreadfully wrong. The public feels 'burned' or 'seared' by the experience and 'cool' to future US military adventurism – at least for a time.

US foreign policy, like all policy, is a product of domestic politics. Many 20th-century political theorists regarded public meddling in foreign affairs as a problem (Lippmann, 1925). They wanted to see foreign policy as some sort of technocratic exercise with objective answers. There are good reasons, however, to be doubtful that there are objective answers. Like all policy, in a democracy, foreign policy should be a product of contestation and debate among citizens and their representatives. It is not simply a technocratic exercise. Those who fear the consequences of these deliberations might wish to consider the even greater risks of alternative forms of political organization.

6

Interest Groups, Religion and Money

The vast sums of money in US politics are a regrettable example of how the US is 'exceptional' – in the sense of being an empirical global outlier. US political campaigns are the most expensive in the world (Powell and Wilcox, 2010), and the 2020 election was the most expensive electoral contest in world history. Spending across all levels of elections that year reached nearly $11 billion, about the same as the total GDP of Armenia (OpenSecrets.org, 2020). The average House seat cost $1.3 million to win; a Senate seat cost, on average, $10.4 million. Total spending in the 2018 midterm elections exceeded $5 billion (OpenSecrets.org, 2018). The 2014 congressional midterm elections, in which 94.5 per cent of election-seeking incumbents were re-elected, cost an estimated $3.8 billion.[1] Sums like these are unheard of in the rest of the democratic world. In 2017, the French presidential election cost $90 million and the UK general election cost $55 million (The Electoral Commission, 2019). The total income of German political parties, which, unlike those in the US are publicly funded, was just under $200 million (Niedermayer, 2020).

Perhaps unsurprisingly, a range of academic studies has shown that affluent Americans have a disproportionate influence on policy outcomes (Broz, 2005; Massey, 2007; Jacobs and Druckman, 2011; Gilens and Page, 2014; Bartels, 2016). While the political influence of organized economic elites has strengthened in recent years (Winters, 2011; Domhoff, 2015; Hacker and Pierson, 2020), the countervailing strength of the organized working class, especially the labour movement, has atrophied (Western and Rosenfeld, 2011). If we really want to understand the domestic roots of US foreign policy, we need to take seriously the relative strengths of organized capital and labour.

The scale of money in politics is one example of American political exceptionalism, but so, too, is the role of religion. Ironically for a country that has a constitutional prohibition on religious establishment, religion plays a more active role in US politics than in nearly any other advanced, industrialized country. Religiosity is far higher in the US than in countries with similar levels of wealth and education. Religious groups form key electorates in both main political parties. White evangelicals are perhaps the single most important constituency in the Republican Party. African-American Christians and Jewish Americans are vital constituencies for the Democratic Party.

This chapter analyses the (distorting) influences of organized capital, labour and religion on US foreign policy outcomes. First, the chapter analyses the numerous 'lobby shops' in Washington, DC that provide services for domestic and foreign actors in attempts to gain influence in the foreign policymaking process. Explored in the next section is the role of think tanks and foundations, ostensibly not-for-profit organizations that nonetheless advance policies that often reflect the views of a wealthy donor class. Third, the influence of organized labour will be inspected. The trade union movement is a true mammoth of US politics: once one of the most influential **interest groups** in Washington, its influence has now evolved into a weaker, more submissive form. Finally, the role of religion and religious groups will be evaluated.

Diplomacy, Inc

Traditionally, diplomacy is conducted by public officials, such as foreign ministers and ambassadors, who formally represent their country on the world stage. Negotiations happen at the highest levels of politics, between members of respective executive branches. Yet, over the years, many countries have found this form of diplomatic wrangling to be challenging and ineffective. With the rare exceptions of the UK and Israel, many countries find it difficult to gain access (and influence) to the US Congress and the executive branch through their embassies in Washington, DC. Increasingly, countries are turning to private lobbying firms to advocate for their interests. John Newhouse calls this trend the 'privatization of diplomacy' or 'Diplomacy, Inc' (2009: 73).

A lobbyist is specified in the Federal Regulation of Lobbying Act of 1946 as anyone who 'solicits, collects, or receives money … to be used to aid in the passage or defeat of legislation by the US Congress' (Zeller, 1948: 244). The Lobbying Disclosure Act of 1995 instructs individuals and firms that are involved in lobbying to register with the

Secretary of the Senate and Clerk of the House of Representatives and to submit quarterly reports about their expenditure. This framework helps to track, to some extent, the activity of lobbyists, but these reports are brief, and it is difficult to ensure that they provide full accuracy. On this measure, there are about 11,000 lobbying firms and groups in Washington, DC, which together employ about 17,000 individuals (McCormick, 2008).

The real number of people engaged in lobbying in Washington is much higher than the reported amount. This is because the Lobbying Disclosure Act contained a loophole, sometimes known as the 'Daschle Loophole' after the Democratic Senate Majority Leader Tom Daschle. The law allowed individuals who spent less than 20 per cent of their time working on lobbying activities to claim that they were not 'lobbyists' at all, so they did not need to register any of their lobbying activities. For example, under the Lobbying Disclosure Act's rules, Senator Daschle did not need to register as a lobbyist until 2016, in spite of having formed his own lobbying and consulting firm (the Daschle Group) not long after losing his Senate seat in 2004 (Wilson, 2016). Nigel Bowles and Robert McMahon estimate that there may be more than twice as many lobbyists in Washington when we take into account those individuals who lobby on a part-time basis and who are therefore exempted from public reporting requirements (Bowles and McMahon, 2014: 255).

At bottom, lobbyists seek to achieve policy change (or block policy change) in ways that maximize benefits for their clients and minimize US-government imposed costs. To do so, they must influence those who create and implement policy. 'Influence' is an amorphous concept. Direct corruption in the US, such as direct cash payments for votes or policy change (quid pro quo), is illegal. So influence must be gained through more subtle and complex means. Lobbyists most often achieve influence by acting as 'service bureaus' for members of Congress and the executive branch. Lobbyists make politicians' lives easier: they provide technical information and policy analysis; they help to write speeches; they draft bills and amendments; they furnish politicians and their staff with 'talking points' and media training. Being well funded, lobbyists have numerous resources at their disposal, often more than a politician can devote to any single issue with his or her publicly funded staff. Lobbyists, in a sense, become 'adjuncts' to formal congressional staff (Bowles and McMahon, 2014: 261).

Lobbyists also provide fundraising services for members of Congress. In a system of largely unregulated, extremely expensive, privately financed campaigns, members must spend a large proportion of their time raising money from a variety of sources. My earlier research entailed conducting interviews with senior staff of candidates for the US House of Representatives and Senate (Johnson, 2020a). These conversations revealed the exhaustion felt by politicians who spend time going through long lists of potential donors pleading for financial support over the phone. One finance director recalled that her candidate 'dialled for dollars every day. Candidates spend a lot of their time needing to raise money. I would be listening to his conversations, recording his conversations, briefing him before a call about why someone was interested in the campaign' (Johnson, 2020a: 391). 'Dialling for dollars' seems to be a universally hated task. A communications director for a state-wide candidate recalled exasperatedly that one of 'the hardest things we had to do was to keep her on the telephone raising money and she completely rebelled against that. She had no interest in doing that, and she would [only] do it because we told her that it had to be done' (Johnson, 2020a: 392). An aide for another Senate candidate informed me, '[My client] is like any other politician; no one likes to raise money. No one wants to sit there pick up the phone and you certainly don't want to do it hard-core for six years, picking up the phone and calling people to say hey I need US$1,000. I need whatever. And I am sure that burnt him out a bit' (Johnson, 2020a: 392).

Lobbyists can help ease this strain by facilitating events that assist members of Congress in raising much-needed campaign funds. Newhouse (2009) describes how fundraising events were held for Senate Foreign Relations members, such as Joe Biden, Dick Lugar, John Kerry and Hillary Clinton, by groups advocating for improved business relations between the US and India, including the Asian American Hotel Owners Association, the American Association of Physicians of Indian Origin, the Indian American Friendship Council and the US–India Business Council. If individuals at such events give money without having to be 'asked' or given the 'hard sell', they reduce the need for candidates to undertake agonizing hours 'dialling for dollars'.

Lobbyists also build up interpersonal networks. Experienced and well-connected lobbyists can provide politicians with political intelligence: a combination of gossip, rumour and insider knowledge about the latest political developments. They can brief members of Congress about internal party machinations, inform them of regulation likely to be implemented by a new presidential administration, and alert members to news stories on the horizon. A certain degree of trust should, therefore, exist between lobbyists and members of Congress.

Lobbying firms usually hire senior former political officials who already have those pre-existing relationships. Former members of Congress, their staff and other figures who have worked in government are likely to be the best informed and connected people in Washington. It is no surprise, therefore, that they are well remunerated for their services once they become lobbyists. Half of retiring members of Congress go on to become lobbyists, as do their staff. In 2010, the average salary paid to a former congressional aide joining a 'K Street' lobbying firm was $350,000 (Bowles and McMahon, 2014: 271). Former Speaker of the US House of Representatives John Boehner, the most powerful Republican in Washington for much of the Obama presidency, has served as a 'senior strategic adviser' for the firm Squire Patton Boggs since 2016, one year after he retired as Speaker.[2] Washington is a city to which many are attracted, but few wish to leave.

Lobbyists do not, of course, provide these services for free; they operate on behalf of paying clients. Washington lobby shops are paid vast sums by foreign governments, international businesses and other international actors (such as political parties or even private foreign citizens). The aforementioned former Senator Daschle has represented the government of Turkey (discussed in Chapter 7) and Japan (to assist Japan in the Trans-Pacific Partnership trade negotiations). The former Democratic leader also worked for representatives of Taiwan and a right-wing Macedonian political party (VMRO-DPMNE), both seeking greater diplomatic recognition from the US for their countries. Their status has been disputed by other international actors: the People's Republic of China and Greece, respectively.[3]

Some of the most prominent lobbying firms in Washington include Squire Patton Boggs, Akin Gump Strauss Hauer & Feld, and the BGR Group (Newhouse, 2009). In 2013, Squire Patton Boggs's revenue was $40 million; Akin Gump's was $34 million; and the BGR Group brought in $15 million. In 2016, BGR's biggest clients were the governments of Ukraine, India and Bangladesh. Squire Patton Boggs lobbied on behalf of a Jordanian bank, a Romanian-based gas company and the British firm BAE Systems. Akin Gump's clients included French wine manufacturers, Canadian health products suppliers and a consortium of Mexican businesses. Even poor countries spend money on hiring lobbying firms rather than using normal diplomatic channels. In 2016, the Democratic Republic of the Congo, with a per capita GDP of $483, paid the BGR Group $875,000 for a four-month lobbying contract.

The US political system is porous and open, if not equal. Lobbying firms exploit the chaotic structures of the system to advance policies in ways that are beneficial to their clients (Winters, 2011). In order to achieve legislative policy change in the US, a bill must receive approval from three sets of lawmakers with disjointed electoral mandates: the House of Representatives, the Senate and the president. They must also withstand scrutiny from the US Supreme Court, which can invalidate any law passed by Congress that a majority of justices deem to be incompatible with the US Constitution. This high number of 'veto players' in the US system has been linked with high levels of inequality (Stepan and Linz, 2011).[4] According to Gilens and Page, these veto players generate a 'strong status quo bias built into the US political system' (2014: 576). Jacob Hacker and Paul Pierson (2010) have also linked this 'policy drift' with growing wealth inequality. They write, 'Pundits often see gridlock as equal-opportunity stalemate.... But gridlock is not so neutral' (2010: 171). Lobbying firms simply need to persuade just one veto player to throw off track an entire piece of legislation. These veto players can hold the others to ransom. The Senate could say to the House, pass the bill with a certain tax regulation removed or the bill won't pass at all. The simultaneously sclerotic and porous nature of the US political system is a staging ground for powerful elites to block policies preferred by democratic electorates, as well as providing opportunities for powerful elites to win concessions for their favoured policies.

In exchange for contracting the services of lobbyists, foreign governments and businesses expect a variety of policy outcomes. Favourable business regulations, trade deals and diplomatic recognition are common objectives. For example, former US Republican Senator Bob Dole was a lobbyist for Verner, Liipfert, Bernhard, McPherson & Hand at the age of 93 in 2016. Dole's clients included Taiwan, Kosovo and Slovenia. On behalf of Taiwan, after the 2016 election Dole set up a phone call between President-Elect Trump and Taiwanese President Tsai Ing-wen. This call was a breach of US diplomatic protocol, as the US recognizes the communist People's Republic of China rather than Taiwan (the Republic of China) as the rightful government of China. Dole's other client Kosovo has employed several firms to support it under the umbrella of the Alliance for a New Kosovo. Many commentators believe that it was through effective lobbying that Kosovo persuaded US policymakers to recognize Kosovo's independence from Serbia. The US was one of the first eight countries to recognize Kosovo after it declared independence in 2008.

The politics of sanctions is another area where foreign governments, businesses and individuals rely on the service of private lobbies to achieve favourable policy change. One striking example of such activity is the circumstances surrounding sanctions on Russian elites passed by Congress during the fourth year of the Obama Administration. In the lame-duck session after the 2012 election, substantial bipartisan majorities in Congress passed a law revoking the visas of 18 Russian officials and freezing their assets. The Magnitsky Act, as it was called, was passed in retaliation for the 2009 death of Sergei Magnitsky, a prominent critic of the Putin government who died in a Russian prison after being blocked from receiving medical care. In retaliation to the Magnitsky Act, the Russian Duma (Parliament), by a vote of 400 to 4, voted that same month to ban US citizens from adopting Russian children (the Yakovlev Act). This was a significant move, given that the majority (70 per cent) of the 60,000 internationally adopted Russian children since the end of the Soviet Union had been taken to the US (Jacobs, 2013).

Those affected by the Magnitsky Act turned to lobbyists to reduce or eliminate these sanctions. Lawyers representing Denis Katsyv, whose business interests had been harmed by Magnitsky's activities, founded an organization entitled Human Rights Accountability Global Initiative Foundation (HRAGIF) in February 2016 (Loop et al, 2019). In April 2016, the Foundation hired Rinat Akhmetshin, a Soviet-born naturalized US citizen and registered lobbyist, to advocate on its behalf.[5] The Foundation also employed the services of lobbying firm Cozen O'Connor.[6] It seems that one of HRAGIF's key initiatives was to repeal the Magnitsky Act (Eckel, 2016).

HRAGIF's lobbyist Rinat Akhmetshin described his job as 'a mercenary': 'I spend other people's money here to achieve other people's goals' (quoted in Manson, 2007). In May 2016, Akhmetshin met with Republican Congressman Dana Rohrabacher, Chair of the House Subcommittee on Europe, the day before the House Foreign Affairs Committee was scheduled to consider a second Magnitsky Act, known as the Global Magnitsky Act, which extended travel and asset sanctions against a variety of officials associated with human rights abuses around the world.[7] Akhmetshin was joined by Ron Dellums, a former self-described socialist congressman from California, who sought out senior Democrats on the committee.[8] Enlisting retired members of Congress to meet with incumbent members of Congress is a common lobbying technique. In the subsequent mark-up of the Global Magnitsky Bill, Congressman Rohrabacher proposed an amendment to strike out Magnitsky's name, disassociating Russia from the new legislation (Arnsdorf and Oreskes, 2016).

The lobbying continued into June 2016, when Katsyv's organization arranged for the premiere of an anti-Magnitsky Act film in the

Newseum in Washington, DC. That same month, Donald Trump's son Don, son-in-law Jared Kushner and campaign chair Paul Manfort met at Trump Tower with Akhmetshin and Natalia Veselnitskaya, Katsyv's lawyer. It appears that they managed to swing the meeting on the promise of providing damaging details about Hillary Clinton.[9] In reality, the purpose of the meeting appears to have been to advocate repealing Magnitsky so that Russian adoptions would be reopened to US citizens.[10] Veselnitskaya had also enlisted Mark Cymot of the law firm BakerHolter to help lobby members support Rohrabacher's amendment (Gray, 2017).

The activities of Rinat Akhmetshin and colleagues, just over a three-month period of work, offer a window into the activities of the thousands of lobbyists operating in Washington, DC. Seeking out persuadable lawmakers, making the case to politicians on behalf of clients and attempting to change the climate of opinion are all part and parcel of the lobbyist's job. In this instance, the aforementioned actors were unable to repeal the Magnitsky Act or stop the passage of the Global Magnitsky Act. Their activities came to light due to the Mueller investigations into Russian interference in the 2016 US election and congressional hearings on related matters, but they should not be seen as particularly unusual in the wider context of lobbying in Washington, DC.

There is legislation that is supposed to limit the extent to which foreign actors can exploit the US political system for gain. In 1938, Congress passed the Foreign Agents Registration Act (FARA). On the eve of the Second World War, US policymakers became increasingly concerned by lobby groups that were formed to advocate on behalf of Nazi Germany, such as the Friends of Nazi Germany, the German American Bund and the Silver Shirts. In 1939, 20,000 people attended a pro-Nazi rally at Madison Square Garden in New York organized by the German American Bund.

FARA places stricter requirements on those who lobby on behalf of foreign clients than those who lobby on behalf of domestic clients. However, enforcement is 'notoriously lax', and since it was amended in 1966, FARA has resulted in only 12 successful convictions.[11] Part of the problem is that it may be diplomatically awkward for the US to pursue FARA prosecutions, especially of allies. However, FARA does get used to threaten actors into 'voluntary' compliance, and has been used as the basis of some successful settlements, limiting improper behaviour.

Think tanks and foundations

There are about 2,500 **think tanks** in the US, most of them centred in Washington, DC (Abelson, 2009). These organizations, along with sundry research and advocacy 'foundations', putatively exist to better inform the policy debate. Many do, and some have a non-partisan, public good commitment at the heart of their organizational mission. However, many are funded with the deliberate aim of shifting the policy debate in the preferred direction of those who fund them. They are another example of organized elite influence in US politics. Alexander Hertel-Fernandez and colleagues (2018) call these groups 'donor consortia'.

Think tanks have had a long and storied role in US foreign policy (Abelson, 2004; Parmar, 2004; Stone and Denham, 2004). Some of the oldest think tanks in the US had a foreign policy dimension, including the Carnegie Endowment for International Peace (founded in 1910), the Hoover Institution on War, Revolution, and Peace (founded in 1919) and the Council on Foreign Relations (founded in 1921). Others include the Brookings Institution and the Carnegie Foundation, whose policy remit straddles both domestic and foreign policy (Anderson, 2017). In principle, think tanks exert their influence by publishing timely and relevant studies. Many of these institutes support high-quality research and have sterling reputations.

Think tanks employ researchers and commission research to influence public policy. They are funded by a mix of member subscriptions, contracted research services, donations and endowments from wealthy funders. Knowing who funds these think tanks is important. While think tanks are usually 'not-for-profit', tax-exempt organizations, their funders might expect research output that benefits them and the causes they care about. At the very least, a think tank can amplify the perspectives of their wealthy donors. Hertel-Fernandez et al believe that think tanks and foundations funded by wealthy donors ultimately 'magnify the values of the wealthy by concentrating the financial clout of like-minded privileged people' (2018: 160).

In principle, think tanks exert their influence by publishing timely and relevant studies. However, it is difficult to know how well think tanks *actually* influence public policy. There are various ways to measure think tank influence statistically: frequency by which think tank staff are interviewed by the media, frequency of references to think tank reports by the media, number of downloads of publications, number of publications, number of staff appointed to government posts and citation of reports by public officials in speeches. However, as with lobbyists, true 'influence' is amorphous and manifests in ways that are very difficult to measure, such as 'trust' and 'credibility'.

Today, the most powerful foreign policy think tanks include the Center for Strategic and International Studies, the Center for Security Policy and the RAND Corporation (discussed in Chapter 3). Other think tanks with a broader output than just foreign policy have nonetheless produced influential foreign policy research, the Heritage Foundation and the Brookings Institution being the most notable. In addition to these think tanks, two 'neoconservative' think tanks have been identified as being influential in post-9/11 US foreign policy: the Project for the New American Century and the American Enterprise Institute (AEI).

The Project for the New American Century has received perhaps the most attention by people who look at the role think tanks played in directing President George W. Bush's foreign policy (Abelson, 2009). It was established in 1997 by commentators who are often described as 'neoconservatives', which is really a form of aggressive IR liberalism. In September 2000, the think tank produced a 90-page document called 'Rebuilding America's Defenses'. The document reflected on the previous decade (the 1990s). The authors argued that the decade's status of relative peace and prosperity was unlikely to last or sustain itself. They recommended that the US use its military might to entrench its leadership in the world, arguing that the US should not reduce its armed forces but instead bolster its defences, engage in 'multiple, simultaneous major theatre wars' and pursue 'constabular duties associated with shaping the security environment'. The document was supported by people who became important figures in the Bush Administration the following year: Vice President Dick Cheney, Secretary of Defense Donald Rumsfeld, Deputy Secretary of Defense Paul Wolfowitz and Cheney's Chief of Staff 'Scooter' Libby. The ideas in the document are very similar to those that became known as the **Bush Doctrine**. The Bush Doctrine is said to consist of four elements: pre-emption, military primacy, new multilateralism, and the spread of democracy.

The 'Rebuilding America's Defenses' document has assumed an infamous status because it contains the following line: 'the process of transformation, even if it brings revolutionary change, is likely to be a long one, absent some catastrophic and catalyzing event – like a new Pearl Harbor'. Many people have argued that the September 11, 2001 attacks were the 'new Pearl Harbor' that the document desired. While some fringe conspiracists have argued that this shows that the Bush Administration had a 'motive' for the 9/11 attacks, more sensible heads can at least agree that it showed that figures in the Bush White House appreciated the potential that a 9/11-like event would have for reshaping the US's foreign policy in the direction set out in the document. It is not so much the case that the Project for the New American Century or the 'Rebuilding America's Defenses' document had a direct influence on the Bush Administration. It was, in some sense, an expression of the beliefs of people who already worked in the administration (Abelson, 2006: 215–16). Think tanks, especially those that have a clear ideological predisposition, preach to the converted (Rich, 2004: 25–6).

Think tanks were an intimate part of the Bush White House's foreign policy strategy. A more direct example of influence comes from the AEI. Soon after 9/11, Deputy Secretary of Defense Paul Wolfowitz contacted the AEI's President Christopher DeMuth. He asked DeMuth to organize a private conference to discuss the US's foreign policy strategy in reaction the 9/11 attacks. The AEI met at a secure conference centre in Virginia in November 2001 to discuss the plan. The seven-page document that it produced, recommended, among other things, confrontation with Saddam Hussein. According to Bob Woodward in his book *State of Denial* (2006: 83–5), President Bush, Vice President Cheney and National Security Advisor Condoleezza Rice all found the document persuasive.

Many people credit the AEI with pushing the US government to embrace a 'surge' strategy in Iraq in 2007. As the situation worsened in Iraq, the Bush Administration sought advice on how to turn the situation around. The AEI made the timely and important choice to write a study entitled *Choosing Victory: A Plan for Success in Iraq*. The study was authored by Frederick Kagan, scholar in residence at the AEI (2011). Jack Keane, a retired general, was deployed by the AEI to brief key Bush Administration officials. He met with Dick Cheney in December 2006. The following month (5 January 2007), Kagan presented the plan to US Senators John McCain and Joseph Lieberman. Five days later, the Bush White House announced the surge. The AEI report was said to be pivotal in persuading senior White House and congressional figures of the strategy, even though it was politically unpopular.

Organized labour

During the Second World War and the Cold War, one of the biggest interest groups involved in American defence policy was the American labour movement. Kevin Boyle writes that during this period 'the labor movement had occupied a preeminent place in national politics' (1995: 1). The proportion of American workers in a union during the Cold War was much higher than today. In the mid-20th century, 37 per cent of the non-farming private sector was unionized (Dinlersoz and Greenwood, 2016). In 2019, only 6.2 per cent of private sector workers were members of trade unions in the US.[12] While organized labour has not disappeared entirely from the American political landscape, its political influence is much shrunken from what it used to be.

In 1939, after six years of the New Deal's peaceful jobs programmes to combat the Great Depression, the American unemployment rate was still a stubborn 15 per cent of the workforce (8 million people). By the end of 1941, when the US entered the Second World War, unemployment had fallen to less than 5 per cent. By 1945, the US was at virtually full employment (1.2 per cent). During the war, trade union strength rose. The National War Labor Board placed restrictions on wage bargaining, but unions could focus on supplemental ('fringe') benefits, such as healthcare, holidays and pensions. Indeed, union-negotiated, employer-provided healthcare became a foundational element of the US healthcare system (Brown, 1997). Still today half of Americans receive their healthcare through their employer or the employer of a close family member. Many companies with low union density also adopted these 'fringe' benefits, partly to thwart successful union balloting in their organizations (Brown, 1997).

As the Second World War came to a close, many American workers feared that peace would bring unemployment (Barnard, 1982). For example, Boris Shishkin, who was a secretary for the AFL-CIO (American Federation of Labor and Congress of Industrial Organization, similar to the Trades Union Congress [TUC] in the UK), wrote a paper entitled 'The Next Depression' in 1944 warning that the end of the war could spell disaster for the American worker. These fears were not entirely unfounded. After the First World War, many Americans returned from service abroad to find few job opportunities at home. This continued well into the 1920s. Long before the Wall Street Crash of 1929 and the Great Depression, thousands of war veterans were left in poverty and unemployment. By the time the Great Depression was under way, in 1932, 43,000 veterans and their dependants marched on Washington, DC to demand pensions for their service in the First World War. They were known as the 'Bonus Army', trying to redeem their 'bonus' for wartime service. President Herbert Hoover reacted by setting the army on the veterans, which led to violence, resulting in the death of two protestors and over a thousand injured.

After the Second World War, demobilization did affect American workers. For example, almost immediately after VJ Day (Victory in Japan Day), there were 300,000 manufacturing job redundancies in Michigan. By 1949, unemployment had ticked up to 7.9 per cent. The unions needed to reverse the tide. Foreign policy offered a solution to these domestic ills. Union leaders enthusiastically signed onto the Truman Doctrine, the idea that the US should contain the spread of communism anywhere in the world. Secretary of State George Marshall, author of the Marshall Plan, became the first secretary of state to address a union meeting when he was an honoured speaker at the CIO conference in 1947. In 1950, from the perspective of American labour, the Truman Doctrine paid its first dividends. President Harry Truman sent 300,000 US troops to Korea. The war helped reverse the domestic economic situation. By 1953, the final year of the Korean War, unemployment had fallen to 1.8 per cent.

What was fuelling these low unemployment figures? One factor was, of course, the mass mobilization of American men through the draft. But the draft only captured a particular segment of the American workforce. The wars did not simply provide jobs through enlistment; they also provided jobs back home through an expansion of defence-related industries. Between 1950 and 1951, the US defence budget grew from $14 billion to $34 billion, an astonishing 10 per cent of GDP. For the most part, these high levels of spending persisted

Figure 6.1: US unemployment rate (%), 1920–54

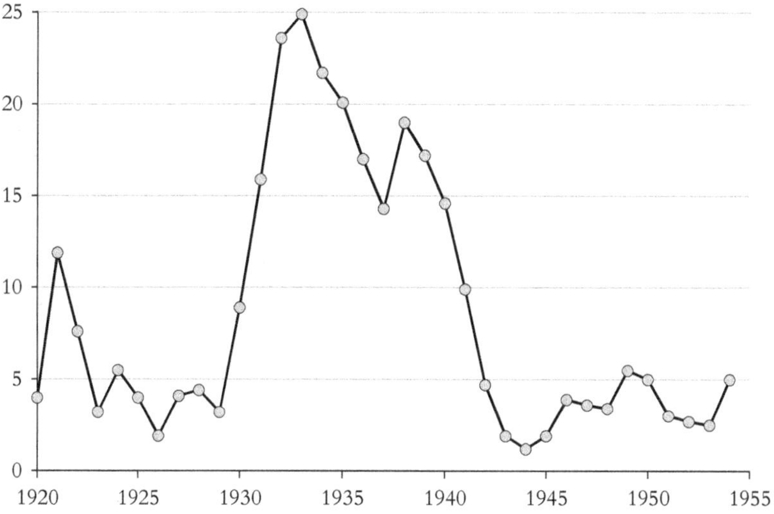

Source: Data based on Lebergott (1957)

through the Cold War. A substantial proportion of this enormous budget was spent on US manufacturing jobs. In 1960, about one-tenth of the entire US workforce relied directly or indirectly on the defence budget (7.5 million jobs) (Barnard, 1982). In the 1960s, in seven states, more than 20 per cent of manufacturing jobs were tied to the military budget (The Economist Intelligence Unit, 1963). In some US states, these new defence jobs came at the perfect time. As traditional manufacturing jobs were fading due to technological change and imports, Department of Defense contracts provided new, well-paid factory jobs. For example, in Connecticut, as its old textile mills declined and closed, new factories building submarines took their place. The first nuclear submarine, the USS *Nautilus*, and the first ballistic missile submarine, the USS *George Washington*, were built by General Dynamics Electric Boat in Groton, Connecticut in the 1950s. These submarines were built by a 100 per cent unionized workforce (Barnard, 1982).

In the mid-20th century, it was clear to many that American labour had become dependent on high levels of defence investment. Democratic Congressman Jamie Whitten told the House Subcommittee on Appropriations, 'It is a very, very sincere statement on my part about a real fear that I have. In other words, the Department of Defense is the greatest buyer and greatest employer. It is the source of day-to-day prosperity in a district'.[13] In this, the trade union movement saw opportunity for bolstering strength. The unions encouraged higher defence spending, with union publications encouraging members to vote for pro-defence (hawkish) candidates (Barnard, 1982). Unions trumpeted big defence projects. The AFL, for example, was extremely supportive of building the *Nautilus* nuclear submarine. A similar situation arose recently in the UK where the left-wing union Unite, otherwise a strong supporter of the anti-nuclear, former Labour leader Jeremy Corbyn, was staunchly in favour of renewing the Trident nuclear submarine programme because of the defence jobs associated with it.

Some left-wing intellectuals were deeply unhappy with this alliance between organized labour and the defence industry. Labour activist Sidney Lens (1959) wrote that the CIO had the makings of being a radical union, but its radicalism was 'bought' by the prospect of good Cold War defence jobs. Lens's book was entitled *The Crisis of American Labor*, perhaps an odd title when organized labour was in its heyday, but Lens was reflecting on what he regarded as the moral and ideological crisis of the union movement. Union leaders had betrayed the international class struggle in exchange for the delivery of particularized benefits for union members, even if this meant bolstering immoral industries and foreign policy positions. Union leaders were strong backers of the defence establishment's anti-communism. In 1949, the CIO banned communists from holding union office. In 1959, AFL-CIO President George Meany refused to meet with Soviet premier Nikita Khrushchev on his visit to the US. He locked the doors of the AFL-CIO headquarters in Washington, leaving Anastas Mikoyan, the Soviet deputy premier, to press his nose against the glass trying to get in (Barnard, 1982).

American trade unions were, by and large, supportive of the war in Vietnam in its early stages because their members wanted the jobs that came through military contracts and increased defence spending (Foner, 1984). In 1965, George Meany declared that the American labour movement would support the war in Vietnam 'no matter what the academic do-gooders may say, no matter what the apostles of appeasement may say' (*Hartford Courant*, 2004). Jacqueline Smetak (1994) writes, 'the Vietnam war, so long as the body count remained low, could be seen, and was seen, as a positive benefit' for American workers. As the situation in Vietnam worsened, organized labour turned against the war. The AFL-CIO's National Peace Action Coalition sponsored marches in American cities, with posters reading 'The Vietnamese never froze my wages', a reference to Richard Nixon's executive order in August 1971, which froze wages for 90 days (Cushing, 2011: 291). It was the first time a president had frozen wages since the aforementioned wage stabilization of the Second World War.

There has been a precipitous decline in trade union density in the US in the last half-century. Only about 10 per cent of American workers in 2020 were unionized, compared to about 25 per cent in the mid-1960s.[14] Some occupations, especially public sector jobs such as teachers, firefighters and the police, are highly unionized, but these are the exceptions rather than the rule (Western and Rosenfeld, 2011). While the size of organized labour has been in decline in the US for decades, their influence on individual members of Congress is not insignificant. Many commentators link the political power of organized labour in proportion to union density (see, for example, Edsall, 1985; Goldfield, 1987; Moody, 1988). Boyle sullenly concluded in the wake of the anti-union Reagan presidency, 'the American labor movement is little more than a hollow shell, unable to defend its members from corporate **retrenchment**, powerless to affect national policy, and devoid of political clout' (1995: 1). Yet it should be noted that during this putatively worst decade in organized labour's history, Congress passed, with bipartisan veto-proof majorities, the Worker

Adjustment and Retraining Notification Act of 1988, which required unions, workers and local officials to be given two months' notice before mass redundancies, and the Employee Polygraph Protection Act of 1988, which prohibits the use of lie detector tests by management against employees.

The concept of uniform 'decline', therefore, is not particularly helpful in studying the political power of the American labour movement due to the segmentation of unions and issue agendas (Form, 1995; Dark, 1999). The political strength of few other groups in society is measured solely by their share of the population. The story must be recast with greater nuance and precision. For example, some unions increased their budgets even as membership declined, by maximizing income from their assets. Thus, a union with a smaller membership could, in fact, spend more in elections and political campaigning. Unions exert an influence, especially within the Democratic Party, through campaign contributions, independent political spending, voter mobilization, rallies, lobbying, information provision, briefing on substantive policy matters and communications. Indeed, many of the techniques used by private sector lobbying firms are also deployed by American trade unions to ensure their continued influence in Washington.

Unions still play a role in some areas of US foreign policy, especially in trade and tariffs. When the US–Korea Free Trade Agreement was being negotiated during the presidency of George W. Bush, the United Auto Workers (UAW) was particularly active in trying to restrict the importation of Korean-produced cars, such as those made by Hyundai, into the US market. The president of the UAW, Ron Gettelfinger (nd), called for the deal's rejection. However, under the Obama presidency, the trade agreement was revised, this time with the involvement of organized labour in the negotiations. Obama secured delays to automobile tariff reductions on automobiles, as well as winning greater access to the Korean market for US-made automobiles. This time, the UAW cheered: 'The UAW fully supports this trade agreement because the automotive provisions, which are very different from those negotiated by President George W. Bush in 2007, will create significantly greater market access for American auto exports and include strong, auto-specific safeguards to protect our domestic markets from potentially harmful surges of Korean automotive imports' (King, 2011). An Obama official remarked that 'It has been a long time since a union supported a trade agreement' (Schneider, 2010).

While the union movement is not quite extinct, it is a poor resemblance of the mid-20th-century mammoth it once was. The political role of organized labour has undoubtedly declined. This decline is significant because, as Hacker and Pierson write, 'labor is the only organized interest focused on the broad economic concerns of those with modest incomes' (2010: 186). An unequal economy directly relates to an unequal politics. The distortions of modern capitalism are deeply interconnected with distortions in US policy outcomes.

Religious groups

The US is an exception among most developed Western democracies in that the prevalence of religious practice and professed religious belief is particularly high. In a country where nine in ten people profess a belief in God and four in ten count themselves as evangelical Protestants, it seems not only likely, but also almost certain that its politics will be influenced by religion (Marty, 2002).

In the 1830s, Alexis de Tocqueville remarked on a perceivable affinity between religious belief and political practice. In the late 19th and early 20th century, American Protestant missionaries were some of the most internationally active of any group of American citizens (Hutchinson, 1987; Preston, 2010). While the ethical record of these missionaries is at best patchy, they had a demonstrable impact on the course of world affairs. Were it not for American missionaries, Sun Yat-sen's nationalist revolution in China may not have been as well resourced as it was (Schiffrin, 1968; Seagrave, 1985).

Since the 1970s, commentators have remarked on a growing trend in American religious history – the politicization of the 'Christian Right' (Phillips, 2006). According to the dominant narrative, in the wake of the social upheavals of the 1960s, culturally conservative Christian leaders began to rally their flocks to participate in politics in an unprecedentedly organized fashion (Wills, 2007). A major effort by political parties to court religious segments of the population began in the 1970s. After the resignation of Richard Nixon in 1974, Republican political operatives began to look for new ways to revive the party. In the 1972 election, Republicans had been successful in aligning Democrats with objectionable elements of the 1960s protest culture, and Republican political strategists were confident that they could create an abiding chasm between a Republican-voting conservative, Christian majority and a Democrat-voting progressive, secularist minority. Conservative Christians were ripe for wooing for several reasons. Christians had already formed well-organized institutions with robust links with local communities, but they had traditionally shied away from electoral politics. Traditionally, matters such as sexuality, reproduction, schooling and gender had been the purview of the family unit. With the cultural upheavals of the 1960s where the personal became the political, conservative Christians began to feel increasing government encroachment into the family sphere. Religious elites such as Jerry Falwell, Pat Robertson and Jim and Tammy Fae Bakker formed 'special purpose groups' in the 1970s and 1980s that attracted wide followings and that were, in part, efforts to mobilize conservative Christians to support a particular religious agenda through political means (Davis and Robinson, 1996).

The Reagan presidency did not reward religious evangelicals to the extent that they had hoped. Apart from occasional lip service to 'traditional' values, there was no deliberate effort on the part of the Reagan White House to implement the major policy changes on the Christian Right's agenda. In response, Pat Robertson, an ordained minister, ran for the Republican presidential nomination in 1988 to challenge Reagan's Vice President George H.W. Bush. With Reverend Jesse Jackson vying to lead the Democratic Party ticket, the nomination campaigns on both sides proved to be the most overtly religious in recent American political history (Noll and Harlow, 2007).

It appeared that evangelical Protestants voted for right-wing candidates on the sole basis of shared religious values, regardless of other important considerations. The electoral success of George W. Bush in 2004 presents the strongest prima facie case from the past 40 years that the religious credentials of the presidential nominee were an important factor in the election outcome. This claim is typically based on several factors, including a high proportion of voters who cited 'moral values' as the most important issue facing the country in a national exit poll, same-sex marriage referenda in several key 'battleground' states and the alleged increase in turnout by evangelicals. From this information, commentators concluded that Bush's victory over John Kerry was a vindication of Karl Rove's strategy to mobilize the Christian Right to vote Republican, and a culmination of the efforts of Republican strategists who had been tapping Christian groups for political support since the 1970s.

The George W. Bush and Donald Trump presidencies have been policy boons to religious conservatives. By executive order in 2002, President George W. Bush created the Center for Faith-Based and Community Initiatives within USAID. Donald Trump renamed the organization the Center for Faith and Opportunity Initiative in 2018. The agency was designed to encourage conservative evangelical organizations to deliver aid on behalf of the US federal government, although it officially purports to offer a 'level playing ground' to all faiths. Under President Bush, evangelical organizations received over a billion dollars through the initiative, including the evangelical aid group World Vision ($374 million), Rev Franklin Graham's Samaritan's Purse ($31 million) and Rev Pat Robertson's 'Operation Blessing' (Marsden, 2008: 130). Kirsten Evans, director of the agency under Donald Trump, was previously executive director of In Defense of Christians. President Trump skilfully made the State Department an important instrument of 'delivering' for evangelical Christians, a constituency that comprised nearly half of his voters in the 2016 and 2020 presidential elections.[15]

These faith-based initiatives have not been limited to Republican presidents. In 2013, Barack Obama created the Office of Religion and Global Affairs (OGRA) within the State Department. It was established to assist in the implementation of President Obama's 'US Strategy on Religious Leader and Faith Community Engagement'. The Strategy's objective was to ensure that 'religious literacy' became an integral part of the training at the Foreign Service Institute and the Department of Defense (Marsden, 2018). Obama appointed Shaun Casey, a professor of Christian ethics at Wesley Theological Seminary, to lead the OGRA. In spite of Casey's Christian background, Obama also created new positions to engage with Jewish and Muslims groups around the world: the Special Envoy to Monitor and Combat Anti-Semitism, the Special Representative to Muslim Communities and the Special Envoy to the Organization of Islamic Cooperation. These appointments, implicitly, recognized not only the importance of Jewish and Muslim people in global affairs, but also as key voting constituencies within the Democratic Party. The Trump Administration abolished the position of the Special Representative to Muslim Communities in Trump's first year in office (Lynch and Gramer, 2017).

The politics of religion cannot be fully understood without taking race and **ethnicity** into account, as with so many other dimensions of American political behaviour. In spite of sharing similar religious beliefs, black Christian fundamentalists and white evangelicals differ starkly in their political behaviour (Emerson and Hawkins, 2007). In 2020, roughly 7 in 10 African-American evangelicals voted for Democrat Joe Biden, whereas about the same proportion of white evangelicals supported Republican Donald Trump.[16] Political division of these religiously similar groups suggests that race is of superseding importance. Even among white Christian voters, ethnicity can still play a decisive role in predicting political behaviour. Phillips has persuasively argued that ethnic divisions in the upper-Midwest in 2000 and 2004 were much better predictors of voting behaviour than religious affiliation. He specifically examined the voting habits of Lutherans, who make up a sizeable proportion of Christians in the region. Phillips found that Lutherans with a German background tended to vote in favour of Bush, but those of Norwegian background tended to vote for Gore and Kerry, suggesting that other cultural dynamics were influential in their decision-making (Phillips, 2006: 391). These racial and ethnic dynamics will be examined in the next chapter.

Conclusion

This chapter has explored the role played by organized interests in American politics. Interest groups take many forms. As an object of study in political science, interest groups simply refer to the coalitions by which people with common material aspirations organize collectively to pursue their goals through politics. They are a way for citizens and motivated publics to express their views with greater coherence, focus and effect. Yet, if interest groups are unrepresentative of the mass public, then their impact can 'distort' the political process. They can undermine the democratic ideal of one person, one voice. We might ask, are interest groups legitimate?

In 2014, political scientists Martin Gilens and Benjamin Page reviewed nearly 2,000 policy issues over a 20-year period, testing four theories of who governs in American politics: average citizens (democracy), the rich (plutocracy), elite interest groups (oligarchy) or mass interest groups (polyarchy). They found little evidence for rule by the average citizen or mass-based interest groups, such as organized labour. The rich and organized business interest groups held a set of policy preferences that did not correlate with the views of the mass public, yet they substantially correlated with actual policy outcomes. This led Gilens and Page to conclude, 'In the United States, our findings indicate, the majority does *not* rule – at least not in the causal sense of actually determining policy outcomes. When a majority of citizens disagrees with economic elites or with organized interests, they generally lose' (2014: 576; original emphasis). Unusually for an academic political science article, especially one with the banal title 'Testing theories of American politics', their research had an explosive effect. The article was widely covered in the press. *The New Yorker* asked, 'Is America an oligarchy?' (Cassidy, 2014). The BBC answered, 'Study: US is an oligarchy, not a democracy' (2014). The Princeton and Northwestern University professors were even invited on to the *Daily Show* on Comedy Central to speak about their academic research.[17]

Gilens and Page's research was powerful because of the quantitative sophistication behind it, but it echoed a refrain from decades of political science writing (Freeman, 1955; Mills, 1956; Schattschneider, 1960; Cater, 1964; Lowi, 1969). Hedrick Smith (1988) wrote about the 'iron triangle' of policymaking in Washington, whereby the bureaucracy, Congress and interest groups form a mutually reinforcing and supportive policy loop that locks out non-specialists and the public from influence (hence the 'iron'). E.E. Schattschneider famously captured this view in his book *The Semi-Sovereign People* when he wrote, 'The flaw with the pluralist heaven is that the heavenly chorus sings with a strong upper-class accent' (1960: 35).

7

Race, Diasporas and Ethnic Politics

The US is a diverse country, home to a wide variety of diasporic communities. A **diaspora** refers to a population who live in a location that is different from the one from which they originated. Many diasporas are composed of immigrants or descendants of immigrants, but the terms 'diasporic community' and 'immigrant community' are not synonymous. Some lack an immigrant history, such as descendants from slavery, forced deportation (for example, penal colonies) and forced migration. Nearly every ethnic group in the world has some diasporic community in the US. Some of these are modest in size, but many are very large, sometimes much larger than the population who have remained in the territory of origin. For example, there are six times as many Americans who identify as 'Irish American' than there are people living in Ireland. Historically, diasporic groups have been politically important in terms of domestic policy. Ethnic and racial identities have formed the backbone of political behaviour throughout the history of US elections. It is difficult to explain or understand US politics without taking into account race and the subdivisions within racial groups, known as 'ethnicities' (King and Smith, 2005).

Many diasporic groups have formed organizations that aim to influence US foreign policy vis-à-vis their country of origin. These are often referred to as 'ethnic lobbies'. This chapter explores four major sets of ethnic 'lobbies': the Irish lobby, the Cuban lobby, the Armenian lobby and the Israeli lobby. These have been chosen because their major financial and political arms, such as the American Israel Public Affairs Committee (AIPAC), the Cuban American National Foundation (CANF), the Armenian National Committee of America (ANCA) and the Irish Northern Aid Committee (NORAID), have had detectable impacts on the content and focus of US foreign policy.

This chapter will also study the role of the African-American community in the construction of US foreign policy. African Americans cannot readily be understood as an *immigrant* diasporic community because, for most black people in the US, theirs is a history of forced transportation and enslavement. Nonetheless, African Americans have played an important role in shaping US foreign policy, and the Congressional Black Caucus (CBC) has taken on an important role in advocating for social justice causes in Africa. There is also a non-trivial immigrant black population in the US (about 1 in 10 black Americans).

Ethnic lobbies are internally diverse. Advocates within the lobbies do not always operate in concert. Sometimes, their influence has been exaggerated, and they are a favourite culprit of political conspiracists who consider them to be 'all powerful' (Lieberman, 2009). Nonetheless, diasporic communities constitute major 'issue publics' in US foreign policy (see Chapter 5). Just as domestic US politics cannot be properly understood without taking race and ethnicity into account, the same is true for US foreign policy.

The languages of race and ethnicity

Race and ethnicity are social constructs, and therefore defy objective specification.[1] Lawrence Bobo and Cybelle Fox define racial categories as 'historically contingent social constructions' whose 'distinctions or categorizations will vary in configuration and salience over time' (2003: 319). A person with a particular background or set of physical characteristics may be racialized one way in a particular time or place but differently at another juncture or locality (Hoetink, 1967). To say that race and ethnicity are social constructs is not to say they are meaningless or detached from differences in appearance, but that their meaning requires some kind of social recognition. They are not 'natural' or biological in the sense that these categories are neither fixed throughout time nor universally intelligible. Debra Thompson writes that racial classifications are 'shifting, contested, and ultimately rather fragile' (2015: 115). Indeed, without having been 'socialized' to understand meaningful physical and morphological distinctions between people who look black, white, Asian, indigenous or Latino, we might very well see completely different physical markers as socially relevant (or none at all). Ta-Nehisi Coates describes race as 'the child of racism, not the father' (2015: 7). Noel Ignatiev summarized: 'people in Africa were not enslaved because they were black; rather, they were defined as black because they were enslaved' (1995: 215).

Race and ethnicity are also *political* constructs in that the government provides the officially sanctioned vocabulary of race. The state gives ultimately 'fictitious boundaries' an air of 'administrative legitimacy' (Thompson, 2015: 116). This is especially true with the census, which has been conducted in the US without interruption every 10 years since 1790. The census categories for race and ethnicity have varied considerably over time, often in response to political demands or social mores. The US government considered 'Mexican' to be a separate racial category until it became important for the US to establish warmer relations with Mexico in the lead-up to the Second World War, as part of Franklin Roosevelt's Good Neighbor Policy. In 1940 the US census transferred 'Mexican' from being a separate race to being an ethnic subcategory within the 'white race' (Gross, 2008). By doing so, Mexicans in the US gained access to privileges that had hitherto been limited to whites, including the right to become naturalized US citizens. People of Asian birth were not permitted to become naturalized US citizens until 1952 (Johnson, 2020b). Still today, the US census declines to consider Hispanics/Latinos as their own racial group. US diplomatic imperatives helped to shape the officially sanctioned, domestic language of race.

In 1977, the Office of Management and Budget declared in Statistical Directive 15 that there were four races in the US: American Indian or Alaska Native, Asian or Pacific Islander, Black, and White (Thompson, 2015: 126). The contemporary census offers six categories of racial identity: White, Black, Native American, Asian (Indian, Chinese, Filipino, Japanese, Korean, Vietnamese, Other), Pacific Islander (Hawaiian, Guamanian, Samoan, Other), or 'Some other race'. A person filling out a census form is also allowed to tick more than one of these races to indicate that they are mixed race. Yet in the US there is a relatively low take-up of people who identify with two or more races (just 3.1 per cent in the 2010 census). Governments have sometimes had incentives to minimize mixed race identification. In the US, under the racial apartheid system known as Jim Crow (1870s–1960s), people with 'one drop' of African ancestry (in practice, usually at least one black great-grandparent) were racialized as black and therefore excluded from white institutions, social spaces and legal privileges. In Canada, the Crown had a fiduciary obligation to those who were classified as 'Indian' (that is, indigenous/First Nations). Thus, the Canadian government had an incentive to deem mixed race indigenous Canadians as 'white' in order to eliminate eligibility to various legal protections owed to First Nations people, such as land rights (Thompson, 2015). There can also be strong social pressures to discourage mixed race identity. Civic groups structured around racial or ethnic identity may have an incentive to minimize mixed race identification because a growing identification with 'mixed race' could plausibly weaken or distort solidaristic and organizational ties structured around particular racial categories.

'Race' and 'ethnicity' are sometimes used interchangeably in popular contexts, but they have slightly different meanings. **Race** refers to broad categories structured (imperfectly) according to physical characteristics and regional origin. 'Ethnicity' operates within racial groups and is often determined by a combination of markers such as national origin, religion or language. For example, a person who is of Irish heritage in the US would today be understood as racially white and ethnically Irish. A person who is of Korean heritage would be identified as racially Asian and ethnically Korean. But racial and ethnic categories are not fixed. Some 'races' have become 'ethnicities' over time, as the example of Mexican Americans shows. In the 19th century, Irish immigrants to the US were treated in custom and law as a separate, non-white race. Indeed, at that time, it was common for people to refer to a variety of different European 'races', such as Slav, Italian, Greek, Irish, German or French. By the 20th century, these groups became ethnic categories under the overarching racial category of 'white' (Jacobson, 1998). Some historians argue that these groups ultimately 'became white' through expressing their superiority to African Americans (Ignatiev, 1995; Roediger, 2005). Toni Morrison wrote 'the move into mainstream America always means buying into the notion of American blacks as the real aliens. Whatever the ethnicity or nationality of the immigrant, his nemesis is understood to be African American' (1993). Personalizing this experience, James Baldwin reflected, 'I had my fill of seeing people come down the gangplank on Wednesday, let us say, speaking not a word of English, and by Friday discovering that I was working for them and they were calling me nigger like everybody else. So that the Italian adventure or even the Jewish adventure, however grim, is distinguished from my own adventure' (Baldwin and Mead, 1971: 67–8). In the other direction, the growing identification of Hispanic/Latino Americans as 'some other race' suggests that the Hispanic/Latino ethnicity may be evolving into a distinct racial category, rather than as a mostly white ethnicity.

The terms 'Hispanic' and 'Latino' are used to refer to people from Central and South America. The term 'Hispanic' was first used by the federal government in the 1970s. In 1976, Congress passed a resolution mandating the federal executive to 'develop methods' to collect 'data relating to Americans of Spanish origin or descent'.[2] Hispanic is a flawed term because not everyone from the region is of Spanish heritage or speaks Spanish, such as Brazilians. Latino is a more encompassing term, which refers to geography: people from Latin America.[3] However, 'Latino' is less commonly used than 'Hispanic' by those in the US who originate from Latin America. According to a 2015 Pew Research poll of people of Latin American heritage, 32 per cent say they prefer the term 'Hispanic', just 15 per cent say they prefer the term 'Latino' and the remaining majority (51 per cent) say that they have no preference between the two.[4] Some people object to the term 'Latino' because it is a masculine noun in Spanish. Some commentators use the terms 'Latinx' or 'Latinidad', which are gender-neutral. But a 2019 survey found that over 76 per cent of Latinos had never heard of the word 'Latinx', and of the 23 per cent who had heard the term, only 3 per cent said they would use it (Lopez et al, 2020). Ironically, a term designed to be 'inclusive' seems to be used by only a very narrow set of the population.

Hispanics/Latinos are often treated as a separate race in popular commentary, but according to the US census, they constitute a (pan-) ethnic group. The census asks whether a person is 'of Hispanic, Latino, or Spanish origin'. The census then leaves it to individual respondents to specify their racial identity. A majority view themselves as white. In the 2010 census, 53.0 per cent of Hispanics/Latinos identified as 'white' racially. As Table 7.1 shows, 36.7 per cent identified as 'Some other race', which constituted 96.8 per cent of all respondents who filled in that category. In other words, 'Some other race' seems to have been almost exclusively used by Hispanics/Latinos who could not find a satisfactory label in the 'race' question on the census; 2.5 per cent

Table 7.1: How do Hispanics/Latinos identify racially?

	Population	% of Hispanics/ Latinos	% of racial category
White	26,735,713	52.97	11.95
Some other race	18,503,103	36.66	96.84
Two or more races	3,042,592	6.03	33.77
Black	1,243,471	2.46	3.19
American Indian and Alaska Native	685,150	1.36	23.37
Asian	209,128	0.41	1.43
Native Hawaiian and Pacific Islander	58,437	0.12	10.82
Total	50,477,594	100	–

Source: Based on data from the 2010 US Census (US Census Bureau, 2012)

of Latinos identified as black, which constitutes about 3.2 per cent of black Americans.

These subtle racial differences within the Latino community appear to have political implications. In the 2020 presidential election, Donald Trump improved his support among Latinos overall relative to 2016, but performed disproportionately well among Latinos who identify as white. Figure 7.1 shows a data analysis of the 20 most heavily Latino counties in the US, all of which are at least 80 per cent Latino. I analysed the proportion of Latinos in those counties who identified in the 2010 census as racially white, which ranged from 53.3 per cent of Latinos (Mora County, New Mexico) to 98.6 per cent (Starr County, Texas). Trump increased his vote most in the counties that had the highest proportion of white-identified Latinos. For example, Trump's vote increased by 18.9 per cent in Mora County but by 59.7 per cent in Starr County.

To recognize that racial and ethnic categories are socially and politically constructed and, therefore, to some extent arbitrary, is not to say that they are irrelevant or that they should or could be simply 'wished away'. The Howard School international relations theorist Alain Locke astutely observed in 1916, 'Race as a unit of social thought is of permanent significance.... Too much social thinking has gone into it for it to be abandoned as a center of thought or practice.' One of the paradoxes of diverse nations, like the US, is that, on the one

Figure 7.1: Increase in Trump support in the most heavily Hispanic/Latino counties in the US, related to proportion of Hispanics/Latinos in the county who identify racially as white, 2016–20

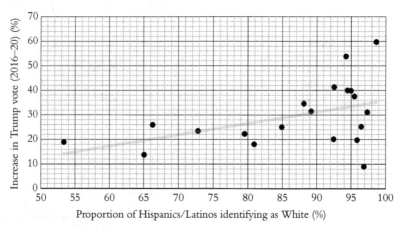

Source: Based on data from the 2010 US Census (US Census Bureau, 2012) and 2016–20 US presidential election results (*The New York Times*, 2016, 2020)

hand, ideal democratic theory teaches that racial distinctions should have no weight in the treatment of others. On the other hand, the racial status quo is unequal. Recognition of historic and material racial distinctions is essential in remedying and, ultimately, eliminating racial difference. To be 'colour blind' in a world of racial inequality is no virtue. It is to be wilfully 'blind' to racial injustice.

Explanations of influence

There is strong evidence that many ethnic and racial minority communities have 'punched above their weight', numerically speaking, to shape the direction of US foreign policy. There are several, potentially overlapping explanations for the successful influence of ethnic lobbies. These include the structures of the US policymaking process; electoral influence; economic leverage; descriptive representation and affective solidarity; and the alignment of ethnic group interests with perceptions of US national security and prosperity.

First, organized ethnic groups are able to take advantage of many of the structural features of the US policymaking process that have been leveraged by other interest groups, as discussed in the previous chapter. The US's high number of institutional 'veto players' and the relatively open access of US political institutions to lobbyists give ethnic lobbies ample opportunities to influence policy. In Congress, for example, the lobbies organize **caucuses**, which are essentially clubs that members of Congress agree to join (often for a fee) to express their support for particular causes.

Ethnic lobbies also provide unique opportunities for foreign governments and other foreign actors to influence US policymaking. Chapter 6 described how foreign governments contract the services of private lobby shops to advance their interests, a tactic that is often viewed as more efficacious than the traditional modes of 'embassy' diplomacy. If a lobbyist works directly for a foreign government, he or she must register with the Foreign Agents Registration Act (FARA). As discussed previously, former Senate Majority Leaders Tom Daschle and Bob Dole were compelled to publish their lobbying activities for Taiwan, Turkey and other nations as part of FARA disclosure rules. Ethnic lobbies offer a different, more subtle entry point. Organizations that are allegedly lobbying on behalf of the concerns of an ethnic group in the US (rather than directly for its home country) are not subject to FARA restrictions. A group representing 'Russian Americans' might ultimately be advocating for a cause that the Russian government also supports, but the domestic ethnic interest group will have fewer restrictions than would the Russian government or a lobbyist acting on their behalf.

Second, ethnic groups use their leverage within the electoral process to shape US foreign policy. Three factors explain their differing levels of success through electoral politics: partisan loyalty, geography and unity. Some ethnic groups are principally identified with one party over another and use their influence *within a party*, such as through primary elections, to achieve policy leverage. For example, the Irish were traditionally associated with the Democratic Party. On St Patrick's Day 1976, Democratic candidate for president Jimmy Carter marched down Fifth Avenue in New York wearing a badge emblazoned with the slogan 'England, get out of Ireland'.[5] The state's Democratic primary was three weeks later. Carter's brazen support for a united Ireland was clearly a ploy to the Irish Catholic electorate within the Democratic Party.

Then there are the more general electoral explanations for ethnic group influence: geography and group unity. Throughout US history, examples can be found of ethnic groups shifting their votes *en masse* in accordance to approval or disapproval of a presidential administration's foreign policy approach. Samuel Lubell (1952) found that in the 1940 election, the biggest swings against President Franklin D. Roosevelt were in counties with large German-descended populations, while strong support was recorded in counties with Norwegian and Polish-descended populations. Although the US was technically still neutral in November 1940, it was obvious that Roosevelt was antipathetic towards Germany and had undertaken measures to assist resistance efforts in Norway and Poland, which had been invaded by Hitler's Germany.

Some ethnic groups are numerous in the US population, but size isn't everything. Stephen Saideman (2002) argues that, being a 'small' community is not as much of a disadvantage as might first appear. In fact, a relatively small diasporic community may be better equipped to mobilize rapidly, achieve higher levels of community unity, and focus on a more limited (and therefore focused) set of policy issues. Smaller communities are less likely to have diffuse priorities and intragroup conflicts. Some groups with relatively large populations in the US have struggled to make their mark on the US's foreign policy development. People of Mexican descent make up more than 11 per cent of the US population (36 million people), but the Mexican lobby is relatively disorganized and not very prominent in foreign policy discussions. Two main organs of the Mexican lobby, the National Council of La Raza and the Mexican American Legal

Defense and Educational Fund, are mostly focused on domestic policy, in particular the conditions of Mexicans in the US rather than on the US's policy to Mexico or political affairs within Mexico itself (McCormick, 2008).

The unusual features of the US political system, such as equal state representation in the US Senate and the electoral college to choose the president, give some groups greater impact on electoral outcomes by virtue of their geographical distribution. Under the electoral college, voters in some states are much more critical to a presidential election's outcome than voters in other states. In the last eight elections, Florida has been decided by about 5 percentage points or less each time. The state carries 29 electoral college votes, 10 per cent of the total needed to win the presidency. Since 1964, Florida has been captured by the overall electoral college winner in every election except for two (Clinton in 1992 and Biden in 2020). The electoral college system means that minority groups that would numerically be trivial in a nationwide, popular election (as is the case in most presidential democracies outside the US) can become extremely significant in deciding the next election winner of the electoral college. This has been especially true for two communities in Florida: Jews and Cubans – 654,000 Jews are estimated to live in Florida, bigger than the winning margins of every presidential candidate in the state since 1992. One in ten Jews in the US live in Florida, more than any other state except for California and New York. There are 1.2 million Cubans living in Florida, two-thirds of the entire Cuban population in the US. The next biggest Cuban population is in California, with only 88,000 Cubans.

A third way in which ethnic groups exert their influence on US foreign policy is through their economic clout. As Chapter 6 established, the exceptionally high levels of privately raised campaign contributions in US elections mark the country as an international outlier. Well-resourced diasporic communities can use their financial power to help them make an outsized impact in the US political process. There are about 5.7 million Jews in the US, roughly 2 per cent of the electorate. In 2012, Jews made up 18 per cent of Barack Obama's donors and 7 per cent of Mitt Romney's donors. In 2016, they made up 20 per cent of Hillary Clinton's donors and 3 per cent of Donald Trump's donors (Hersh and Schaffner, 2016). The Indian-American population is another electorate that is numerically small (just 1 per cent of the US population) but economically powerful. Indians in the US are highly educated – 70 per cent of Indian-American adults have university degrees (Desilver, 2014) compared with just 35 per cent of white Americans (Duffin, 2021). They are a largely affluent group. Their median income is double that of the overall US median. Indian Americans also have powerful business ties, with one in five Silicon Valley firms estimated to be owned by an Indian American (McCormick, 2008). Vice President Kamala Harris is the first Indian American to be elected to national office.[6] The Indian lobby is mainly represented by the US India Political Action Committee, but there are also professional lobbies for Indian Americans such as the American Association of Physicians of Indian Origin and the Asian American Hotel Owners Association. The Congressional Caucus on India and Indian Americans has over 100 members, but until 2017, none of them were Indian American. This shows wide interest from members of Congress in Indian affairs, a recognition of their importance, in spite of their modest size in the overall electorate.

A fourth set of explanations is based on affective solidarity. Descriptive representation can make a difference (Mansbridge, 1999). Members of Congress who share an ethnic background may be more inclined to listen to the perspective of a particular **ethnic lobby**. Some ethnic groups have prominent leaders within parties or in high-placed government roles, which can help to provide an 'in' for them in the institutions of power. Historically, Greek Americans were well placed for a community of their size. Vice President Spiro Agnew, Governor and presidential candidate Mike Dukakis, Senator and presidential candidate Paul Tsongas and members of Bill Clinton's White House, such as his Communications Director George Stephanopoulos and Chief of Staff John Podesta, were all of Greek heritage. During this period of prominence in American government, Greek lobbying organizations such as the American Hellenic Institute helped push the US government to impose an arms embargo on Turkey in response to the invasion of Cyprus in 1974.

Minority ethnic lobbies can also form coalitions with other interest groups to grow their clout, using moral or affective solidaristic ties. Both the Israel and Armenian lobbies attract a great deal of support from Christian evangelicals who sympathize with those countries, one as a Jewish country and the other as a Christian country, against what they perceive to be a threat from Islam.

A final way in which ethnic lobbies might exert influence is by appealing to realist inclinations of American foreign policymakers. The end of the Cold War prompted the emergence of lobbies advocating on behalf of former Eastern bloc countries. The most prominent of these is the Central and Eastern European Coalition, founded in 1994, and which has worked to add former Eastern bloc countries to NATO (McCormick, 2008). John Newhouse (2009) credits these lobbying groups with persuading the US Senate in 1998 to support bringing Poland into NATO. Another example of a realist approach is the appeal to lawmakers on the basis of using ethnic communities to open access to new markets. The Indian lobby is perhaps the most successful example of this.

Ethnic and diasporic lobbies

This section details four case studies of ethnic interest lobbies in the US that have had demonstrable influences on the content and direction of US foreign policy: the Irish lobby, the Cuban lobby, the Armenian lobby and the Israeli lobby.

Ethnic lobbies are often composed of émigrés and sympathizers who take harder-line stances than the political mainstream of the countries from which they originate. Irish-American politicians' support for leaders of the IRA (Irish Republican Army) and Sinn Féin often put them on the most militant and extremist wing of the Irish republican movement. The Cuban lobby is composed of anti-Castro émigrés, whose animosity towards the communist government that ejected them does not necessarily encourage US officials to take a balanced approach towards Cuba. The Israeli lobby is said to have a much harder anti-Palestinian, pro-settlement position than the mainstream of Israeli public opinion or American Jews (not all of whom are especially interested in Israeli affairs).

Ethnic lobbies' interests may sometimes conflict with the US's broader national security and diplomatic interests. In the 1980s, the Israeli lobby was strongly opposed to the US's continued sale of arms to the Saudi regime. As a consequence, in 1988 the Saudi regime gave up on an effort to buy weapons from the US and decided to purchase $30 billion of arms from the more pro-Arab UK instead (McCormick, 2008). In 2006 the Indian lobby persuaded Congress to lift restrictions on the nuclear fuels trade with India, even though this violates the Treaty on the Non-Proliferation of Nuclear Weapons (McCormick, 2008).

The Irish lobby

Arguably the oldest ethnic lobby in the US is the Irish-American lobby. It gained renewed attention in 2020 with the election of President Joe Biden, who has regularly highlighted his ancestral Irish ties and affinities for Ireland.

In the 19th century there was an enormous inflow of Irish immigrants to the US after the Potato Famine in the 1840s. The Famine depleted the Irish population by a quarter in just six years, due to either starvation or emigration. This was a major global refugee crisis of its day. The result is that today over 30 million Americans identify as being of Irish descent. By comparison, the population of Ireland is 4.9 million. In other words, there are six times as many people in the US who claim to be Irish as who live in Ireland itself.

Historically, the Irish-American population has been fiercely anti-British (Jacobson, 1995). In the 1860s, a group of Irish immigrants tried to provoke war between the US and the UK by occupying British fortifications in Canada. While largely unsuccessful in driving a wedge between the US and the UK at a diplomatic level, grassroots US public support has been a key source of strength for the Irish nationalist cause (Jacobson, 1995). In 1919, Éamon de Valera escaped from prison in England and was made president of the Dáil Éireann (Assembly of Ireland). That summer, he travelled to the US to try to persuade the US government to recognize an independent Ireland. De Valera spent six months in the US giving speeches to a variety of audiences in defence of Irish separatism from the UK. He raised an astonishing $5.5 million from supporters in the US, equivalent to $85.6 million in

Figure 7.2: Number of Irish arrivals in the US, by decade

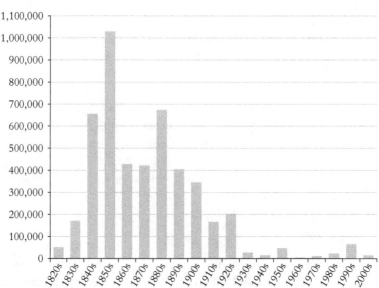

Source: Based on data from *2018 Yearbook of Immigration Statistics*, Department of Homeland Security, Table 2

2021 dollars.[7] The source of his strength was the Irish diaspora. Over 50,000 supporters attended a rally for the Irish nationalist at Fenway Park in the heavily Irish-American city of Boston. *The Boston Globe* oozed over de Valera's visit: 'To say it was thrilling is putting it mildly – it was electric' (30 June 1919). *The Globe* said the reaction to de Valera's visit was 'a reception as only the head of a nation is accorded', but de Valera was unable to persuade policymakers in Washington to recognize the Irish republic. US recognition came only in 1924 at the end of the Irish Civil War.

Although de Valera was unsuccessful in persuading the US government to recognize an independent Irish state, he was able to exact his revenge on the Wilson Administration. In September 1919, de Valera addressed the Massachusetts State Board (MSB) of the American Federation of Labor (AFL). The MSB had a significant section of its members who were of Irish heritage. De Valera was able to persuade the board to come out against the League of Nations, an organization rejected by Irish nationalists because of the exclusion of Ireland as an independent member. According to Rhodri Jeffreys-Jones (2010: 66), 'immediately' in the wake of de Valera's speech, Massachusetts Senator Henry Cabot Lodge, the powerful chair of the Senate Foreign Relations Committee, issued a list of reservations to the League proposal. He was soon followed by Massachusetts's other Senator David Walsh, who came out against ratifying the League of Nations Treaty. A few weeks later, on 19 November 1919, the US Senate voted down the League of Nations Treaty, a humiliation for President Woodrow Wilson, himself an anglophile.

As de Valera discovered, US presidential administrations have historically substantively tended to side with the UK, whom the US has considered as a more valuable and more important strategic partner, while also offering a degree of symbolic affirmation for the Irish republic, given the widespread affection for Ireland among many segments of the American public. This symbolic lip service continues today. Every year the Taoiseach (prime minister) of Ireland celebrates St Patrick's Day not in Ireland but by flying to Washington to meet with the US president. This tradition ensures that the Irish Taoiseach is the only head of government in the world who is guaranteed an annual in-person meeting with the US president. There is also typically a grand luncheon held for the Taoiseach at the US Capitol, attended by some of the most important leaders in the US legislature.

The Irish lobby comprises several groups with quite diverse political agendas. Unlike the Cuban lobby, which is dominated by one large lobby group, there is a multitude of Irish-American organizations.

Most of the Irish lobby organizations were founded during 'The Troubles', a period of violence between unionists and nationalists in Northern Ireland that erupted in the late 1960s and continued into the 1990s, claiming the lives of thousands of soldiers and civilians on both sides of the sectarian divide. There was also a campaign of violence waged by Irish nationalists in Britain, which left dozens of British civilians dead.[8] Several British Members of Parliament were assassinated by Irish republicans, and two UK prime ministers (Margaret Thatcher and John Major) survived IRA bombings intended to kill them.

The most 'militantly republican' group of the Irish lobby was Irish Northern Aid (NORAID), founded by Michael Flannery in 1970 (Guelke, 1996: 524). Flannery was originally from County Tipperary, where the first shots of the Irish War of Independence were fired in 1919, and had been a member of the IRA during the Irish Civil War in the 1920s. In the US, Flannery used NORAID to fund the efforts of the Provisional IRA during The Troubles. A 1981 judgment from the Southern District of New York ruled, 'the uncontroverted evidence is that defendant [NORAID] is an agent of the IRA, providing money and services for other than relief purposes'.[9] Flannery would throw fundraising events, many of them attended by prominent American politicians, on the basis of their shared Irish roots. Between 1970 and 1986, NORAID raised $3 million for the IRA, in particular for Catholics in Northern Ireland whose relatives had been killed in the struggle or who were in prison. NORAID was quite socially conservative and anti-communist, which sometimes put it at odds with the IRA's political voice Sinn Féin, a democratic socialist and socially moderate party. Some of the other Irish lobby groups, such as the Irish National Caucus, tried to model themselves around civil rights groups, looking for inspiration in the US civil rights movement and the South Africa anti-apartheid movement, to frame the desire for Irish unification in terms of a struggle for human rights.

The Irish lobby groups were supported by prominent American officials who claimed Irish ancestry. The most notable were colloquially known as the 'four horsemen': the Speaker of the House of Representatives Tip O'Neill, Senator Ted Kennedy, Senator Patrick Moynihan and Governor Hugh Carey. All Democrats, the 'horsemen' were able to persuade US presidential administrations to take action in favour of Irish republican causes, in spite of protest from the British government. In 1986, Ronald Reagan signed legislation that provided for $50 million of aid to Ireland – both the Republic of Ireland and Northern Ireland. In 1994, Bill Clinton reluctantly agreed to grant Sinn Féin leader Gerry Adams a 48-hour visa to come to New York to speak at a conference, in spite of strong opposition from the British government. Irish lobby groups such as Americans for a New Irish Agenda, founded by the Connecticut Democratic Congressman Bruce Morrison, and the Irish American Labor Coalition were crucial to persuading Clinton to take this position even though it offended the British government. Bruce Morrison subsequently served as a representative of Irish Americans on the National Democratic Ethnic Coordinating Committee, and was a superdelegate for Hillary Clinton.[10]

In the 1980s and 1990s, the Irish lobby had power and presence not just in Congress, but also in state legislatures. Between 1985 and 1992, the Irish lobby persuaded 13 states with large Irish populations, as well as the AFL-CIO and the National Council of Churches, to boycott firms that discriminated against Catholics in Northern Ireland. As a result, Margaret Thatcher's government passed the Fair Employment (Northern Ireland) Act in 1989 that brought an end to sectarian hiring practices.

The role of the Irish lobby has gained renewed attention in recent years. Before the UK secured a free trade agreement with the EU in December 2020, members of the US Congress threatened to block a US–UK trade deal unless the UK–EU agreement maintained an open border between the north and south of the island of Ireland. The House Committee on Ways and Means, which would scrutinize a US–UK trade deal, was chaired by Democrat Congressman Richard Neal. Neal is co-chair of the Friends of Ireland Caucus, founded in 1981 by the three Irish 'horsemen' in Congress at the time of the IRA prisoner hunger strikes. Nancy Pelosi, the incumbent Democrat Speaker of the House of Representatives, told the Irish Dáil in 2019, 'As you face the challenges posed by Brexit, know that the United States Congress – Democrats and Republicans in the House and in the Senate – stand with you.' She recalled affectionately, 'For generations, Ireland has been the emerald thread in the fabric of American history and national life' (Pelosi, 2019).

Most US presidents make some claim to Irish ancestry. With the exception of Donald Trump, the son of a British immigrant to the US, nearly every president of the last half-century has identified as Irish, even when the evidence of such a link has been tenuous. Bill Clinton, for example, claimed to be descended from Irish immigrants, but there is no record to link him with any Irish immigrants. Barack Obama claimed Irish ancestry through his mother's line. His mother's great-great-grandfather had been born in Moneygall in County Offaly in 1831. Most US presidents make at least one visit to Ireland. When

Obama visited Ireland in 2011, he made sure to visit his ancestor's home and drink a pint of Guinness. There is now an Obama Cafe and an Obama ancestral home in this tiny Irish village. A book and a film called *Obama: The Road to Moneygall* chronicles Obama's 'homecoming' to Ireland. President Joe Biden is the most strongly identified Irish-American president since President John F. Kennedy. Both men were practising Roman Catholics and raised by their families with a keen sense of Irish identity, but neither of them had particularly close Irish ancestry. It had been generations since a direct ancestor had been born in Ireland. Indeed, the Irish ancestors of Kennedy, Obama and Biden all left Ireland within a decade of each other, during or just after the Irish Potato Famine (Burns, 2020). The last ancestor of Joe Biden to be born in Ireland was his great-great-grandfather, born in 1832, one year after Barack Obama's closest Irish ancestor.

President Biden has shown strong personal sympathies with Irish nationalism. Biden was one of the US senators in the 1990s who urged Bill Clinton to ignore British objections and grant Gerry Adams a visa (Sawer, 2020). As vice president and as a candidate for president, Joe Biden made jokes about banning the colour orange from his house (the colour of Northern Irish unionism),[11] refused to speak to a BBC reporter by saying 'The BBC? I'm Irish', and met with the former Sinn Féin leader Gerry Adams to discuss, as Adams put it, 'UI' (a united Ireland). While Biden's symbolic affections are clear, in practice there is no sign that President Biden wishes to endanger the UK–US relationship, or adopt an outwardly sectarian position on the question of Northern Ireland's future within the UK.

The Cuban lobby

One of the most successful lobbies in the US has been the Cuban lobby (Gibbs 2010). The main organization within the Cuban lobby is the Cuban American National Foundation (CANF). The central goal of CANF is to use US foreign policy power to bring an end to communism in Cuba. It is comprised mainly of Cuban émigrés who defected from the regimes led by Fidel (1959–2006) and Raúl (2006–18) Castro (Haney and Vanderbush, 1999). The Cuban lobby has made maximum leverage of two key factors: its anti-communism and the electoral strength of the Cuban community in the key swing state of Florida.

Following the US victory in the Spanish–American War of 1898, the former Spanish territories of Puerto Rico and Guam became US colonial possessions, the US purchased the Philippines for

$20 million and the US government placed Cuba under military rule (Immerwahr, 2019: 72–3). However, Congress had passed the Teller Amendment in 1898 stating that Cuba could not become an official US territory. The debate over Cuba's entry into the US was highly racialized. Newspapers that favoured Cuba's presence in the US depicted Cubans as white. Newspapers that opposed Cuba's presence in the US depicted Cubans as black. It was eventually decided that Cuba would be made an independent republic, albeit under the supervision of the US, especially for foreign affairs. According to the Platt Amendment of 1901, Cuba needed to agree to a degree of subservience to the US in order to end the US military occupation of the island. The US retained possession of one piece of land on the island of Cuba, Guantanamo Bay, which remains a (infamous) US military base and prison camp today.

In 1959, the US-backed military government in Cuba fell to the communist forces of Fidel Castro. The following year, in October 1960, Republican President Dwight Eisenhower imposed a trade embargo with Cuba after the Cuban government nationalized US-owned industries on the island without compensation. Three months later, just before leaving office, Eisenhower severed diplomatic relations with Cuba entirely. In February 1962, Democratic President John Kennedy tightened the embargo by prohibiting the use of third countries to traffic in Cuban goods. In February 1963, after the Cuban Missile Crisis of October 1962, Kennedy banned all travel to Cuba by US citizens. In the 1970s, there was some attempt to relax relations. Jimmy Carter made several policy shifts towards normalization (Gibbs, 2010). Carter reversed his predecessors' bans on travel to Cuba and allowed a 'US interests section' to operate within the Swiss Embassy in Havana (Haney and Vanderbush, 2008). The Carter Administration also reached an agreement with the Castro government on fishing and maritime boundaries (Haney and Vanderbush, 1999).

Carter was defeated in the 1980 election and replaced by stridently anti-communist Ronald Reagan. It was in this context that CANF was founded in 1981, on the advice of Reagan's National Security Advisor Richard Allen (Haney and Vanderbush, 1999). The Reagan Administration was sympathetic to CANF's conservative ideological positions and geostrategic aims. Reagan reversed many of Carter's efforts, including strengthening the embargo (Haney and Vanderbush, 2008). He also agreed to the creation of a US-funded radio station that would broadcast anti-Castro, pro-American propaganda to the Cuban public, known as Radio Marti. Radio Marti was run by CANF activists and received millions of dollars from the federal government.

In this way, the US government was using public money to fund a voice-piece of an ethnic lobby group (Haney and Vanderbush, 1999). Under Reagan's successor, George H.W. Bush, funding for Radio Marti continued and was expanded even further to include the creation of Television Marti. Television Marti proved to be a massive waste of American taxpayers' money, as the station's broadcasts were blocked by the Cuban government – very few people in Cuba were actually able to watch the bespoke broadcasts (Snyder, 1995: 235).

For many years, CANF was directed by the charismatic Jorge Mas Canosa. It was widely described during Mas Canosa's tenure as one of the most powerful ethnic lobbying organizations in the US. CANF's political fundraising arm, the Free Cuba PAC, operated with tactical precision against supporters of normalization. In 1988, they helped fund Democrat Joe Lieberman against Republican Senator Lowell Weicker, who had met Castro in Cuba and championed better ties between the two countries (*The New York Times*, 1980; Gibbs, 2010). On the same day that Republican President George H.W. Bush won Connecticut by more than 5 percentage points, Weicker lost to Lieberman by just 0.8 per cent of the vote, a warning shot to other congressional supporters of normalization.

Legislatively, the Cuban lobby achieved two major victories in the 1990s. The first was the Cuban Democracy Act of 1992. The Act made it illegal for companies to trade with Cuba and the US at the same time. Additionally, any country that traded with Cuba risked being cut off from US international aid. The legislation was an attempt to weaken the Castro government at a key time of vulnerability. The Soviet Union had dissolved the previous year. This was a potentially catastrophic development for the Cuban government, which had relied on Soviet subsidies in the face of the US embargo. The Cuban Democracy Act was designed to discourage Western companies from filling the financial void left by the former USSR in hopes that a global economic boycott would cripple the Cuban economy and bring the government to its knees. The result of the Act was, indeed, a terrible economic recession throughout the 1990s, punishing many ordinary Cubans, but the Castro government survived. Although President George H.W. Bush initially opposed the legislation, he eventually succumbed to pressure from the Cuban lobby to sign it, which he did so a week before the presidential election in 1992. Although Bush lost the election, he did carry the state of Florida by 1.9 per cent over Bill Clinton.

The most important piece of legislation in US–Cuba relations and, indeed, CANF's most important legislative victory is the Helms–

Burton Act of 1996, which placed the US embargo in statute. Until 1996, the US embargo on Cuba had been an executive order, first issued by President Eisenhower and maintained (and sometimes strengthened) by every president from Eisenhower to Clinton. Executive orders are weaker than legislation because they can be overturned by a simple stroke of a president's pen. Some members of Congress, such as Republican Congressman Lincoln Diaz-Balart, speculated that Clinton was preparing to remove the embargo after the 1996 elections (Haney and Vanderbush, 2008). Clinton had already ended the US embargo on Vietnam in 1995. Helms–Burton means that the US embargo on Cuba can only end if Congress passes a new law to repeal it. Bill Clinton's Secretary of State Warren Christopher had warned Clinton not to sign the bill, and Clinton's Under Secretary of State Peter Tarnoff testified against the bill in the Senate. Yet political strategists in the Clinton White House were concerned that Clinton would be punished electorally in 1996 if he continued to oppose the bill. Clinton had only won 22 per cent of the vote in the predominantly Latino precincts of south Florida in 1992 and lost the state overall (Gibbs, 2010). Jessica Gibbs argues that Bill Clinton chose to be 'guided by his domestic political advisers rather than his foreign policy team' (2010: 148). Clinton reversed his position on Helms–Burton and signed the embargo into law in March 1996. Clinton went on to win Florida that November, boosting his support by 9 percentage points from 1992.

Although Helms–Burton impairs presidents' ability to undo the embargo, the Act did not hamstring the US president entirely. Under Barack Obama, the US implemented what became known as the 'Cuban thaw', or a warming of relations between the US and Cuba. Within Helms–Burton (Section 112) there is some leeway for the president to ease restrictions on travel and remittances (money sent by people in the US to family members in Cuba). Obama announced that he would use his authority to lift these bans. He also announced that he would reopen the US Embassy in Havana and invited the Cubans to open their embassy in Washington. This happened in 2015, the first time either country had an embassy in the other's country since 1961. In 2016, President Obama made the first presidential visit to Cuba since 1928 and met with Raúl Castro.

Obama's final act of the 'Cuban thaw' occurred in his final week as president in January 2017 when he ended special immigration privileges for Cuban arrivals to the US. The Cuban Adjustment Act of 1966 grants the right of permanent residency, after one year in the US, to any Cuban arriving in the US by any means, legal or illegal. Thus,

Cubans do not need to demonstrate the kinds of criteria demanded of other immigrants to the US: economic self-sufficiency, family or economic links to the US or evidence of arrival through a legal port of entry. The law also exempts Cubans from US immigration quotas. Over three-quarters of a million Cubans have immigrated to the US under its provisions.

For nearly three decades, 'arrival' in the US was understood to mean presence in US coastal waters. Cuba is 90 miles (144 km) south of Florida. For reference, the shortest distance between England and France is 20 miles (33 km). In spite of the relatively close distance, few Cubans have the capacity to charter boats to sail over to Florida, and the waters brim with sharks and jellyfish. As a result of the severe economic recession in Cuba in the 1990s, thousands of Cubans attempted to enter the US by crossing the dangerous Florida Straits. In 1994, 65,000 Cubans attempted to enter the US on a variety of makeshift rafts and homemade boats. Many of these boats were not seaworthy, but once they passed out of Cuba's territorial waters (12 miles out),[12] they could be intercepted by the US Coast Guard and brought safely to the US (Santiago, 2014). In 1995, after discussion with the Cuban government, President Bill Clinton announced that the US would stop admitting people intercepted in these waters. A Cuban caught in the waters between the two nations (with 'wet feet') would summarily be sent home or to a third country. A Cuban who made it to shore ('dry feet') would have the ability to remain in the US, qualifying for expedited 'legal permanent resident' status and ultimately US citizenship. Clinton's change in policy led to the famous Elián González incident in 1999, when fishermen found a five-year-old Cuban boy floating in an inner tube three miles from Florida. The boy's mother had perished in the dangerous journey. Under the 'wet feet, dry feet' policy, Clinton explained that González needed to be returned to Cuba. This provoked outrage from the Cuban community in Florida, which was only exacerbated when frightening images of federal agents apprehending the boy from his cousins' home in Miami in April 2000 were published. The images showed a federal agent pointing a machine gun at the crying child. González was, nonetheless, flown back to Cuba where he was greeted by Fidel Castro and became a national celebrity. Bill Clinton's Vice President Al Gore was criticized for supporting the deportation. His Republican opponent George W. Bush won 81 per cent of the Cuban vote in Florida that November.[13] Given the closeness of the result in Florida, it is feasible that Clinton's Cuban policy may very well have cost Gore victory in Florida and with it, the presidency. William

Schneider, in *The Atlantic*, wrote after the election, 'Elián González defeated Al Gore' (2001).

The 'wet feet, dry feet' policy encouraged Cuban migrants to enter the US via Mexico. This meant that while migrants from Central America had to wait in long queues (often literally) for admission to the US, Cubans had a fast track (Preston, 2016). One week before leaving the White House, Obama abolished this fast track.[14] Cuban migrants would not be 'let in' the US by the Mexican border on terms different from other migrants. They would now either need to enter furtively or claim asylum on entry to become eligible for the Cuban Adjustment Act benefits after one year. 'By taking this step, we are treating Cuban migrants the same way we treat migrants from other countries', announced Obama.[15] The Obama policy represented a major blow to the mission of the Cuban lobby, which had seen the special status of Cuban migrants in the US as a source of community strength.

What does this tell us about the continued strength of the Cuban lobby? Some people argue that the Cuban lobby is losing its potency as the Cuban electorate becomes more politically heterogeneous. While first-generation Cuban immigrants were staunchly anti-communist, younger generations – those who were born in the US – are more open to cooperation. Yet it should be noted that some of Obama's changes did not outlast his presidency. In 2017, President Trump announced that he would be introducing new restrictions on travel to Cuba, and that American financial transactions to entities owned by the Cuban government, which include hotels, tourism agencies, some shops and some bars, would be prohibited under US law.

Unlike most other Latino groups, Cubans tend to lean more to the Republican Party, partly a reflection of their anti-socialist politics and historic class position. However, to some extent, the Cuban vote is 'up for grabs', which makes ambitious politicians, including members of the Senate Foreign Relations Committee, take a keen interest in Cuban affairs. Support for the Cuba embargo has been bipartisan, with one of the fiercest opponents of Obama's 'Cuba thaw' being New Jersey Democratic Senator Bob Menendez (LeoGrande, 2013).

After underperforming among Cubans in the 2016 election, Donald Trump attempted to win back support from the Cuban population. To do this, he in effect adopted the traditional CANF positions. He rolled back many of Obama's normalization policies, and adopted staunchly anti-communist rhetoric. Trump's tough language against the socialist Venezuelan government can, in part, be understood by the importance of the Cuban diaspora to his re-election strategy. In February 2020,

Trump invited Juan Guaidó, anti-socialist pretender to the presidency of Venezuela, to be a guest at his State of the Union address and entertained Guaidó at the White House. Guaidó was recognized by 50 countries as the legitimate president of Venezuela, but by this time it was quite clear that Guaidó's efforts at removing the socialist President Nicolás Maduro from power had failed. Yet, as Josh Rogin wrote, 'it's great politics, especially in Florida – where Latino voters lean heavily anti-Maduro' (2020). In his State of the Union speech, Trump tied the struggle against the socialist Maduro government with the effort to dislodge the power of communists in Cuba: 'We are supporting the hopes of Cubans, Nicaraguans and Venezuelans to restore democracy.' During the 2020 election, Donald Trump ran advertisements that showed Maduro apparently saying positive things about Joe Biden and even calling him 'Camarada [Comrade] Biden'.[16] Ultimately, Trump won 59 per cent of the vote in Florida precincts where at least a quarter of voters were of Cuban ancestry. In 2016 Hillary Clinton won 54 per cent of the vote in these precincts.[17] While Trump lost the election overall, his victory in the traditionally crucial swing state of Florida is creditable in large part to the advances he made with voters of Cuban ancestry.

The Armenian lobby

The Armenian population in the US is not numerically large. According to the 2017 American Communities Survey, there are about 486,000 Armenian Americans, just 0.14 per cent of the US population. In spite of their size (or perhaps because of it), the Armenian lobby is politically powerful. Milner and Tingley describe the Armenian lobby as one with 'disproportionate influence' (2015: 99). They have succeeded in winning financial and symbolic support for the South Caucus nation.

The first major wave of Armenians to the US occurred in the late 19th and early 20th century. By the time that their numbers were restricted by the Immigration Act of 1924, about 90,000 had arrived in the US during the first two decades of the 20th century (Zarifian, 2014: 505). A second wave of Armenians arrived in the post-war period. Armenians are concentrated in a few areas of the country, in particular in California, New York and Massachusetts. Armenians' concentration in these uncompetitive, Democratic states deprives them of the kind of pivotal electoral advantage enjoyed by the Cuban community. Perhaps partly a reflection of this, there has been minimal attention to Armenian causes at the presidential level.

While the Armenian lobby has been generally unsuccessful at gaining influence in the executive branch, their efforts at lobbying members of Congress have been more successful.

The main organization of the Armenian lobby is the Armenian National Committee of America (ANCA), which has existed for over a century. It operates under a 501(c)(4) status, which enables it to participate in extensive lobbying. It has also helped to facilitate the creation of the Congressional Caucus on Armenian Issues, which has about 150 congressional members, making it one of the largest ethnic group caucuses in Congress. To attract congressional support, ANCA highlights Armenia's Christian heritage and portrays the country as one under siege from its Muslim neighbours, much like the Israeli lobby has done (Stephens, 2010). ANCA regularly trumpets Armenia as 'the world's first Christian nation'.[18]

The Armenian lobby has a few core issues. The foremost was its desire to pass a motion against Turkey for its role in massacring over 1 million people of Armenian descent in 1915, which it achieved in 2019. A second is to secure greater development aid for Armenia. In 2019, the federal government spent $41 million on aid to Armenia, about $13 for each person in a country of just under 3 million inhabitants.[19] Julien Zarifian writes that 'the support of the lobby and of its friends in Congress has made Armenia one of the most important recipient countries of US per capita foreign direct aid' (2014: 509).

The other priorities revolve around Armenia's adversaries, Azerbaijan and Turkey. The ANCA advocates for a 'free, united, and independent' Armenia. This, in effect, means the restoration of certain historically Armenian territories held by Armenia's neighbours. Armenia has lobbied to reduce US aid to Azerbaijan, and it continues to lobby for recognition of the independence of Nagorno-Karabakh (also known as the Republic of Artsakh), a region in Azerbaijan that is overwhelmingly ethnically Armenian and Christian. In 2010, the House Appropriations Subcommittee on Foreign Operations allocated $10 million in aid to Nagorno-Karabakh, which had been left out of President Obama's budget proposals, a victory for Armenian lobby influencers (Milner and Tingley, 2015). They also ensured that Armenia received an equal amount of military assistance to Azerbaijan even though Obama's original proposals had only allocated about half as much to Armenia as to Azerbaijan.

In 2020, Armenia and Azerbaijan went to war over the Nagorno-Karabakh territory. Over 30 members of Congress, led by the Armenian Caucus Chair Frank Pallone (a New Jersey Democrat), introduced a motion siding with the Armenians against the Azeris.[20]

Secretary of State Mike Pompeo condemned Turkish support for Azerbaijan. Congressman Brad Sherman, whose southern California district has a reasonably sizeable Armenian population, called for imposing the Global Magnitsky Act on Azeri officials.[21]

The most high-profile policy objective of the Armenian lobby has been a congressional resolution condemning the 1915 genocide. While the diaspora has historically been divided internally due to divisions in the Soviet era, this pre-Soviet slaughter of a million Armenians by the Ottoman Turks operates as the 'political cement' of the Armenian community (Zarifian, 2014: 509). At state level, 40 US states have supported genocide recognition resolutions, but at federal level, passage was more fraught for geostrategic reasons.

The campaign for recognition of the Armenian genocide had been a difficult one because of Turkey's important strategic role in the Middle East and as a NATO ally. The US has depended on Turkey to facilitate US incursions in Iraq and, later, to host millions of Syrian refugees who had been driven out of their country by civil war. It seemed objectively harmful to damage US–Turkey relations for the sake of commentary on an historic tragedy in the early 20th century. Indeed, the executive branch has typically been wary of any use of the 'g' word. In 2006, George W. Bush recalled the US ambassador to Armenia, John Evans, because it was revealed that Evans had used the word 'genocide' in a talk on the subject at UC Berkeley. Bush replaced Evans with Marie Yovanovitch, who later gained notoriety as the ambassador to Ukraine recalled by Donald Trump. Yovanovitch avoided using the word 'genocide' during her term as ambassador to Armenia (Zarifian, 2014: 510).

In 2010, the Democratic-controlled House Committee on Foreign Affairs nodded through a motion recognizing the 1915 genocide. Some on the Committee expressed their concerns that the bill would endanger US troops who relied on supportive treatment from the Turkish government to complete US missions in the Middle East. One of those who raised concerns was Indiana Congressman Mike Pence, who later became vice president under Donald Trump. In spite of Pence's opposition, the bill passed in Committee by 1 vote (23 to 22). In response, Turkey withdrew its ambassador to the US (McCormick, 2008). The Obama Administration had urged the House Foreign Affairs Committee not to pass the resolution. Secretary of State Hillary Clinton stated, 'the Obama administration strongly opposes the resolution that was passed by only one vote in the House committee, and we'll work very hard to make sure it does not go to the House floor'. The Obama Administration was successful in persuading the House leadership, which at the time was controlled by the Democrats under Speaker Nancy Pelosi, not to put the bill to a vote of the full House, thus killing the resolution. An irony had been that as a US senator, Barack Obama wrote a letter to Secretary of State Condoleezza Rice condemning the dismissal of Ambassador Evans for using the term 'genocide'. Obama wrote in his 2006 letter, 'The occurrence of the Armenian genocide in 1915 is not an allegation, a personal opinion, or a point of view. Supported by an overwhelming amount of historical evidence, it is a widely documented fact.'[22] Obama had also promised to recognize the genocide when he ran for president in 2008, but after taking office he studiously avoided use of the term and blocked any genocide resolutions from passing in Congress.

In 2019, large bipartisan majorities in both chambers of Congress finally passed resolutions formally affirming and recognizing the Armenian genocide in 2019.[23] The resolution's success was, in part, a reflection of the fading status of Turkey. President Trump had enabled Turkey to launch an offensive against the US's hitherto Kurdish allies in northeast Syria, which sparked outrage across the chambers. The passage of the genocide resolution was at once a credit to the persistence of the Armenian lobby and for the motion acting as an easy tool for the US Congress to voice its displeasure at present-day Turkish policy.

The case of the Armenian lobby demonstrates the conflicts that diasporic lobbies can generate for US foreign policymakers. Turkey and Armenia do not have formal diplomatic relations with each other. Through their diasporas, US foreign policy becomes a proxy war between the two countries, with members of Congress as unwitting foot-soldiers. While Turkey is a sworn enemy of Armenia, it is also a NATO ally of the US. Some commentators have suggested that Armenia's policy influence has not necessarily benefited US national interests. A resolution against Turkey for its role in a 1915 genocide undoubtedly means a great deal to Armenian Americans and Armenians in Armenia, but from the perspective of the US, it might not be the most advantageous decision to damage diplomatic relations with Turkey over a point of historical interpretation regarding an event that occurred over a century ago.

The Israeli lobby

The most high-profile diasporic lobby in the US is the Israeli lobby. It is distinctive from many other ethnic lobbies in that its relevant diasporic community is more difficult to define. Domestic US actors who advocate on Israel-related matters are mostly not Israeli immigrants or their descendants. As the lone Jewish state in the world, Israel has special resonance for the Jewish diaspora in the US – 69 per cent of American Jews say that they feel emotionally attached to Israel (Pew Research Center, 2013). The proportion is even higher for religiously practising Jews (76 per cent). Only 12 per cent of Jews say that caring about Israel is 'not an important part of being Jewish'. In spite of a clear majority of Jews professing interest and affection for Israel, the Jewish diaspora is diverse. A non-trivial minority of American Jews feel little or no connection with Israel (Rynhold, 2015), especially non-religious and young Jews (but see Waxman, 2017). Additionally, some of the biggest proponents of a pro-Israel US foreign policy are neither Jewish nor Israeli, but the large proportion of mostly (but not exclusively) white Christian evangelicals in the US. Therefore, while Jewish Americans are a major and important constituency of the Israeli lobby, they are not synonymous and should not be conflated. The Israeli lobby simply refers to 'a loose coalition of individuals and organizations that actively works to move US foreign policy in a pro-Israel direction' (Lieberman, 2009: 5).

Israel receives military and diplomatic support from the US that is unrivalled by most other countries. It is the largest cumulative recipient of US foreign assistance since the Second World War (Sharp, 2020). Each year, the US sends $3.8 billion to Israel, nearly all in the form of military assistance. The US phased out economic assistance to Israel in 2007, in recognition of the country's status as a prosperous, industrialized economy (Sharp, 2020). With the exception of Iraq and Afghanistan, no other countries in the world come close to receiving the level of aid that Israel does. In fact, aid to Israel (one country) is one-fifth of the entire US military foreign assistance budget. Ironically, a plurality of Israelis (47 per cent) believes that the US gives their country too much aid (Mearsheimer and Walt, 2007: 48). Israel not only receives exceptionally high levels of aid, but it also has fewer strings attached to that aid than most other countries. Most recipients of US military aid are required to spend the money on products from US military contractors. This is one of the ways in which US foreign aid supports US domestic industries. Israel is exempted from this requirement (Mearsheimer and Walt, 2007: 28).

John Mearsheimer and Stephen Walt (2007, 2011) present a forceful account of what they see as the significant influence of pro-Israel interest groups on US politics. The most powerful is the American Israel Public Affairs Committee (AIPAC). In 2015, AIPAC had a total revenue of $88.5 million, virtually all of which came from fundraising. When AIPAC was founded in 1963, the US was a supporter of Israel, but not an unequivocal one. It was France, not the US, which was Israel's main arms supplier until 1967 (Mearsheimer and Walt, 2007: 53). In 1956, the US had sided against Israel in the conflict over the Suez Canal. Yet, over the next few decades, the US became – and has remained – Israel's best and most loyal ally.

The annual AIPAC Policy Conference is one of the largest political conferences in the US. In 2016, about 20,000 people attended as delegates. AIPAC's Conference has become a must-go-to event for aspiring political candidates. It has also been the source of some controversy – in 2006 it was accused of passing sensitive US intelligence onto the government of Israel. While APAIC is the most powerful lobbying arm, there are other conservative pro-Israel organizations such as Christians United for Israel and the Conference of the Presidents of Major American Jewish Organizations. The Israeli lobby is not ideologically monolithic, however. There are smaller, more liberal lobbying groups such as the Israel Policy Forum and J Street.

Although founded in 1963, AIPAC only achieved the financial and political clout necessary to sway congressional opinion from the 1970s. In 1975, President Gerald Ford proposed a 'reassessment' of the US's position towards Israel vis-à-vis other Middle East countries. This was in the context of the Yom Kippur War in October 1973, during which Israel had handily seen off Egyptian, Jordanian and Syrian invasions. Ford was frustrated by what he regarded as Israel's lack of willingness to agree to a peace treaty. In his frustration, he sent the following message to Israeli Prime Minister Yitzhak Rabin:

> I wish to express my profound disappointment over Israel's attitude in the course of the negotiations.... Failure of the negotiation will have a far reaching impact on the region and on our relations. I have given instructions for a reassessment of United States policy in the region, including our relations with Israel.... You will be notified of our decision. (Rabin, 1979: 256)

Rabin responded by mobilizing AIPAC against the president. Confronted with opposition from both houses of Congress, Ford rescinded his 'reassessment'.

In the 21st century, the influence of AIPAC and other pro-Israel organizations has continued to be demonstrated across both

Republican and Democratic administrations. In 2004, AIPAC and other groups managed to persuade 89 US senators to write a letter thanking President George W. Bush for refusing to meet with Yasser Arafat. They organized a motion in the House of Representatives condemning 'the ongoing support and coordination of terror by Yasser Arafat' by 352 votes to 21.

At the start of President Obama's first term, he nominated former US Ambassador to Saudi Arabia Charles Freeman to be the chair of the National Intelligence Council. Freeman had been a critic of Benjamin Netanyahu and members of the Israeli coalition government, including the far-right Foreign Minister Avigdor Lieberman. After the naming of Freeman, there were various stories in the DC-based press that accused him of being anti-Israel and pro-Arab. The Zionist Organization of America, a pro-Israeli lobby, released a press statement that called on Obama to rescind the nomination:

> The Zionist Organization of America (ZOA) has expressed shock and deep concern at President Barack Obama's invitation to anti-Israeli former diplomat and pro-Arab lobbyist Chas W. Freeman Jr to be Chairman of the National Intelligence Council and has called upon the President to rescind the invitation. (Klein, 2009)

Two months later, Freeman withdrew from consideration for the position. He cited the 'Israel lobby' in a statement about his removal:

> The tactics of the Israel Lobby plumb the depths of dishonor and indecency and include character assassination, selective misquotation, the willful distortion of the record, the fabrication of falsehoods, and an utter disregard for the truth. The aim of this Lobby is control of the policy process through the exercise of a veto over the appointment of people who dispute the wisdom of its views, the substitution of political correctness for analysis, and the exclusion of any and all options for decision by Americans and our government other than those that it favors.

Both parties express strong commitment to Israel. Resolutions and legislation supporting Israel tend to pass with little or no dissent. The US–Israel Free Trade Agreement of 1985 passed the House of Representatives by a margin of 422–0. The US–Israel Strategic Partnership Act of 2015 passed the House with a vote of 400–1. The

2016 Republican Party platform pledged 'unequivocal' support for Israel, and the Democratic platform assured that the party's support for Israel was 'ironclad'.

Jewish Americans are a strongly Democratic constituency. Jews have voted at least 60 per cent Democratic in every election since 1928, except for one;[24] 65 per cent of Democratic Jews express personal emotional attachment with Israel, and 86 per cent of Democratic Jews say caring about Israel is an important part of being Jewish (Pew Research Center, 2013). Democratic Party leaders typically express strongly pro-Israel sentiments. President Biden has expressed strong antipathy for Palestinian leaders, stating that he is 'tired of everybody giving the Palestinian Authority a pass ... as if they're not continuing to foment all of this'. Biden also said, 'They continued to insist on baiting everyone who is Jewish, saying they would not sign a deal with a Jewish state' (quoted in Barrow, 2019). Democratic Senate Leader Chuck Schumer likened the Palestinian Liberation Organization (PLO) to the Taliban, just weeks after 9/11 (Edozien, 2001). Some figures on the left of US politics have been critical of the amount and nature of US assistance to Israel, but they do not enjoy widespread support in their party. For example, during the 2020 Democratic primaries, socialist Senator Bernie Sanders argued that US military aid to Israel should come with preconditions about Israeli treatment of Palestinians. Vice President Joe Biden, the eventual Democratic nominee and future president, called Sanders's comments 'bizarre' (Barrow, 2019).

Christian evangelicals have been perhaps an even more ardently pro-Israel constituency than American Jews. Unlike Jews, white evangelicals lean heavily towards the Republicans, with roughly four in five voting for Donald Trump in both 2016 and 2020. Elizabeth Stephens (2010) writes that pro-Israel Christian groups have successfully framed Israel as a democratic nation under siege from its authoritarian Muslim neighbours. Additionally, some evangelical Christians view the re-establishment of a Jewish state in Israel as a precondition to the end times known as the Rapture, when the souls of true believers in Jesus Christ will be saved (Hagee, 2007). The capture of the Old City of Jerusalem and the site of the Temple during the Six Days War in 1967 signified the hastening of the Rapture.

Donald Trump was one of the most pro-Israel presidents in US history. Trump broke decades of precedent by outwardly siding with Israel in the Israel–Palestine conflict. He recognized Israeli sovereignty over the disputed Golan Heights (Landler and Halbfinger, 2019). The Israeli government then named a section of the territory 'Trump

Heights' in his honour (Holmes, 2020). Trump took Israel's side on the disputed status of Jerusalem, moving the US Embassy from Tel Aviv as a sign of official US recognition of Jerusalem's status as Israel's capital (Landler and Halbfinger, 2017). It should be noted that relocating the US Embassy to Jerusalem had been official US policy since an act of Congress in 1995, but Presidents Clinton, Bush and Obama had all deferred the implementation of the decision due to its potentially explosive implications for the peace process. Secretary of State Mike Pompeo rescinded a 1978 State Department memorandum, which had stated that Israeli settlements in the West Bank violated international law (Jakes and Halbfinger, 2019).

The Trump Administration also brokered historic normalization accords between Israel and a number of Muslim-majority nations, including the UAE, Bahrain and Sudan. These accords broke with half a century of Arab solidarity to the Palestinian cause. The Trump Administration took a series of punitive steps against Palestinians, including eliminating all US funding for the UN Relief and Works Agency that provides aid to Palestinian refugees (Wong, 2018). The Trump Administration also cut nearly $300 million of federal funding for the Palestinian Authority through USAID and for other projects in Palestine, such as security and medical projects (Halbfinger, 2020). The Administration evicted the PLO from its offices in Washington, DC (Ryan et al, 2018).

Critics of the Israeli lobby argue it causes the US government to support policies that are almost entirely driven by domestic interest group politics rather than a rational calculation of the US's security and international needs. Israel has acted against the US, yet receives minimal punishment. For example, Israel has been accused of selling US military technology to China (Mearsheimer and Walt, 2011). Israel attacked the USS *Liberty* in 1967, killing 34 US soldiers (Mearsheimer and Walt, 2007: 368). Israel is known to conduct extensive surveillance of US officials through espionage. One such example was the case of Jonathan Pollard, an analyst for the US Navy. Pollard, a Jewish US citizen, passed secret military intelligence from the US to Israel. Pollard was described as 'one of the most prolific spies in US history' (Cheeseman, 2020). He was sentenced to life in prison, but was released for good behaviour after 30 years. Parole was lifted by the Trump Administration, allowing Pollard to immigrate to Israel, which had granted him citizenship while in prison.

It is difficult to know the degree of direct influence of the Israeli lobby on US foreign policy. This is a constant problem with measuring interest group influence in general. Robert Lieberman (2009) has criticized Mearsheimer and Walt (2007) on the basis that they fail to establish the *causal* connection between the Israeli lobby and pro-Israel US foreign policy. While Lieberman accepts that the US has a generous foreign policy disposition towards Israel, he is not convinced that Mearsheimer and Walt show that *ceteris paribus* the absence of the strongly organized Israeli lobby would mean that the US would have a more balanced approach to Middle East geopolitics. Elizabeth Stephens sides with this critique. She believes that US public and elite opinion is already highly sympathetic to Israel, and that the lobby 'could not function effectively in an environment that was hostile to its activities' (2010: 132).

The cultural affection between the US and Israel is a deep one (Stephens, 2010). Israel's defenders point out Israel's precarious situation as the only non-Muslim country in the Middle East. Many believe that this makes it uniquely vulnerable and requires special support from the US. There are legitimate continuing reasons for the US to support Israel today: shared political values, common cultural linkages and an historic debt to ensure a safe homeland for the Jews after the Holocaust and thousands of years of persecution. But ultimately, both countries are settler-colonial states whose popular cultures value 'pioneering peoples' irrespective of their impact on the indigenous population (Stephens, 2010: 126).

African Americans and US foreign policy

The racial divide between people of European and African descent – known as the black–white colour line – has been socially and politically enforced in the US for centuries. The historian John Hope Franklin wrote that by the 20th century, 'the color line was as well defined and as firmly entrenched as any institution in the land. After all, it was older than most institutions, including the federal government itself. More important, it informed the content and shaped the lives of those institutions and the people who lived under them' (1993: 36).

Black people have been living in the present-day US for as long as white people, arriving as early as 1619 in Virginia (Allen, 1975). Unlike nearly all other ethnic groups in the US except for Native Americans, African Americans are, by and large, not descendants of 'immigrants'. Slavery and the forcible removal of African people from their homes are the common experience that unites the vast majority of black people in the US. This makes the US black population quite unlike, say, the black population in the UK where many black people have recent family ties to a particular country (Nigeria, Jamaica,

Trinidad, and so on). Barack Obama, the son of a Kenyan, is unusual in most African-American circles in having a direct tie to a particular African country. Indeed, some people in the African–American community initially questioned Barack Obama's legitimacy as the first black candidate for president in the US because he lacked that descent from American chattel slavery that unifies the experience of the vast majority of African Americans (Johnson, 2017). For that reason, African Americans are not the same as other 'ethnic lobbies'. The vast majority of African Americans do not have a particular country in Africa to which they can claim common descent in the same way in which Armenian Americans, Irish Americans, Cuban Americans, Indian Americans and many other groups of Americans can.

There is an important exception that must be highlighted: black people in the US who are immigrants or descendants of immigrants. They constitute a relatively small proportion of the black population in the US (about 10 per cent). Since the liberalization of US immigration law in 1965, eliminating racial quotas, just 3.3 per cent of all immigrants to the US have been black. Mary Waters (1999) writes that many black immigrants in the US struggle because they have a strong sense of their ethnic/national identity, but they are primarily seen through their racial identity by outsiders. Almost without exception, African immigrants are assigned a 'black' racial identity in America's dichotomous white–black racial order, whereas other immigrants, such as Latinos and Asians, have, at various points in American history, been able to straddle these boundaries and, at times, found themselves classified as 'white'.[25] As many anthropologists who have studied black immigrant communities in the US have pointed out, black immigrants must accept the state/society-imposed category 'African American' while holding a desire to preserve a separate national or regional identity, especially due to perceptions of African Americans' subordinate status in American society.[26]

This lack of a family history of immigration for most African Americans has led some commentators to assume that African Americans are broadly uninterested in foreign affairs. This is simply not the case. The first black person to win the Nobel Peace Prize was the African American Ralph Bunche in 1950. Bunche received the prize for his role in mediating between Israel and the Arab States on behalf of the UN. In 1957, Martin Luther King and his wife Coretta Scott King went to Ghana to attend the country's official independence ceremonies. In the 1950s, the handful of African-American members of Congress became involved in foreign policy, partly as a way of boosting their status in the House (Tillery, 2011: 133). In his second term in office, Michigan Congressman Charles Diggs joined the House Foreign Affairs Committee in 1957. Diggs later explained that showing ability in foreign affairs was unthreatening to white members of Congress but also demonstrated a real aptitude that would become helpful in future policy efforts.

Some commentators argue that African-American elites were reluctant to become overly involved in the decolonization movement out of fear of being seen as pro-communist (Borstelmann, 2001). The Council on African Affairs tended to offer harshly critical, left-wing critiques of US foreign policy, which Carl Watts (2010) believes limited their appeal during the Cold War struggle. In contrast, mainstream civil rights groups like the NAACP (National Association for the Advancement of Colored People) broached foreign policy with some trepidation. Other black leaders regarded foreign policy as something of an indulgence that needlessly antagonized the Kennedy and Johnson Administrations, which had otherwise been supportive in the domestic sphere (Noer, 1985: 169; Borstelmann, 2001: 168)

Some groups, however, engaged with foreign policy and had access to policymakers. The American Committee on Africa (ACOA) provided funds and publicity for anti-colonial African campaigners to make speeches in the US and at the UN. The ACOA provided legal and welfare assistance to political prisoners and their families. However, the ACOA was dominated by white leadership, which led to the formation of the black-led American Negro Leadership Conference on Africa (ANLCA) in 1962 (Watts, 2010). Initially, the ANCLA had serious access to high-level officials during the Kennedy Administration, but they were sidelined by the Johnson Administration. Watts (2010) explains that the Johnson Administration wanted to resist getting dragged too far into the Rhodesia situation (see also Lake, 1976; Brinkley, 1992: 315–27). Thomas Borstelmann summarizes, 'The Johnson administration in 1965 believed that its record on racial discrimination was quite strong, and it had no interest in besmirching that reputation by a high-level engagement with the racially explosive situation in southern Africa' (2001: 196).

In 1977, the Congressional Black Caucus (CBC) supported the formation of the lobby group the TransAfrican Forum, founded in order to lobby in support of black independence movements in Africa and the Caribbean. That same year, President Jimmy Carter announced that the mayor of Atlanta Andrew Young would be the first black US ambassador to the UN, the most high-ranking ambassadorial nomination that a president makes. It was a significant statement from the Carter Administration for the US to be represented to the rest of the world by an African American, especially one of Young's stature who, in addition to his role as mayor of Atlanta, had also been a close confidante of Martin Luther King.

Perhaps the most powerful expression of black power in US foreign affairs occurred during the 1980s over the question of sanctions on apartheid South Africa. For years, black members of Congress had been agitating for sanctions to be used against the white regime in South Africa. The CBC had proposed legislation to prevent the US supporting IMF loans to countries that violated human rights, specifically to block a proposed loan to apartheid South Africa. The first sanctions bill was proposed in Congress in 1972 by Ron Dellums, a left-wing African-American congressman from Oakland, California. Although initially unsuccessful, by 1988 Dellums garnered bipartisan support for the bill despite being a self-proclaimed socialist, at a time when such a label was particularly taboo given the ongoing Cold War (Mallinson and Johnson, 2021). The Comprehensive Anti-Apartheid Act even had enough support to override the veto of President Ronald Reagan, who feared instability in South Africa following sanctions. Reagan instead preferred a policy of 'constructive engagement', involving creating strong socioeconomic ties between South Africa and the US to slowly liberalize the country and end apartheid (Fatton, 1984). The Comprehensive Anti-Apartheid Act of 1988 banned all new US trade and investment in South Africa, ended direct air links between the countries and required various federal agencies to stop the flow of funds to South Africa. The sanctions lasted until Nelson Mandela's release from prison in 1990.

Some commentators would argue that African-Americans' involvement in African political affairs is demonstrative of affective bonds driven by a pan-African identity (Weisbord, 1973; Walters, 1987). In this regard, black Americans are motivated by a sense of **linked fate** with African people. Linked fate refers to the degree to which people feel that what happens to a group at large also affects them individually due to their membership of that group (Dawson, 1994). In Tillery's (2011) analysis of black newspapers (such as *The Chicago Defender*, *New York Amsterdam News*, *The Pittsburgh Courier*), there was more coverage of Ghanaian independence in 1957–59 (352 articles) than there was of India's independence (189 articles), whereas the opposite trend was observed in *The New York Times* that had nearly twice as many articles about Indian independence as it did Ghanaian independence. This does not necessarily show linked fate, but it certainly shows a greater interest among African Americans in the affairs of Africa. During the black power movement, there was a certain degree to which African Americans embraced a pan-African identity. Jack Valenti, a political adviser to Lyndon Johnson, observed in 1965, 'The United States is inescapably involved in Africa by reasons of its large, increasingly politically conscious Negro minority. A Zionist type of emotional concern, affecting local voting, could emerge' (Horne, 2001).

However, Alvin Tillery (2011) argues that material domestic politics should not be written out of our understandings of African-American foreign policy involvement. Tillery (2011) demonstrates that there are times when black members of Congress have put the interests of their (mainly black) constituents over the interests of Africans writ large. A key example of this is the African Growth and Opportunity Act (AGOA). The Act provides trade preferences into the US for certain goods, especially textiles and clothing, as well as raw materials, such as oil. The deal allows the US president to decide which countries in Africa should be eligible at different times. Although the CBC initially welcomed the deal, some black members of Congress voiced their strong opposition. Many spoke of their own constituents' jobs being put at risk, especially those who represented districts with large cotton, textile and clothing manufacturers. In fact, Tillery (2011) found that the number of jobs tied to the textile industry in a black Congress member's district was directly correlated to whether or not they would vote for the bill. The average number of textile jobs in a district of a black AGOA opposer was three times that of a black AGOA supporter.

Conclusion

Ultimately, race and ethnicity are social and political constructs, whose meanings and identifiers change according to time and place (Omi and Winant, 1994; Fredrickson, 2002). National identities are products of history, myth, ideology, culture and politics (Anderson, 2006). Because of the US's diverse immigrant makeup, ethnic groups play an important role in directing US foreign policy. While no single ethnic group dominates all of US foreign policy, particular ethnic groups have lobbied effectively to shape US foreign policy towards the particular country or region from which they or their ancestors come. Ethnic groups seek to use their leverage within parties to control the agenda on certain issues.

Ethnic and racial identities are major cleavages in US electoral politics. Canny politicians who wish to win favour with some of these electorates may decide that signalling their support on a foreign policy issue is a less costly form of electoral appeal than a substantive domestic policy commitment that might entail the distribution of most harshly contested material resources. Foreign policy is ripe for 'positioning taking', which David Mayhew identified as a central activity of members of Congress in his seminal 1974 study. Yet, there are serious questions to be asked about the role of ethnic interest groups in the construction of US foreign policy. Some critics argue that these lobbies cause the US to undermine its own national interests and undermine its credibility around the world.

PART IV

The Goals of US Foreign Policy

8

Realism: Order, Security
and Prosperity

The final two chapters of this book revert to the conventional themes of international relations scholarship: realism and liberalism. Realist IR theory emphasizes individual countries' pursuit of their own material interests, especially security and prosperity, even at the expense of others in the international system. Liberalism takes a positive–sum view of the world, where the spread of democracy and capitalism, bolstered by international institutions, will bring security and prosperity. It is sometimes argued that the US has pursued a kind of 'liberal realism'. The US has constructed a particular global order, ostensibly around a set of liberal values, which, at the same time, serves material US interests. This is sometimes known as the US-led 'security community' or US-led order. The bargain is as follows: America provides states with security and access to American markets, technology and supplies within an open world economy. In return, countries agree to be reliable partners providing diplomatic, economic and logistical support for the US as it leads in this 'unipolar' world order. **Unipolarity** refers to when one state enjoys an overwhelming advantage in relative capabilities to all other states in the international system (Brooks and Wohlforth, 2008: 13).

While seemingly a 'liberal' order, there are critics who claim that American unipolar hegemony is merely window-dressing for its realist outlook. In reality, this so-called liberal order is a realist vehicle for US self-interest. The US breaks the very rules that it has made whenever such rules interfere with the US's own security and economic interests. This chapter, therefore, will view the international order constructed by the United States after the Second World War through a realist lens.

Others contend that the US-led order is crumbling due to both assault from external factors and also from internal neglect. The Obama and Trump presidencies, in different ways, saw the US withdraw from some of its earlier adventurism. While the US is often viewed as an impenetrably powerful imperial power, it has, in fact, been quite unsuccessful at compelling countries to come to its heel in recent years. The US has lost most of the major wars in which it has participated in the post-Second World War period of its supposed hegemony.

Finally, this chapter considers what the rise of China means for US power in world politics. For decades, estimations of the death of US global leadership have been gravely exaggerated. The Soviet Union, Japan and the EU were each identified as likely world powers to 'overtake' the US at some point in the decades following the Second World War. Yet none of these challenges came to pass, in part due to structural flaws within the challengers' domestic economies and political systems. To appreciate the nature of China's 'challenge', scholars must take seriously the constraints imposed by China's own domestic politics.

The US-led order

The concept of order has inappropriately been conflated with the concept of peace. Although a peaceful world will almost certainly be an ordered world, the relationship is not essential. Hedley Bull, one of the most prominent academics in the English School of International Relations, provides the following definition: order consists of 'those patterns or dispositions of human activity that sustain the elementary or primary goals of social life among mankind as a whole' (Bull, 1977: 19). There is no mention of peace in Bull's definition. In fact, if war was taken to be one of the elementary goals of social life, then order could be built around conflict.

In his essay 'The Great Powers', Leopold von Ranke explained that a country assumes the status of a 'great power' when it is 'able to maintain itself against all others, even when they are united' (1981: 140). A great power has power capabilities (both hard and soft), spatial constraints and status considerations (the need to preserve legitimacy in the eyes of other states). These are the extent and limits to its capacity to maintain order. Some commentators would argue that great powers recognize that they have certain rights and duties in the international system by virtue of their status. A great power will enjoy the rights to assert its own will (to an extent) in shaping and promoting the common interests of the international system, but it will also be responsible for a number of duties including peacekeeping and providing development aid.

Many commentators regard the 20th century as the rise of the US as a 'great power'. In this understanding, for the first 150 years the US had enjoyed a broadly non-interventionist poise towards global affairs, with a few key exceptions, as an independent state. However, after its entry in the Second Word War, the US took on the mantle of global leadership befitting of a country with its economic and military might (Kindleberger, 1989). In the post-Second World War period, the US is said to have fashioned a 'liberal' world order in which it acted as a benevolent hegemon, ensuring the expansion of markets and liberal values through a US-guaranteed security network (Ikenberry, 2001, 2004b, 2011). Recent commentators have looked askance at late political developments in the US and raised the alarm about the decline of US global leadership (Dueck, 2015; Ikenberry, 2018).

There are many ways to interpret this narrative, but at its core it tells a story of the US's rise to leadership as a benevolent world power on whom world prosperity and security rely. Many commentators portray the 19th century as being an isolationist period in US foreign policy while the 20th century was characterized by a 'rise to globalism', as Stephen Ambrose and Douglas Brinkley (2012 [1971]) call it. Ian Bremmer summarizes the narrative as follows: 'US policymakers have broadly agreed that two World Wars and the struggle with expansionist Soviet communism offered indisputable proof that American leadership is both good for the world and for national security' (2019).

A strong candidate for Year 0 for the US-led order is 1945. That year, there were over 12 million active duty troops in the US military (see Figure 8.1). The strength of the US military was unmatched. It was a moment when the US stood at the apogee of its power in the world. The war had been brought to a decisive close by the nuclear bombings of the Japanese cities of Hiroshima and Nagasaki in August 1945. These bombings killed a civilian population of about 200,000. The dropping of these bombs constituted tremendous, indeed terrifying, displays of American technological and military power. They were made possible as a result of a deep relationship between the federal government and scientific research, discussed in Chapter 3. Indeed, it might be argued that this relationship, which endures today, was one of the Second World War's most economically significant legacies (Hughes, 2004; Giroux, 2007).

Gar Alperovitz (1994) has persuasively argued that the bombings of Hiroshima and Nagasaki were not necessary to bring the war to an end. He writes that 'Japan would almost certainly have surrendered' when the USSR declared war, as planned, on 15 August 1945 (1994: xi). The threat of a Soviet land invasion, rather than its reality, was

Figure 8.1: The size of the US military, 1801–2014

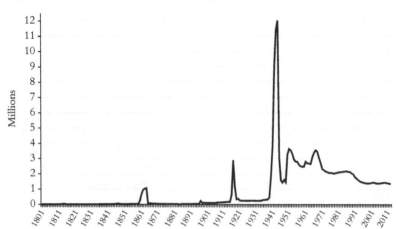

Note: Absolute number of active duty service personnel.

Source: 1801–1997, Department of Defense (1997, Table 2.13); 1997–2014: History in Pieces (nd)

the sufficient precondition to bring about victory in Japan. According to Alperovitz (1994), based on his extensive archival and interview research, President Harry Truman thought that it was essential that the US was credited with victory in Japan, rather than the Soviet Union. He decided to rush forward with the bombings of these two Japanese cities, one week before Stalin's planned declaration of war.[1] Dwight Eisenhower, Supreme Allied Commander in Europe, reflected towards the end of his life, 'the Japanese were ready to surrender, and it wasn't necessary to hit them with that awful thing.... I hated to see our country be the first to use such a weapon' (quoted in *Newsweek*, 1963).

The decision whether or not to drop the atomic bomb had little to do with war strategy in Japan and much more to do with positioning the future relations of the US against the Soviet Union in the post-Second World War era (Bernstein, 1974; Messer, 1982; Herken, 1988). President Truman timed the test of the nuclear bomb in late July 1945 to coincide with the Potsdam Conference in order to give him a more powerful hand negotiating with the Soviet Union about the future of the post-war order. Truman believed that his predecessor, Franklin Roosevelt, who had died in April 1945, had been too soft with Soviet leader Joseph Stalin in his final months (Alperovitz, 1994: 54).[2] Yet Truman's decision may have backfired, causing the Soviet Union to harden its stance against the US, and appalling US allies in turn. British General Hastings Ismay, who became the first NATO Secretary-General, recalled his 'revulsion' at the news of the Hiroshima bombing (1960: 401). White House Chief of Staff Admiral William Leahy reacted similarly: 'My own feeling is that in being the first to use it, we had adopted an ethical standard common to the barbarians of the Dark Ages…. I was not taught to make war in that fashion, and wars cannot be won by destroying women and children' (1950: 439). Ultimately, realist politics led Truman and his advisers to support the unnecessary killing of 200,000 civilians in order to gain diplomatic leverage against the Soviet Union.

After committing one of the greatest ever acts of military destruction in Japan, the US soon embarked on one of the greatest acts of humanitarian intervention in Europe. In the Marshall Plan, the US provided $13 billion (over $130 billion in 2017 dollars) to aid in the reconstruction of Western Europe after the Second World War. Over one-quarter of these funds went to the UK, more than any other country, including West Germany. Western Europe saw it in its interests to encourage the US to maintain its position of leadership over this new order rather than retreat to its interwar position (Cox, 1987). President Harry Truman was more than happy to oblige, and in 1947, he declared a commitment to contain the spread of communism throughout the world. In what became known as the 'Truman Doctrine', President Truman promised that the US would offer aid and support to any nation that was engaged in a struggle to protect a liberal democratic constitution from a communist revolution. In a sense, the US was offering to drape the liberal democracies of Western Europe – and beyond – in the US security blanket. The Truman Doctrine reflected a commitment to an American hegemonic order. **Hegemony** is one model to maintain international order, referring to when one actor sustains an international order.

This courtship precipitated the signing of the North Atlantic Treaty in 1949, which created the intergovernmental military alliance NATO. NATO has provided ballast for America to assert its control over the Western world from a security standpoint, with NATO countries accounting for 70 per cent of global military expenditure. The US alone accounts for nearly half of global military expenditure, making it by far NATO's most important contributor.

Thus, the starting date of the so-called 'US-led liberal order' is typically said to be 1945, when the US sat at the height of its power, but we should be careful not to fall for a teleology that sees America as having been on a path of inevitable rise (Lieven, 2005: 74). Its place in global affairs has been the product of choices, sometimes serendipitous choices, but there is no sense in which we should assume that American power in the world is preordained or irreversible.

American post-war benevolence came as a consequence of several domestic contingencies. In the 1930s, the US military was only just over 400,000 strong. In 1941, Congress nearly failed to pass the essential extension of the Selective Service Act, which was responsible for growing the US military to its largest number ever (Ambrose and Brinkley, 2012 [1971]). The bill passed the House of Representatives by one vote (203–202). Similarly, the success of the **Manhattan Project** was not preordained. It was completed only after victory in Europe had been achieved. President Harry Truman called it 'the greatest scientific gamble in history'. The Marshall Plan faced bitter opposition in Congress and would perhaps not have passed had there not been a communist coup in Czechoslovakia in February 1948. The fall of European nations to communism helped to 'scare the hell out of the country', as Senator Arthur Vandenberg insisted was necessary.

From 1945 until the early 1990s, the US was understood to operate in a bipolar global environment. The US stood on one side as the leader of a capitalist, liberal, democratic world order while the Soviet Union stood on the other side as the leader of a communist, fraternal world order. In this bipolar world, the US became a kind of 'lender of last resort' for democracy. Daniel Deudney and Jeffrey Meiser write (with no small hubris), 'had it not been for American power and purpose between 1940 and 1990, liberal democracy might well have been eliminated from the planet' (2012: 33). Colin Dueck (2006: 2) argues that US foreign policy in the modern era has been shaped 'by a set of beliefs that can only be called "liberal"'. He asserts implausibly that 'classical liberal ideas' which are 'unique to the United States' have been the major contributing force to the US-led order. Whatever values can be ascribed to US hegemony, the material reality is that it has required enormous investment from the US, not least in its level of defence spending and willingness to expend American lives in far-flung military adventures around the world. Before the Second World War, the US public had tended not to support such grand entanglements of the US, except in periods of perceived existential threat. John Thompson (1992) argued that bipolarity assisted in exaggerating the sense of American vulnerability during the Cold War. Reflecting on the period, he wrote that 'the full and effective deployment of that power has required from the American people disciplines and sacrifices that they are prepared to sustain only if they are persuaded that the nation's safety is directly at stake' (1992: 43). Perry Anderson echoes this when he writes that policymakers were 'Masking strategies of offence as exigencies of defence'. In Anderson's assessment, 'no theme was better calculated to close the potential gap between popular sentiments and elite designs' (2017: 30).

Post-Second World War US global leadership was understood to be an institutionally based, rule-following order underpinned by free trade, expanding alliances and liberal democracy. Hillary Clinton described it as a 'long-standing bipartisan tradition of global leadership rooted in a preference for cooperating over acting unilaterally, for exhausting diplomacy before making war, and for converting old adversaries into allies rather than making new enemies' (2007: 3). The liberal order was premised on a putative commitment to (1) a world composed of democratic states that (2) are commensurate with self-determining nations and (3) supportive of an open, capitalist economic system (Cox and Stokes, 2012).[3]

To achieve these goals, the US helped to construct multinational institutions that would provide the framework of good global governance. These included institutions such as the IMF and the World Bank, the WTO, and various bilateral and multilateral organizations. Although multinational in form, in spirit the US has always played a dominant or outsized role. Liberal theorists have defended the unequal power of the US in this liberal order using the concept of **primacy**. Primacy emphasizes the need for the US to be the pre-eminent power in world politics because the US is uniquely equipped to guarantee the stability of the international system and its institutions. On quite the opposite end is the theory of **offshore balancing**, which welcomes multipolarity. Proponents of 'offshore balancing' are broadly critical of the US's attempts to lead through power alone. They argue that the US is overstretching itself and that global stability is achieved through alliances and constraint (Schwarz and Layne, 2002).

After the fall of the Soviet Union in 1991, the US found itself in an unprecedented position. For the first time in post-Second World War history, and perhaps in modern history, a great power existed with no rival or potential rivals with which to contend. The world had moved from multipolarity before the Second World War to bipolarity during the Cold War to the exceptional condition of unipolarity. John Ikenberry marvelled, 'For the first time in the modern era, the world's most powerful state can operate on the global stage without the counterbalancing constraints of other great powers. We have entered the American unipolar age' (2004b: 609). Francis Fukuyama famously described this moment as 'the end of history' (Fukuyama, 1992). By this, he meant that liberal capitalist democracy had won out at the final form of human production and governance: 'the universalization of Western liberal democracy as the final form of human government'

(Fukuyama, 1989: 4). History was over because the 'final' (and most superior) model of human organization had been decided on: the US model.

The end of the Cold War also saw the repurposing of the IR discipline, especially in the US. Tony Smith observed in 1994 that some of his colleagues were 'almost wistful about the loss of the perfect clarity' that the Cold War had afforded (1994: xi). No longer was the focus on the logic of nuclear destruction or defeating the Soviet Union. Instead, focus shifted to explaining (and defending) US 'liberal hegemony'. John Ikenberry (2004b) is one of the great academic defenders of American hegemony. With its position as a global hegemon, he viewed the US's responsibility to be a 'producer of world order' (Ikenberry, 2004b: 609). The 'American Project', as he conceived it, pursues a protean order that is distinctly open and rules-based. It is built on liberal values: the provision of security and economic goods, mutually agreeable rules and institutions and interactive political processes that give weaker, subordinate states some opportunities to voice concerns.

As it turned out, the early years of the unipolar order (the 1990s) was a period of great complacency for the US. From 1989 until 2001, America seemed to be unchallengeable. It had unmatched economic, military and cultural power. Its military interventions – the Gulf War, Haiti and Bosnia – were won quickly and, from the US perspective, with minimal loss of life. The US economy was booming. And with all this backdrop, polls showed that Americans expressed very little interest in foreign affairs. Yet the US had not really retreated in any meaningful way from its Cold War posture, which had, until that point, been justified on the basis of existential threat posed to the US by the Soviet Union (Thompson, 1992). The US maintained thousands of troops around the world in over one hundred countries. Although US defence spending declined after the fall of the USSR, it only declined to the levels that it had been in the 1970s before Ronald Reagan's defence build-up (see Figure 8.2). By the 21st century, the US was spending more on defence than at any time since the Second World War. The attacks on New York and Washington, DC by the al-Qaeda network on 11 September 2001 provided the basis for a new sense of existential threat, which undergirded military expansion.

Some would say that this transition was an epochal shift from *pace d'equilibrio* ('peace of equilibrium') to *pace egemonica* ('hegemonic peace') (Parsi, 2003: 196). Advanced democracies operated within a 'security community' where the threat of force was unthinkable between them (Ikenberry, 2004b: 611). Indeed, the US still provides

Figure 8.2: US defence spending (millions of dollars), 1976–2019

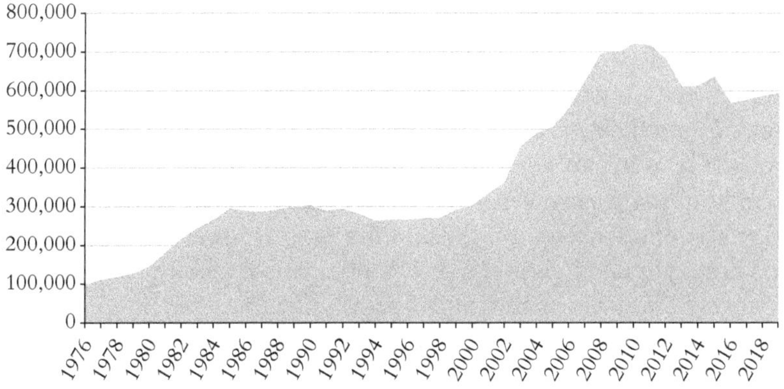

Note: Numbers for 2014–19 are estimates.
Source: US Government (2015)

security and protection to many states around the globe – from Palau to Germany and Japan. Disputes may still occur – over trade, law, human rights – but military retaliation is not an option.

Champions of the *pace egemonica* worried that President Donald Trump's foreign policy represented an abdication of US global leadership and, therefore, a potentially disastrous destabilization of the US-led order. John Ikenberry likened the election of Donald Trump to the citizens of Rome deciding to tear down their empire in a fit of madness. Writing in 2006, Colin Dueck asserted that the belief that the US should reduce its military footprint and strategically disengage from its international entanglements was 'considered beyond the fringe of mainstream political discourse' (2006). In this light, Trump's critical stance to US military entanglements seems like a huge discontinuity. Trump's foreign policy adviser Michael Anton was indeed fiercely critical of policymakers whom he believed 'remain besotted with the post-World War II "Present at the Creation"' order (Anton, 2019). Aaron Ettinger assessed that, as president, Trump 'eschew[ed] the universal values expounded by his predecessors.… This vision is new among presidents in the post-1945 era' (2019: 423). Ettinger went on to argue that Trump's foreign policy 'marks the most pronounced ideational discontinuity in US foreign policy since the end of World War II' (2019: 428).

This is probably hyperbole. US support for interdependence was always conditional on ultimate US sovereign autonomy and the protection of interests. The US's failure to ratify numerous UN treaties over the decades is evidence that US policymakers believed that their own country played by different rules from other actors in the international community, even those that operated within the aforementioned institutions of global governance the US itself had constructed (see Table 8.1). John Ikenberry strongly criticized the administration of George W. Bush because 'it offered the world a system in which America rules the world but does not abide by the rules. This is in effect empire' (2011: 22). Ikenberry's description is not wrong in the narrow sense, but it is flawed in its application. While Ikenberry presents the Bush Administration as some aberration from US foreign policy, all post-war US presidential administrations have followed a fundamentally similar path – one that Patrick Porter calls 'self-interest dressed up as moral universalism' (2020: 22).

Whatever the empirical veracity of the idea that the US has 'stopped' playing by the rules, the core contention of a declining ability of the US to assert world leadership has merit. Attributing this decline wholly to Trump, however, is historically short-sighted. Some commentators argue that decline began long before Trump. Immanuel Wallerstein (2003) contends that the US has been in decline as a global leader since

Table 8.1: Selected UN treaties not ratified by the US

Treaty	Year	US response	Number of party UN states
UN Convention Against Discrimination in Education	1960	Unsigned	106
UN Convention on the Elimination of All Forms of Discrimination Against Women	1981	Not ratified	189
UN Convention on the Rights of the Child	1990	Not ratified	196
UN Convention on the Law of the Sea	1994	Unsigned	167
Comprehensive Nuclear-Test-Ban Treaty	1996	Not ratified	168
Ottawa Treaty (Anti-Personnel Mine Ban Convention)	1997	Unsigned	164
Kyoto Protocol	1997	Not ratified	192
Rome Statute (International Criminal Court)	2000	Signature withdrawn	123
Optional Protocol to the Convention on Torture	2002	Unsigned	90
UN Convention on the Rights of Persons with Disabilities	2008	Not ratified	181
UN Convention on Cluster Bombs	2010	Unsigned	108

Source: http://hrlibrary.umn.edu/research/ratification-USA.html

its defeat in Vietnam in the 1970s, perhaps even earlier. In the five major wars the US has fought since the Second World War – Korea, Vietnam, Kuwait, Afghanistan and Iraq – the US has lost four (Korea, Vietnam, Afghanistan and Iraq), only securing a decisive victory in the Persian Gulf War to liberate Kuwait in 1991.

The Obama presidency was marked by a growing sense of America's limits (Deudney and Meiser, 2012). Obama was more modest in what he wanted to achieve internationally – or at least more modest in the resources he wanted to invest to achieve it – than many of his predecessors. While Obama engaged in some prominent multilateral deals, such as the Iran Nuclear Deal and the Paris Climate Change Agreement, he was also much more reluctant than his predecessors to commit US forces to promote democracy or to protect US interests. Colin Dueck (2015: 14) called these 'gestures of international good will' coupled with 'incremental retrenchment' of US military commitments. The US footprint in the world was by no means absent – the US drone strikes in Yemen during the Obama presidency make that clear – but it was in some sense lighter or less steady than it had been under either Bill Clinton or George W. Bush. In this way, there may have been more continuity than first meets the eye between Obama's and Trump's approach to US foreign policy. Both presidents inherited an increasingly dysfunctional arrangement: permanent war unevenly felt in the public, contending with precisely the kind of unwarranted influences of military, industry and state that Eisenhower had warned about over half a century earlier (Zielinski, 2018). Both were uncomfortable with this status quo but ultimately unable to overturn it.

Critical perspectives of the US-led order

Colin Dueck (2006) argues that the US's political culture constrains the US from engaging in dangerous international interventionism. He writes that America's core principles render some illiberal foreign policy choices 'unthinkable'. This is naive. The US has been more than willing to deploy damaging coercive methods to achieve its foreign policy goals. When Joe Biden told a crowd of reporters in Wilmington, Delaware, 'America is coming back like we used to be: ethical, straight, telling the truth, supporting our allies. All those good things', he was engaging in an act of selective nostalgia (Scherer and Wagner, 2019). Coups, bombing campaigns, economic sanctions and the like are not lapses but instruments of the US-led order. To suggest that the war on terror, drone strikes, CIA black sites and Guantanamo Bay are regrettable aberrations from 'true' American liberal internationalism is reminiscent of the doctrinaire Marxists in the mid-20th century who would argue that the gulag, political suppression and bread lines were unfortunate deviations from 'true' communism (Porter, 2020).

Another criticism of American hegemony is that it proposes to establish a largely 'Western' set of values onto all members of the international state system. Michael Howard (2002) goes so far as to call hegemony 'cultural imperialism', which forces countries to accept a laundry list of Western values. Liberal or not, hegemony interferes with internal sovereign authority – even if it is to a lesser extent than full-scale empire. It is true that the unipolar order finds legitimacy less easily than bipolar or multipolar orders where the concept of the balance of power is quite straightforward. David Rapkin (2005) is convinced that the US readily fits in with the overseas imperial model that Britain exemplified in the 19th century. He cites US defence spending (45 per cent of global defence spending) and the profusion of US military bases around the world as evidence of America's capacity to maintain both an informal and formal empire. The US still maintains nearly 800 military bases in more than 70 countries and territories abroad. American commentators rely on euphemisms such as 'order' or 'hegemon' to describe what is effectively 'imperial'. Hedley Bull famously described the concept of 'order' in the international sphere as 'imperialism with good manners' (1977: 209).

The excuses given as to why the US is different or exceptional from past empires are not convincing. It is a recurring trope of imperial powers to describe *their* empire as liberal or enlightened compared to past empires (Ferguson, 2004). The British Empire justified itself on this basis, underplaying its raw exercise of power (Porter, 2020). Winston Churchill had claimed that the role of the British Empire was to bring liberal values to the world. He saw Britain as 'an enlightened community' that engaged in the 'noble' mission to reclaim populations from 'barbarism' and to 'give peace to warring tribes, to administer justice where all was violence, to strike the chains off the slave, to draw richness from the soil, to place the earliest seeds of commerce and learning, to increase in whole peoples their capacities for pleasure and diminish their chances of pain' (Churchill, 1899: 9). In this vein, American unipolar hegemony is merely window-dressing for an American imperial order which, in fact, undermines the international system of states (Johnson, 2004). The US (paradoxically) relies on unilateralism, coercive domination and divide-and-rule strategies to promote 'liberal' values around the world.

Ikenberry (2004b) answers that the features of American hegemony make it far more benign than critics contend. 'The American Project' cannot be compared to any other order that has previously existed. The features of nuclear weapons, democracy, capitalization and modernization – in addition to its unipolarity – give it an unparalleled character. Ikenberry admits, however, that the imperial critique is understandable. In light of the abuses and arrogance of the Bush and Trump Administrations with respect to the 'rules' of international order, it is easy to see that the US has the power to subvert the international state system and become the international Leviathan. This is a weakness in Ikenberry's formulation. Whether the hegemony of the US is benevolent rests almost entirely on the character of the leaders elected by the American people.

If the US is such a successful imperial power, it might, then, be asked why it has been so unsuccessful at compelling countries to come to its heel in recent years. In the post-Cold War period, the US has issued threats to regimes in Iraq, Libya, Serbia, Afghanistan and Haiti, all warning these countries to heed American demands, but each time these countries simply ignored what the US demanded. This is the dilemma that Dianne Chamberlain takes up in her book *Cheap Threats* (2016). In 2003, Bush issued a clear ultimatum to Saddam Hussein telling him to leave Iraq. Saddam Hussein did not. Why have countries ignored these threats from the world's most powerful country? You might be tempted to say that it's because these threats aren't credible, that they are bluffs. But that's not the case. In all of these instances (Iraq, Libya, the Balkans, Afghanistan and Haiti), the US did carry out its threat. The US made a clear 'escape' clause for the regimes it disagreed with and that it could clearly overpower, but the regimes nonetheless ignored the US.

Chamberlain (2016) suggests that the issue is that threats made by the US might be 'credible' but this does not necessarily make them 'effective'. She thinks that for threats to be effective, countries need to be willing to show 'resolve'. Countries might be willing to bear the burden of pain inflicted on them, even if it meant that their country might be ultimately overpowered by the US. This is because some goals might override simple, rational calculations of power imbalances and even survival. Sometimes 'saving face' is just as important to a political regime as victory (Morrow, 1989). Chamberlain believes that these motives are particularly stark when the threats from the US are 'cheap'. By this she means that the modern US model of war fighting has minimized the human, financial and political costs of deploying troops abroad. Launching military action no longer involves significant US casualties, long-term fiscal sacrifice or serious political blowback.

There are reasons that we might doubt this assessment at first. For example, the Iraq War can hardly be said to fit in these categories, certainly in terms of its fiscal impact, and even more so its political blowback. But even this hard case ultimately vindicates Chamberlain's point. The American public is decreasingly interested in staying in a conflict until the job is done. If the target can be overwhelmed quickly and through a massive display of the US's forces, then that's all for the good. This was very much the public expectation of the 2003 war in Iraq. But if a war involves a high level of US sacrifice, the US public quickly tires. The political resolve evaporates as the wars become costly and the deaths of US troops mount. Threats of an enormous scale might be counterproductive. America's enemies might accept that it is 'credible' that the US could display a massive show of force in their country, but it makes them less likely to want to cooperate with the US. Smaller, more limited demands might be more likely to make countries talk by helping them to save face.

The China challenge

Since the Second World War, the idea that the US was 'falling behind' and would be surpassed by a superior power has been a recurring motif in popular commentary. While sometimes there is a military component to these predictions, more often than not these claims about 'decline' are made with respect to economic output.

In the 1950s and 1960s, American commentators worried that the US economy would be overtaken by the USSR. The USSR was the world's second largest economy and produced more oil and gas than even Saudi Arabia. In the 1970s and 1980s, the fear was that Japan would overtake the US. Japan seemed to be on the cutting edge of a technological revolution. Facilitated by Reagan-era deregulation and currency revaluation, Japanese businesses were able to engage in a buying spree of US businesses. The idea of a Japanese 'takeover' of US businesses was a widespread anxiety of the period. In the 1990s, a recently unified Germany and the EU more broadly were seen as a major economic threat. The further integration of the EU single market, the creation of the single currency, expansion into the former Soviet bloc – all seemed to suggest that the EU would become *the* major global economic powerhouse. Yet, due to their internal political or economic impairments, the US saw off each of these rivals.

In the 21st century, such concerns have been placed squarely with China. China has been growing at a much higher rate than the US or any of its previous competitors. Since 1989, Chinese annual growth has not dipped below 6 per cent annually, whereas US growth rates have not even reached 5 per cent in the same period. China holds over $800 billion in US Treasury bonds and $2 trillion in currency reserves. As a share of global GDP China is rapidly catching up with the US – although part of this is obscured by the fact that these two countries have quite differently sized populations. The Chinese population is more than four times the population of the US. Measuring by per capita GDP, the picture is complicated: both countries have been on a course of steady increase (see Figure 8.3). China's course has admittedly been slightly more accelerated in recent years, but the US is still tens of thousands of dollars ahead of China per capita.

Some commentators argue that China is quietly preparing to overtake the US as the world's dominant economic power. Mao Zedong's successor Deng Xiaoping (1978–89) began a series of dramatic and far-reaching economic reforms, which liberalized the Chinese economy, and, many commentators argue, set the ground for the country's recent economic success. At the end of his tenure as China's president, Deng drafted a 24-character strategy that set out what should guide China's role in the international arena into the future. Deng suggested that China 'stand firmly, hide our capabilities, and bide our time'.

Recent commentators suggest that China has done just this, and it has shown remarkable success economically, for many of the reasons already outlined. It is said that this success has been driven by the so-called **Beijing Consensus**, which includes replacing trust in

Figure 8.3: Per capita GDP growth (adjusted to 2005, US$), 1990–2016

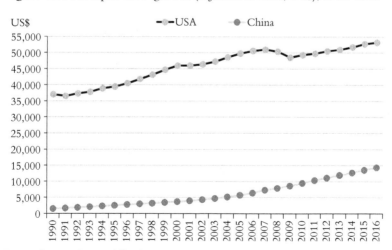

Source: https://data.worldbank.org/indicator/NY.GDP.PCAP.CD

the free market for economic growth with a more muscular state hand on the levers of production; political authoritarianism guided by an unchallenged, ruling political party; and population control, including family planning (*The Economist*, 2009). Chinese officials firmly believe that this combination of authoritarian politics, state-directed domestic economic management and capitalist international economic engagement has been the key to China's success. The Beijing Consensus is a direct challenge to the so-called **Washington Consensus** that refers to the preference for free markets and free political systems with very little state interference.

The Beijing model, its defenders would argue, has lifted hundreds of millions of Chinese people out of poverty. Hugh White (2012) has argued that no government has done more to make poverty history than the government of China. Certain political consequences are likely to rise from China's increased economic clout within Asia. Its economic interdependence with Taiwan (the anti-communist Republic of China) grows, and China may aspire to fulfil Mao Zedong's prediction to Henry Kissinger in 1973. Kissinger asked when Taiwan would become a full part of China. 'After one hundred years', Mao predicted. The present government of China seems to lack such patience. In recent years, Beijing has whittled away the autonomy of Hong Kong. In June 2020, the Chinese government criminalized advocacy for independence for Hong Kong, 'collusion with foreign forces' and 'subversion' (Kuo and Yu, 2020). Hundreds of pro-democracy activists in Hong Kong have been imprisoned (Davidson, 2020).

China has also become economically active outside Asia. It has become Africa's largest trade partner, surpassing the US in 2009. It has greatly expanded its economic ties to the continent. China engages in a form of commercial diplomacy that most other countries cannot match. China is a significant source of foreign direct investment in Africa. Chinese creditors have financed agriculture and infrastructure projects across the continent. The 'Belt and Road' initiative of President Xi Jinping is integral to this growth in China's economic and cultural weight throughout the developing world and beyond.

Commentators are increasingly becoming attracted to the idea that the US and China are falling prey to what has become known as the 'Thucydides trap'. From his perspective as an Athenian and a veteran, the Greek historian Thucydides wrote his masterful treatise *The History of the Peloponnesian War*, which told the story of the conflict between the two great city-states of Athens and Sparta during the 5th century BC. Thucydides explained the context of this conflict:

'It was the *rise* of Athens, and the fear that this instilled in Sparta, that made war inevitable.' Graham Allison (2017) has applied Thucydides' words to 16 cases in the last 500 years where there was a rising power that threatened to overtake the existing power. He found that in 12 of the 16 cases (75 per cent of the time), the rising power and the dominant power went to war. The thing to understand here is that wars are often sparked by small choices (for example, shooting an archduke). These small events are extremely difficult to predict; they are almost random. But the structural factors that lay the foundations or background conditions by which such a spark can ignite an entire conflagration that leads to war are easier to observe.

John Mearsheimer thinks that the only way in which hegemonic powers cede power is through war. They do not voluntarily give up this place. They must be forced to do so. This leads to a dilemma: China and the US are commercial partners, yet the success of China threatens to displace the US. Allison plays out several scenarios by which that spark might be lit (the collision of ships in the South China Sea, the death of Kim Jong-un without an heir, Taiwanese dissidents, and so on). These are all interesting war games to play out, but the point Allison (2017) is making is that the wider structural conditions for war between the US and China area already there, and they are strengthening by the moment. Some people have regrettably got caught up in the 'inevitable' part of this quote. Nothing is entirely predetermined, but what it does tell us is that certain forces can put countries on a path or trajectory to a certain end (in this case, war) that is difficult to avoid unless some other action is taken to change course.

Another concern about China's rise is that China does not reflect the US's values politically. This is not only a challenge in terms of economic clout, but also an ideational challenge. Some commentators would prefer the rise of a country like Japan, India or the EU rather than China because the other countries are all democracies while China is not. One reaction to this dilemma was put forward by Hugh White in *The China Choice* (2012). He argued that there was little that the US could do to stop the rise of China. In his view, the US should accept that it can no longer assert primacy around the entire world. Instead, it should be prepared to *share* power in Asia with China, while not *ceding power*. Aaron Friedberg (2011, 2012, 2020), however, believes that power sharing is little more than a form of appeasement. He believes in the importance of US primacy and fears that ceding power is dangerous. He worries that once the US gives China hegemonic power over Asia or Africa, it might develop an appetite for more.

Still others suggest that most Asian countries are relatively unconcerned about China's rise (Goh, 2005). They tend to pursue a policy of 'hedging', which means that they avoid choosing between the US and China in the hopes that neither will be a regional hegemon. A few Asian countries have not hedged, however. Japan, the Philippines and South Korea have firmly put their eggs in the US basket. North Korea, historically, had done so with China.

There are several reasons why commentators are sceptical of China's rise. One argument is that we've heard this all before. The false warnings about the USSR, Japan and the EU lead some commentators to think that the concerns about China overtaking the US are overblown. All countries need some sort of competitor to keep them economically active, vibrant and dynamic.

Another reason why commentators are sceptical is that China's rise has been dependent on the US. China has done well from the US-led international order. It has used the rules enforced by the US to its own advantage, and it has become prosperous on the backs of US consumers. To upend the dynamic and displace the US might risk China's own ruin. The success of China and the US are linked (interdependent), not separate and antagonistic.

Third, the US is the world's largest economy because it creates most of its own supply and demand. This was a long product of the 19th-century 'American system', discussed in Chapter 5. China is trying to achieve in a matter of a couple decades what took the US the best part of a century. China desperately needs to ensure sustainable internal demand because an export-dependent model, which is aided through artificial currency devaluation, is not sustainable.

Finally, China's prosperity is driven in part by its peculiar monetary policy. China does not have a currency to replace the dollar as the world's reserve currency, which some people would regard as one of the US's major trump cards. The Chinese have serious limits on the amount of money that individuals can take offshore in a given year.

Many commentators conclude that China remains militarily, politically and economically inferior to the US. It seems that if China would like to dislodge the US's hegemony it should continue to follow Deng Xiaoping's advice. With growth of at least 6 per cent for the next quarter of a century, the Chinese economy would be in a position of great strength. Perhaps Napoleon Bonaparte was right when he said in 1817, 'Let China sleep; when she wakes, she will shake the world.'

Conclusion

This chapter has reviewed core concepts of IR realism – security and prosperity – through the frame of the post-Second World War US-led international order. This order is sometimes called a 'liberal' order, and American global dominance has been described in euphemistic terms of 'hegemony' and 'unipolarity'. Motivating these descriptions is a desire to distinguish the US's post-Second World War role from past empires. It would be a paradoxical identity for the US to hold: a liberal democratic empire. It sits uneasily with the US's constructed self-image as a paragon of democracy and freedom at home, as well as its chief exponent abroad. The next chapter engages with this paradox of democracy promotion directly.

Whatever terms might be best suited to describe US global dominance, there is some evidence that the US-led international order is under serious strain. Maintaining a military at the size and scale of the US is exacting. It demands high costs from the American public, and there is some evidence that the public has grown weary of those costs. It is worth contemplating how much the physical, educational and health infrastructure of the US might have benefited from the resources that were expended to support the US occupations of Iraq and Afghanistan in the 21st century.

Politicians of both parties have shared in this weariness. Both Barack Obama and Donald Trump criticized US military adventurism. Neither president launched a major military invasion on the scale of their predecessors (although it would be inaccurate to paint either as 'doves'). Their proposed alternatives to US global dominance differed. Obama wanted more multilateralism, greater humility, and an acceptance of differences of opinion over internal self-government. Donald Trump wanted a focus on 'America First', which meant insisting that US allies assumed more of the burden for maintaining the liberal order that the US had created and underwritten for so long. In spite of these key differences, both Obama and Trump believed that the US could not continue to shoulder the burdens of hegemony (or empire) indefinitely.

President Joe Biden is more bullish about US global leadership, but this may be an echo of the past rather than a portent of the future. Biden originates from an earlier political era than either Obama or Trump. Biden was a creature of the Cold War and a participant in the unipolar 'moment' after the collapse of the USSR. Richard Nixon was president when Biden became a US senator. Biden was born before his four predecessors – Trump, Obama, Bush or Clinton. Biden's enthusiasm for US global leadership may be tempered, however, by challenges faced on the international arena. The choice of whether the US should continue as a global hegemon may not ultimately be for the US to make.

The coronavirus pandemic exposed the vulnerabilities of all economies, yet it did not fundamentally destabilize the basic competitive dynamic in international politics. The US's biggest challenge, both before and after the pandemic, appears to be China. There are good reasons to be sceptical of this challenge. Perhaps we have been here before – as with the supposed challenges of the USSR, Japan and the EU, none of which came to pass. The US dollar faces no serious challenger currency, especially from China. Chinese GDP and growth are impressive, but they are complicated by its population size and internal inequalities.

These may all be false comfort. China has many internal weaknesses, but it is clear that the US also has many internal weaknesses. Its ideational superiority, itself weaker than Americans might like to admit, may not be sufficient to sustain its material dominance. China has invested billions more dollars than the US in infrastructure, education and energy. It has been more proactive in trade and international exchange. President Biden gloomily admitted as much after his first presidential phone call with Chinese President Xi Jinping in 2021: 'If we don't get moving, they are going to eat our lunch.'[4]

Idealism: Democracy Promotion and the Paradoxes of US Foreign Policy

Richard Hofstadter's 1948 book *The American Political Tradition and the Men Who Made It* was the newly minted Columbia University academic's opportunity to play the role of the 'American Gramsci' (Heer, 2020). The book was a collection of unflattering portraits of hitherto revered American personalities: Thomas Jefferson, Abraham Lincoln, Woodrow Wilson and Franklin Roosevelt, among others. Unflinching, caustic and revisionist in its cultural critique, Hofstadter had still not fully shed his Marxist inclinations for the anti-populist, consensus liberalism for which he would become famed in the final decades of his life. In the book, Hofstadter partly lamented that the US was 'a democracy of cupidity rather than a democracy of fraternity'. Rather than a politics composed of great ideological clashes, he saw widespread agreement over 'self-interest and self-assertion'. 'America doesn't have ideologies', Hofstadter wrote, 'Rather, it is one' (1948: viii).

Chapter 2 of this book sketched the contours of this ideology: American exceptionalism. It is a self-image of the US as beacon and guardian of liberty to the rest of the world. The US, it is believed, was 'consciously founded on universal liberal, democratic principles' (Bouchet, 2013: 35). Gary Gerstle writes that the American War of Independence constituted 'the world's first democratic revolution' that aimed 'to break with patterns of elite rule altogether' (2015: 17). Daniel Deudney and Jeffrey Meiser (2012) state that the 'founding documents of the republic' provided the US with 'individual freedom and institutionalized civil rights, popular sovereignty ... [and] rule of law' (2012: 25). They write that the US in the 19th century was characterized by profound social mobility that contributed to 'the widespread economic equality, which was in stark contrast to the extreme socio-economic stratification virtually everywhere in the world' (2012: 27). This solipsistic image of democracy at home has given confidence to Americans that their country can and should spread democracy abroad. American exceptionalism was, in great respects, used to justify and explain the US's role in the post-Second World War era as the leader of the liberal democratic order, as described in the previous chapter.

While this image of the US as a uniquely disposed democracy with the power, and indeed duty, to spread freedom to the rest of the world is widely held, it is also profoundly misconceived. Such an assessment can only be accurate if African Americans and Native Americans are written out of the picture. This cannot be done because the inferior status of black and indigenous people is central to America's founding, its imperial expansion and the paradoxes of its self-ordained role in promoting democracy and freedom around the world.

This chapter will examine putatively contradictory impulses in American foreign policy history and practice: first, the impulse of the US as an imperial power, one that sought to accumulate territory which made it one of the largest nations in the world and, second, the impulse to champion and spread democracy around the world. Sometimes these tendencies are combined: the US leads an empire of liberty, it is sometimes said, made stronger by its internal diversity. Yet, as this chapter will show, there are profound contradictions even in this account, and while the US has occasionally championed democracy abroad, it does so inconsistently. Moreover, its support for democracy abroad has been impaired by serious weaknesses of democracy at home. The inadequacy of American democracy has exposed the US to accusations of hypocrisy from international partners. International pressure, in turn, as authors like Mary Dudziak (2000) have suggested, may have helped strengthen domestic reformers. The promotion of democracy is not unidirectional. It has often been external actors who have brought democracy to the US rather than the other way around.

The US as an imperial power

In order to understand the US's mission in promoting democracy abroad, we first have to interrogate the history of the US's creation. Understanding whether the US was founded on the basis of liberty and democratic values, or whether these have been revisionist accounts, can help us to understand better American imperialism and democracy promotion.

Slaves, land and taxes were central causes for rebellion in the 1770s. While the third factor (taxes) is well rehearsed, the first two are usually ignored. Far from being an exercise in expanding liberty, the American Revolution almost certainly strengthened the institution of slavery. At the time of the American Revolution, slaves made up one-fifth of the population in the 13 American colonies and two-fifths of all enslaved people in the British Empire. By 1820, the US slave population was 2.5 times larger than it had been at the start of the American Revolution.

In the 1772 *Somerset v Stewart* case, Lord Mansfield found that chattel slavery was unsupported by the common law of England. Mansfield declared that 'It is so odious, that nothing can be suffered to support it, but positive law.' Challenging Parliament to pass a law that positively authorized slavery, Parliament declined to do so, confirming that slavery was illegal in England and Wales (Scotland also faced a similar case with the same outcome at the time). Although Mansfield's judgment applied only to England and Wales, the case was watched closely from America. Harry Marchant, a Rhode Island lawyer who attended the *Somerset* hearings, was concerned that Mansfield's findings could become 'plausible pretense ... to cheat an honest American of his slave' (van Cleve, 2010: 37). This fear became even more of a reality when American lawyers started to cite the *Somerset* decision in American colonial courts to justify the freeing of slaves.

American slaveholders became concerned that *Somerset* could eventually be extended to the American colonies. Lacking representation in Parliament, many Americans worried that Parliament could legislate for slavery's abolition in America (as, in fact, it did throughout the remaining British Empire in 1833). A Parliament that could impose taxes could also impose the abolition of slavery. Furthermore, slaveholders argued that the *Somerset* decision represented a loss of their liberty. It meant that American slaveholders could no longer bring their slaves to England for fear that the slaves would seek protection by English courts.

George III also attracted ire for the Proclamation of 1763 that forbade settlement west of the Appalachian Mountains by white, British subjects. The measure was designed to protect Native Americans who were given the exclusive right to inhabit the lands between the Appalachian Mountains and the Mississippi River. This directive was regarded as an act of appalling tyranny by white Americans who wished to push westward and strip the Native Americans of the fertile Ohio River Valley territory. A less popularly quoted passage in the Declaration of Independence is Thomas Jefferson's racist rant against George III for failing to deploy British troops to exterminate the Native Americans in this territory. The Declaration denounces the King who 'has endeavoured to bring on the inhabitants of our frontiers the merciless Indian savages, whose known rule of warfare is undistinguished destruction of all ages, sexes, and conditions'.[1]

These facts complicate the narrative that the American Revolution was fought by sturdy, liberty-loving patriots against the tyrannical, monarchy-loving British. In fact, Alan Taylor (2016) and Holger Hoock (2017) both view the American Revolution as a brutal civil war. The American Revolution was a victory for the slave-holding class, from which George Washington, Thomas Jefferson and James Madison hailed. The American Revolution created more refugees as a proportion of the population than the French Revolution. Loyalty oaths, public executions and recriminations of neighbours were used against those who lacked commitment to the cause long before they became hallmarks of terror in France. The economic turmoil caused by the American Revolution was the worst in American history until the Great Depression.

Among those who fled the 13 colonies in rebellion were former slaves. More than 3,000 black men and women fled to Nova Scotia. The town they founded, Birchtown, quickly became the largest free black settlement in North America. Many of the black refugees from the US went onwards to London and others went to establish Freetown in Sierra Leone. At the end of the American Revolution, in the Treaty of Paris (1783) negotiations, the US government demanded the return of American slaves who had fled during the war, but the British government refused.

In the years to follow, the US expanded from the territories established in the 1783 Treaty of Paris to span across the North American continent. The 'expansion' of the US should not be regarded as some sort of natural process of filling empty space. Sometimes Americans see their country as one would a liquid that fills an empty jar, that jar being the continental US. We should, rather, see the creation of the US as an imperial process, one that shares many characteristics of empire building abroad. Throughout the 19th century, the US was a colonial power. Its colonies were those territories west of the Mississippi River, where it assumed control not of empty space, but over thousands of indigenous peoples.

In this way, for much of the 19th century the US empire was akin to the kind of contiguous empire of the early pre-modern period, such as the Roman Empire. But the fact that US imperial expansion was initially focused on the North American continent does not mean that the US had an 'isolationist' poise in this period. Indeed, the US has never truly been a country removed from international engagements. In the 19th century, the US government and its citizens were involved in the foundation of Liberia, the successful opening of Japan and the unsuccessful opening of Korea to US markets. The US was prepared to engage in armed battle when it felt its interests were threatened, as evidenced by its skirmish with Germany over control of Samoa in the 1880s.

The most significant aspect of US foreign engagement in the 19th century was its concerted attempt to build an American empire through massive territorial expansion and incorporation of new lands and peoples. In the 19th century, the US took lands from Mexico (through war and conquest), Spain (through sabotage and compulsory purchase), France (through purchase), Russia (through purchase), Britain (through treaty) and Native American and Hawaiian communities (through war, purchase and massacre) (Dunn, 2005). In addition, the US invaded Canada in 1812 in a botched attempt to take control of the entire North American continent. The US was defeated by British and Canadian troops in the War of 1812, a conflict that many Americans wrongly see as something other than a US defeat.

In the first half of the 19th century, America's colonial expansion was often linked to slavery. Some of the fiercest battles over Native American removal had occurred in the heart of slave country (Rothman, 2007; Beckert, 2014). Eventually, non-geographically contiguous territories were viewed as possible staging grounds for the American empire because of their ties to slavery. Cuba had long been considered as a possible addition to the US because pro-slavery forces wanted another slave state admitted to the Union (Frymer, 2017).

On the other side of the coin, abolitionists also favoured some form of colonialization. The American Colonization Society existed from 1816 to 1919 and encouraged African Americans to move to Africa. In the 20th century, African Americans sought to establish their own colonies or spaces in Liberia and other parts of Africa through the 'Back to Africa' movement. A leading proponent of the movement was Marcus Garvey, founder of the Universal Negro Improvement Association and African Communities League (Grant, 2008). The black Americans who moved to Liberia did not find life easy, however. Slavery had deprived them of their languages and much of their original culture. They were distinctly American, English-speaking and Christian. It was not clear from where in the continent of Africa they had originated. They were perceived by many in the native population of Liberia as foreign settlers.

Back on the North American continent, the US empire differed in some ways from the empires of other European powers. While 'settler colonial' states were established by European powers, many European governments did not see the creation of a majority-white population in their conquered territories as a public policy goal. This was not the case for the US. When the US expanded in the first phase of its empire, it sought to settle the territories it conquered. This meant the importation of (white) Americans into new colonial possessions and the expulsion of indigenous peoples (through removal via reservations or execution). The US federal government strategically offered land to white settlers in these territories in order to add surplus white populations in critical and contested territories. While this is sometimes presented as an organic or natural occurrence, it was, in fact, a planned state project (Frymer, 2017: 10). The federal government used a variety of laws to provide incentives for whites (but not blacks) to move into the new possessions in the west. There was a legal basis that authorized the giving away of new federal lands for white settlers: the Preemption Act (1841), the Armed Occupation Act (1842), the Donation Land Act (1850) and the Homestead Acts (1862, 1866, 1904 and 1909).

There was also a bureaucracy to regulate and enforce this American empire: the General Land Office, the Bureau of Indian Affairs and the Department of War. Management of new territorial acquisitions was a major aspect of what Congress did in the 19th century. Between 1780 and 1880, Congress passed more than 3,000 statutes pertaining to the regulation of public land in the west (Frymer, 2017). The federal government often lacked full control over the new territories it acquired. It therefore became reliant on third-party actors to help achieve its ends. White militias fought off and, in some cases, systematically slaughtered indigenous people, acting as kinds of arm's-length imperial state actors (Frymer, 2017). By the 1890s, it was believed that the US had successfully subdued the indigenous peoples in its territories. The massacre at Wounded Knee, in which the US government executed as many as 300 Native American men, women and children, was the largest mass shooting in US history. The mass shootings of unarmed Native Americans were a despicable recurrence of 19th-century US history. A hundred and fifty unarmed Cheyenne and Arapaho, mostly women, children and the elderly, were gunned down at Sand Creek in 1865 (Horwitz, 2014). Five years later, about 175 unarmed Blackfeet, the majority of them being women and children, were slaughtered by the US Army (Wylie, 2016).

With the indigenous populations violently suppressed and large numbers of white settlers in their place, the demography of the new territorial acquisitions had changed dramatically. By the time of the Wounded Knee Massacre, the US government was in the final stages of admitting all of its territorial possessions on an equal footing with the older states in the Union. Stefan Heumann (2011) describes this as an 'imperial' process of readying the territories with the appropriate citizenry. The western territories of North America became the US federal government's 'tutelary empire'. By 1912, with the admission of Arizona, the project was complete. Every colonial territory in the North American continent conquered or otherwise obtained by the US government, with the exception of Alaska, had been granted statehood.

The idea that this process was one of colonization is not some sort of retrospective from a wide-eyed 21st-century, critical theorist's reimagining. It was described as such by people at the time. A. Lawrence Lowell, Harvard politics lecturer and president of the American Political Science Association, acknowledged that the US since the War of Independence had undergone a process of colonial expansion:

> For many Americans the word [colony] has disagreeable associations.... [However,] since the Revolutionary War the inhabitants of the United States have increased twentyfold ... and one-half live in communities that have at some time been organized as territories – in other words, that have been founded by the process of colonization.... Therefore, the United States has been one of the greatest and most successful colonizing powers the world has ever known. (Lowell, 1899)

In the 20th century, the US gained territories where the native population was more difficult to displace. After the Spanish–American War, the US won control of Puerto Rico and Guam. The US also bought the Philippines from Spain for $20 million. Walter McDougall argues that the US took control of the Philippines because they wanted to keep out European rivals (for example, Spain, the UK and Germany). This left the US in possession of a colony of about 1.7 million people. If it had become a state, the Philippines would have been the 20th largest US state at the time.

American policymakers were engaged in a contentious debate about what the US should do with the Philippines. Previously, when the US acquired territory, the idea was for the US to import whites who would overpower the local populations and make the territories predominantly white before their admission to the union. There was no possibility that the US would be able to do this in the Philippines, but policymakers also felt (through racist assumptions) that the Filipinos were unable to govern themselves. US control of the Philippines would lead to over 100,000 Filipinos losing their lives (McDougall, 1997a). The Philippines did not gain independence from the US until 1946, but there was never a serious attempt to make Philippines a state within the United States of America.

The challenge that prevented Puerto Rico, Guam, the Philippines, Cuba and the Dominican Republic from becoming integrated into the US was not geography but race. Republican Senator Albert Beveridge, a leading figure in the Progressive movement, argued that these colonies could not become part of the US because (in the case of the Philippines) 'we are not dealing with Americans or Europeans. We are dealing with Orientals ... a barbarous race, modified by three centuries of contact with a decadent race.'[2]

The legal status of these American colonial subjects shared a great deal in common with how Native Americans had been legally treated. In six different cases, in 1901 the Supreme Court adjudicated on the legal status of the possessions acquired by the US from Spain as a result of the Spanish–American War. One of the cases was *Downes v Bidwell*, in which the Supreme Court declared that Puerto Ricans were 'subject to the jurisdiction of the United States' but were 'not of the United States'. They were 'foreign to the United States in a domestic sense'. The case echoed Native American case law, beginning with *Johnson v McIntosh* (1823), where the Supreme Court had ruled Native Americans in 'a state of pupillage' as 'domestic dependent nations' (Grann, 2017). Black theorists argued that, in effect, African-American populations were de facto domestic colonies in the US as well (Locke, 1992 [1916]; Henderson, 2017). Alain Locke, of the Howard School of International Relations discussed in Chapter 1, described 'the internal or home policy of imperialism' towards African Americans (1992 [1916]: 33). Ralphe Bunche (1995 [1929]), who went on to win the Nobel Peace Prize, agreed that 'The organization of Negro society bears, in certain important aspects, a significant resemblance to the organization of society in a colony or a subject nation.'

For all of US expansion, every newly admitted state to the US has been majority white, with one exception. Hawaii is the only predominantly Asian state in the US, and when it was admitted as a state in 1959, it was the only predominantly non-white state in the US. Today, about half of people in Hawaii are Asian American, about one-quarter are white and about one-tenth are native Hawaiian. It is the only non-continental state in the US, setting it apart from the many other island territories and colonies of the US. Geopolitics with Japan – the desire to keep Japan away from expanding its empire closer to the US – ultimately explains Hawaii's admission as a territory in the late 19th century and as a state 60 years later.

The United Kingdom of Hawaii was established in 1795, and in 1840, the Hawaiian Islands became a constitutional monarchy. Over the course of the century, American settlers started private business operations on the islands, making use of the native Hawaiian population for labour and, when they were exhausted, importing migrant labourers from Asia, in particular Japan. In 1887, these American capitalists forced the King of Hawaii (Kalākaua) to adopt a new constitution, known as the Bayonet Constitution, which restricted the franchise only to landowners, disenfranchising most native Hawaiians while putting most power in the hands of white Americans. Kalākaua's successor, his sister Liliuokalani, tried to reverse the forced constitution and restore voting rights to the wider Hawaiian population: Native Hawaiians and people of Asian heritage (Frymer, 2017).

The white American population on the island revolted and called on the support of the US military. The US ambassador to Hawaii, John Stevens, was very sympathetic of the American settlers' cause and helped to coordinate US military assistance. In January 1893, the USS *Boston*, with two companies of sailors, landed in Hawaii, forcing Liliuokalani to abdicate. The monarchy was overthrown and a puppet republic was declared in 1893. Within months, the new government, led by American settlers, petitioned for Hawaii to become part of the US (Frymer, 2017).

The reaction from the US was mixed, in part, once again, due to racial animus. *The New York Times* reported that 'the population of the island is a very mixed one', with a population of Asians who were 'a class wholly unfit to take any part in public affairs' (1893). In 1898, when Congress debated Hawaii's annexation, Republican Representative Joseph Alexander observed that 'the principle objection to annexation seems to be its people' (quoted in Frymer, 2017: 275). Walter McDougall argues that the US did not want to annex Hawaii in part because of its racial diversity. At the time, a majority of Hawaiian residents were Asian. Native Hawaiians also outnumbered whites (see Figure 9.1). Democrat Representative James Clark warned that if Hawaii was made a US territory, in 20 years 'you will have a polyglot House [of Representatives]' with congressmen even from 'the cannibal islands who will gaze upon you with watering mouth and gleaming

Figure 9.1: Racial demographics of Hawaii in 1900

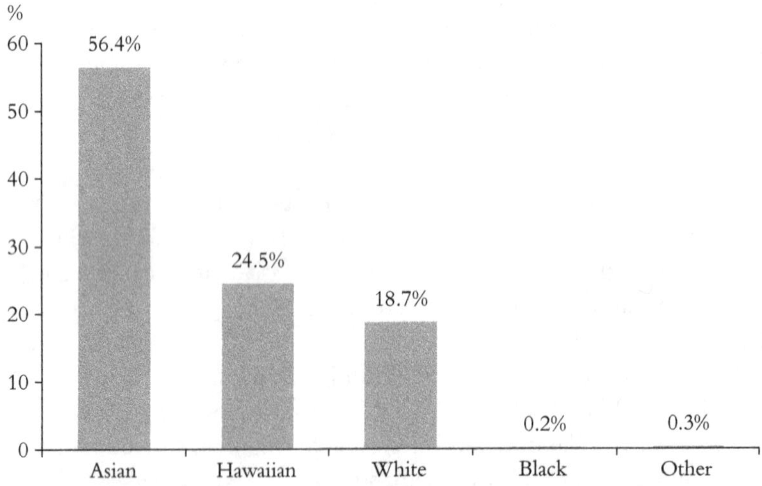

```
%
60 ┐     56.4%

50 -

40 -

30 -
             24.5%
                        18.7%
20 -

10 -
                                    0.2%      0.3%
 0 └──────────────────────────────────────────────
    Asian    Hawaiian    White    Black    Other
```

Source: 1900 US Census

teeth'. *The Congressional Record* (1898) describes the 'great laughter and applause' that met these comments.[3] Democrat Senator Donelson Caffey lamented that Hawaii consisted of 'aboriginal races, incapable of self-government'. But when the Japanese government sent a cruiser to protect Japanese migrants, the US government felt that it needed to annex Hawaii in order to block Japan from gaining control of the islands.

Entering into the early 20th century, some commentators have pointed to Woodrow Wilson's reluctance to bring the US into the First World War (not until 1917) as evidence of US isolationism, but this is a gross mischaracterization. It strains credulity to describe Wilson as approaching anything close to being an isolationist. Before the US entered the First World War, Wilson sent US troops to Mexico, Haiti, the Dominican Republic and China. Indeed, under Wilson, the US occupied the Mexican port city of Veracruz for seven months and began an eight-year occupation of the Dominican Republic (San Domingo) and a 19-year military occupation of Haiti (Calhoun, 1993). In 1916, Woodrow Wilson drafted a speech in which he asserted, 'It shall not lie with the American people to dictate to another what their government shall be.' His Secretary of State Robert Lansing, noting the hypocrisy, jotted in the margin, 'Haiti, S. Domingo, Nicaragua, Panama' (Zimmerman, 2002: 476).

Wilson's reluctance to send US troops to fight in Europe during the First World War had less to do with US 'isolationism' than it did with

Wilson's fear that US entry might unleash 'serious domestic ethnic clashes' among European immigrants and their descendants within the US (Ruggie, 1996: 187). Wilson worried that the US taking sides in the First World War would upset large German and Italian immigrant populations in the US, or set them against Americans of Irish and British ancestry. Not for the last time domestic ethnic politics influenced the direction of US foreign policy (Lubell, 1952). In 1940, Franklin Roosevelt's denunciation of Benito Mussolini for supporting the invasion of France was viewed as a risky electoral strategy, given his need to appeal to Italian-American voters in that election (De Conde, 1971: 237–41; Luconi, 2002).

In conclusion, while empire for most other countries at the time was about resource extraction, for the US, resource extraction usually had to coincide with a guarantee of white dominance. The American empire was not simply about controlling peoples in order to take natural resources from them; it was about spreading 'America' (conceptualized as white Americans) across a continent and then to other parts of the world. The treatment of Native Americans was, in some sense, a model, a prelude to other imperial actions by the US once they had fully conquered indigenous (Native) Americans by the 1890s (Frymer, 2017).

Democracy promotion abroad and at home

In spite of this inglorious past, some would argue that the US turned from being an ethnic, white settler empire in the 19th and early 20th centuries to an 'empire of liberty', with the US being the leading light of guarding and promoting democratic values since the Second World War. Nicolas Bouchet (2013) argues that there is a 'democracy tradition' in US foreign policy. No matter how much presidents seek to distinguish themselves from their predecessors, all US presidents ultimately fall back on the idea that the key ideological motivation for US foreign policy is a desire to spread democracy around the world. Tony Smith surmised that every president since William McKinley, elected in 1896, held the view that 'if democracy were to spread, America's place in the world would be more secure' (1994: xiii).

Since the Second World War, the US has practically committed to helping countries democratize. The first – and in some senses, most successful – precedents of US intervention to establish democracy were in Germany and Japan that moved from autocracy to becoming some of the world's most successful advanced, democratic industrialized countries. During the Cold War, US presidents believed that economic development would lead countries to embrace democracy, which was positive for US security interests. Thus, the US government – especially under the Kennedy Administration – created and funded programmes that were ostensibly about economic development but were, in fact, about promoting democracy: the Peace Corps (State Department), Alliance for Progress (Latin American Economic Development), US Agency for International Development (USAID) and Food for Peace (Department of Agriculture). In the 1980s, President Ronald Reagan continued these efforts with the formation of the National Endowment for Democracy (NED), which receives over $100 million annually from federal government to sponsor 'democratic initiatives' in the US and around the world (Heer, 2018). The NED funds organizations such as the National Democratic Institute for International Affairs, the International Republican Institute, the American Center for International Labor Solidarity and the Center for International Private Enterprise. In the past the Cuban American National Foundation (CANF) received NED funding to support its efforts in overthrowing the Castro government.

As mentioned in Chapter 8, many leading American commentators have argued that US leadership is necessary for sustaining democracy around the world. It is apparently in the US's security interests for other countries to become democratic. With no sense of hyperbole, Dean Rusk, secretary of state to Presidents John F. Kennedy and Lyndon Johnson, declared, 'the United States cannot be secure until the total international environment is ideologically safe' (quoted in Meaney, 2020). Bill Clinton's Secretary of State Madeleine Albright described the US as the 'indispensable nation' in 1998.[4] Bill Clinton himself assessed that 'democracy abroad also protects our own concrete economic and security interests here at home' (quoted in Marsden, 2018: 42). This tradition has enjoyed a bipartisan consensus. George W. Bush's Secretary of State Condoleezza Rice asked, 'Where does America stand?... Since the Second World War, the United States has had an answer to that question. We stand for free peoples and free markets. We will defend and support them.... When friends or foes alike don't know the answer to that question, unambiguously and clearly, the world is likely to be a more dangerous and chaotic place.'[5]

Promoting democracy is popular among the American public, even today when many commentators assert that the US public has turned inward against becoming overly involved in global affairs. Indeed, Americans' desire to help other countries build democracies is nearly as strong today as it was in the early 2000s at the height of the post-9/11 fervour. About three in four Americans believe that it is important for the US to help other countries build democracies (see Figure 9.2).

Figure 9.2: How important is it for the US to be helping other countries build democracies?

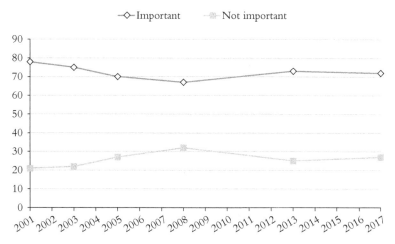

Source: Based on data from https://news.gallup.com/poll/116350/position-world.aspx

Some commentators, however, have wondered whether we have seen a movement away from the 'democracy' tradition. At the start of his presidency, when he visited Cairo, Barack Obama told the young audience, 'America does not presume to know what is best for everyone.'[6] Two years later, he echoed in his speech to the UN General Assembly, 'We believe that each nation must chart its own course to fulfil the aspirations of its people, and America does not expect to agree with every party or person who expresses themselves politically.'[7] When Obama visited Cuba in his final year as president and stood next to the communist leader Raúl Castro, he stated, 'We recognize that every country, every people, must chart its own course and shape its own model' (quoted in Beckwith, 2016). While Obama expressed a preference for democracy, he did not insist that it was a requirement for engagement with the US. He admitted that countries had different paths and different models, and that he, as president, accepted this. Obama's words echoed the 2010 US National Security Strategy:

> America will not impose any system of government on another country, but our long-term security and prosperity depends on our steady support for universal values, which sets us apart from our enemies, adversarial governments, and many potential competitors for influence.... More than any other action that we have taken, the power of America's example has helped spread freedom and democracy abroad.[8]

There did seem to be a consistent line across Obama's presidency: Americans believe strongly in democracy – and will say so – but the US will not expect another country to be a democracy if they do not wish for it to be one. While subtle, this is a shift from the presupposition for much of the post-Second World War period that everyone in the world would want to live in a democracy, if only given the opportunity.

Donald Trump also seemed to depart from the 'democracy' tradition, but in ways that were different from his predecessor. Trump showed a preference for strong authoritarian leaders such as Vladimir Putin in Russia and Rodrigo Duterte in the Philippines. Trump held somewhat pliable views on human rights, expressing an interest in bringing back the use of torture against enemy combatants. When Trump visited Saudi Arabia, he made no mention of the country's political oppression or routine beheadings. Sitting beside Egyptian President Abdel Fattah al-Sisi in the Oval Office, Trump eschewed delivering any public lectures on the widespread jailing of dissidents. US presidents have long balanced outspoken recriminations over human rights abuses with the need to do business with autocratic leaders who run countries that are important US security and trade partners. Trump was no exception in this. But he perhaps more explicitly than some *refused* to criticize the human rights violations of certain countries he believes to be strategically important. Trump said in Saudi Arabia, 'We are not here to lecture – we are not here to tell other people how to live, what to do, who to be, or how to worship.'[9] For this posture, Trump won the accolades of the Chinese state press:

> Unlike other politicians who are stiff and inflexible over political doctrines or political correctness, Trump is planning and adjusting his policies to balance public sentiment and social reality. Therefore, when it comes to the nation's future China policy if Trump is to be elected, he will be most likely to choose a pragmatic approach. Unlike traditional idealistic politicians who tend to place ideological values, such as democracy and human rights, as the priority in their diplomacy, Trump has more realistic interests in mind. As a businessman, he understands the importance of making profit through cooperation. (*Global Times*, 2016)

The two major exceptions to Trump's constitutional relativism were on Cuba and Venezuela, where Trump took a firm line against their democratic failings. Trump said of Cuba, 'While imprisoning innocents, it has harbored cop killers, hijackers and terrorists. It has supported human trafficking, forced labor and exploitation all around the globe.'[10] Trump vowed that sanctions would not be lifted on Cuba until 'all political prisoners are freed, freedoms of assembly and expression are respected, all political parties are legalized and free and internationally supervised elections are scheduled.'[11] The discussion about the Cuban lobby in Chapter 7 provides some explanation for this discontinuity.

Bouchet (2013) suggests that the correct label for US democracy promotion is 'semi-realism'. The US will promote democracy when costs to the US are low or rewards are high. These can include post facto justification for realist intervention (for example, Iraq) or achieving leverage in asserting dominance in international space. As secretary of state, even Hillary Clinton accepted this semi-realist approach to democracy promotion. She asked:

> Why does America promote democracy one way in some countries and another way in others? Well, the answer starts with a very practical point: situations vary dramatically from country to country. It would be foolish to take a one-size-fits-all approach and barrel forward regardless of circumstances on the ground. Sometimes, as in Libya, we can bring dozens of countries together to protect civilians and help people liberate their country without a single American life lost. In other cases, to achieve that same goal, we would have to act alone, at a much greater cost, with far greater risks, and perhaps even with troops on the ground. (quoted in Rubin, 2011)

Paradoxes (hypocrisies) of democracy promotion

One of the prominent stories to flow from the 2016 election was a concern over the extent to which the Russian state had meddled in the US electoral process. Reports show that Russian intelligence agency workers hacked into the email servers of the Democratic National Committee and chose to leak its emails to Wikileaks in July 2016. Russian intelligence groups also hacked the Gmail account of Hillary Clinton's campaign chair John Podesta. Wikileaks released batches of Podesta's emails each day from October until the election in November 2016. While the Russian interference is to be condemned, it would be incomplete of us to ignore the extent to which the US has intervened in the elections of other countries to tip the balance of elections in the US's favour.

In 1947, Congress passed the National Security Act, which established the CIA, as discussed in Chapter 3. Months later, the democratically elected governments of Hungary and Czechoslovakia fell to communist takeovers, helping to precipitate the final passage of the Marshall Plan in March 1948. Only two weeks after the Marshall Plan was passed, Italy was coming up for elections. The Socialist Party and the Communist Party teamed together to create the Popular Democratic Front (Fronte Democratico Popolare, FDP). The FDP had done well in local elections weeks earlier, and it was thought that they were receiving support from the Soviet Union.

The Truman Administration authorized the CIA to provide funds to the Christian Democrats in Italy in an effort to defeat the communists in the 1948 Italian parliamentary elections. The CIA provided direct funds to candidates from the centre-right Christian Democratic Party ('bags of money', as one CIA officer later described, quoted in Weiner, 2006), but also funded propaganda that accused communist candidates of sex scandals and warned of their desire to destroy the Catholic Church. Publicly, the State Department warned the Italians that if they elected a communist government, 'there would be no further question of assistance from the United States', meaning that the Marshall Plan funds were in jeopardy. Italy ended up receiving $1.2 billion ($10 billion, in today's money) in Marshall funds, second only to the UK. So this was not something to sniff at.

Showing the power of the Italian diaspora, there was a massive letter writing campaign from Americans of Italian extraction to their relatives and friends in Italy. Letters were guided by 'sample letters' in newspapers, but soon expanded to mass-produced, pre-written letters with paid postage and accompanying leaflets and posters. An estimated 10 million letters were believed to have been sent by Americans to Italians. This campaign was not a random outpouring, however. It was funded by the CIA. The communists lost the election substantially. The CIA's practice of buying political clout was repeated in every Italian election for the next 24 years. The Christian Democrats won every election between 1948 and 1992, before being supplanted by Silvio Berlusconi's Forza Italia.

Yet it is not simply the practices of the US abroad that make us consider the paradoxes of US democracy promotion. It is also the incompleteness of US democracy at home that impairs the ability of the US to speak for democracies abroad.

However one looks at it, democracy in the US is (and always has been) impoverished. It has some of the lowest participation rates in the democratic world (Lijphart, 1997; Fullmer, 2015). The views of its richest citizens have been shown to correspond with the behaviour of its elected politicians more closely than any other group (Broz, 2005; Massey, 2007; Jacobs and Druckman, 2011; Gilens and Page, 2014; Bartels, 2016). The Constitution has left the country with more veto points than any other country, making it virtually impossible to pass legislation except in rare circumstances of unified control or external crisis (Stepan and Linz, 2011). Before the Voting Rights Act of 1965, access to even this limited manifestation of democratic governance was blocked for millions of non-white American citizens.

Göran Therborn (1977) and others (Mickey, 2015; Gibson and King, 2016; Johnson, 2020b) have argued that the US was one of the last major industrialized nations to democratize, not one of the first. It is worth noting that well after the Second World War access to citizenship and its basic elements was unavailable to millions of Americans.

Until the mid-20th century, essential features of a democratic polity – free and fair elections, multi-party competition, universal franchise, free assembly and speech – were not available to millions of US residents. People of Asian birth were not permitted to apply for US citizenship until 1952 (King, 2000: 238). The secret ballot was not introduced in Georgia or South Carolina until the 1950s.[12] Until the 1960s, some states prohibited public sector workers from joining black civic organizations such as the NAACP (Mickey, 2015: 226).[13] Municipalities passed ordinances barring residents from assembling to promote civil rights or voter registration (Kennedy, 1990). Exploiting the highly decentralized structures of the American government, local white bureaucrats adapted to the post-Civil War constitutional settlement through new, innovative mechanisms of voter suppression. One common tactic was for a registrar to challenge the legal qualifications of an African American who tried to register to vote. Challenges included county residency requirements (six-month minimum), illiteracy and insufficient knowledge (literacy tests that asked applicants to recall sections of the Constitution verbatim or interpret complicated statutes) or poor 'character'. While the grounds were spurious, the challenged voter was forced to go to court to clear their name, a burden that was simply too high for many of the state's impoverished African Americans. The result was that millions of African Americans had no effective right to vote until the 1960s. It was not until the 1970s that all Native Americans could exercise the right to vote.[14]

These facts were somewhat embarrassing for a country that claimed during the Cold War to be the champion of democracy around the world. How could the US be the leading light of democracy when its own house was not on order? Cold War international relations might shed light on some of the impetus behind the civil rights legislation and executive action from the 1940s to 1980s. They can be partly seen as an attempt by American politicians to defend the country from the critiques of the inferiority of American capitalist democracy by ostensibly non-racist communist regimes, to build goodwill from non-aligned countries and to strengthen the credibility of the US's leadership role in the 'free' world.

The 'international gaze' had been called on many times in the history of American civil rights to try to use international pressure abroad to force democratization at home. Frederick Douglass had travelled around Britain seeking the support of the abolitionist movement in the United Kingdom to end slavery. Ida Wells embarked on a similar set of tours around Britain in the late 19th century in order to place international pressure on the US to put an end to the lynching of hundreds of mainly black men each year by mobs.

During the Second World War, over 1.2 million African Americans served in the US Armed Forces. There was an irony in black soldiers fighting for freedom against race-based fascism in racially segregated units, but black leaders supported the war effort.[15] They promoted what they called a 'Double V' strategy – victory for freedom abroad would lead to victory for freedom at home. This strategy proved effective, but its success was not automatic. Black veterans initially returned to southern states where they could not vote, and they could not use the GI Bill to attend their state's top universities or access veterans' housing in white neighbourhoods.

Moments of crisis prompted government action. Photographs of a lynched black veteran's flag-draped coffin shortly after the Second World War were plastered across American newspapers. Mary Dudziak (2000) argues that the poor treatment of black veterans was instrumental in pushing President Harry Truman to desegregate the US military. Truman's *To Secure These Rights* (1947) report marvelled that when a black person came to the national capital, it was as if he or she had 'left democratic practices behind'. The report's findings about segregation in Washington, DC were damning:

> With very few exceptions, [an African American] is refused service at downtown restaurants, he may not attend a downtown movie or play, and he has to go into the poorer section of the city to find a night's lodging. The Negro who decides to settle in the District must often find a home in

an overcrowded, substandard area. He must often take a job below the level of his ability. He must send his children to the inferior public schools set aside for Negroes and entrust his family's health to medical agencies which give inferior service. In addition, he must endure the countless daily humiliations that the system of segregation imposes upon the one-third of Washington that is Negro.[16]

The President's Committee on Civil Rights, which authored the report, warned that, 'our civil rights record has growing international implications'.[17] It worried that America's 'civil rights record had been an issue in world politics'. These sentiments were echoed in an *amicus curiae* brief to the Supreme Court, written by Truman's Attorney General James McGranery in 1952: 'the existence of discrimination against minority groups in the United States has an adverse effect upon our relations with other countries. Racial discrimination furnishes grist for the Communist propaganda mills.'[18]

Racist incidents in the 1940s, 1950s and 1960s – which civil rights groups ensured received media attention – drove further action from the federal government. In 1957, Secretary of State John Foster Dulles pleaded with Alabama Governor James Folsom to halt the execution of a black handyman named Jimmy Wilson, who had been sentenced to death by an all-white jury for stealing $1.95 from an elderly white woman. Folsom relented due to the 'international hullabaloo' and commuted Wilson's sentence to 16 years in prison (Dudziak, 2000: 6). The Wilson case is evidence of how international pressure on civil rights forced change in the US. Wilson's case was not one of systematic change, of course, but it does show how domestic civil rights crises quickly became internationalized which, in turn, influenced the actions of US policymakers.

Early in the spring of 1961, an international incident nearly erupted when William Fitzjohn, Sierra Leone's first ambassador to the US, was on his way to Pittsburgh for a lecture. The ambassador stopped for dinner with his driver at a Howard Johnson restaurant in rural Pennsylvania. Both men were refused service because of their race. In a damage limitation exercise, President John Kennedy invited Fitzjohn to the White House. Kennedy arranged for the president of the restaurant chain to deliver an apology. The mayor of the Pennsylvania town invited Fitzjohn to an elaborate dinner with the municipality's leading citizens.

As newly independent nations emerged from colonialism in Africa, Asia and Latin America, they faced a choice between the American and Soviet models (Cobbs, 1996). Images of lynched veterans, meek seamstresses arrested for riding the bus and children pelted with missiles on the way to school became hugely inconvenient in the US's Cold War strategy (Fraser, 2000). Truman told Congress in early 1948: 'If we wish to inspire the peoples of the world whose freedom is in jeopardy … we must correct the remaining imperfections in our practice of democracy.' In a similar vein, in 1957 Vice President Richard Nixon wrote a memo to President Dwight Eisenhower after a trip to Ghana: 'We cannot talk equality to the peoples of Africa and Asia and practice inequality in the United States. In the national interest, as well as for the moral issues involved, we must support the necessary steps which will assure orderly progress in the elimination of discrimination in the United States' (US Department of State Historical Division, 1957).

The international gaze forced the US into a form of ad hoc crisis management. Many saw the Supreme Court's landmark 1954 school desegregation decision, *Brown v Board of Education*, as part of a Cold War effort to improve America's standing among what were at the time described as 'Third World' countries. Eisenhower was facing intense international pressure to implement the decision. In a conversation with Attorney General Herbert Brownell, Secretary of State Dulles worried, 'This situating is ruining our foreign policy. The effect of this in Asia and Africa will be worse than Hungary was for the Russians.'[19]

International incidents throughout the 1940s, 1950s and 1960s were not enough on their own to push US policymakers to change US laws, but they raised the costs for not doing so. US policymakers responded in two ways. They repressed dissent where possible, but also allowed a certain level of domestic rights advancement. Part of the strategy involved attempts to silence critics such as the black leftists Paul Robeson and W.E.B. Du Bois by confiscating their passports. Voice of America broadcasts and newsreels, films, 'talking points' for embassy personnel or 'approved' speakers were sent on tours overseas that all would present an account of progress, of the triumph of good over evil, and of US moral superiority over communism. These efforts at damage control were of limited success.

Unfavourable international comparisons also caused white Americans to reconsider their racist assumptions. In the spring of 1965, ABC interrupted an airing of *Judgment at Nuremberg* to broadcast images of John Lewis and his Student Nonviolent Coordinating Committee being brutally beaten by the police for daring to cross the Edmund Pettus Bridge in Selma to peacefully march in demand of their voting rights. Gary May explains: 'For many people, seeing the scenes from

Selma after watching a film about Nazi atrocities, they're thinking, "My God, what's happening to America? Are we becoming like Nazi Germany?'" (*USA Today*, 2015). In this context, racial minorities were able to invoke foreign policy as a way of bolstering their own causes at home. Black workers argued that racial discrimination in the workplace mimicked too closely the racial exclusivism of the totalitarian regimes the US was fighting to defeat (Meier and Rudwick, 1979). These dynamics give some credence to Derrick Bell's (1980) convergence theory: whites are most inclined to secure greater rights for non-whites when whites' own interests are threatened.

Conclusion

In his book *America's Mission*, Tony Smith argues that, in some form since its founding in the late 18th century, and in full expression since the presidency of Woodrow Wilson at the start of the 20th, the US has promoted 'liberal democratic internationalism', which Smith defines as 'a world order opposed to imperialism and composed of independent, self-determining, preferably democratic states bounded together through international organizations dedicated to the peaceful handling of conflicts, free trade, and mutual defense' (1994: 7). Smith goes on to assert that it is 'self-evident' that democracy would likely not have survived into the present era had it not been for the US (1994: 9). This liberal democratic internationalism, Smith goes on to write, has been the US's 'most important and distinctive contribution' to world history (1994: 12).

The blind spots in Smith's argument are glaring. Smith asserts that by 1828 the US 'could rightfully call itself the first modern democracy' (1994: 17). This image of the US as a long-standing democracy is astonishingly incomplete. It is only accurate insofar as 'democracy in America' is understood in white terms. Working-class white men have had the right to vote since the early 19th century, but non-whites of all classes won the effective right to vote in living memory. The intensity of racial divisions in the US is perhaps the most dramatic form of American exceptionalism. Many (white) Americans prefer to imagine their country as one of the world's oldest democracies, but, in fact, it only joined the club relatively recently.

Conclusion

When I was first asked to teach a course on US foreign policy, I accepted the challenge with some trepidation. My research background is in American racial politics. Thinking back to my own undergraduate days, US foreign policy seemed detached from the vital concerns of party competition, elections, representations and political institutions that so attracted me to the study of the United States. It was easy to associate US foreign policy with detailed, interesting, but ultimately ungeneralizable historical treatises about memorable summits, grave crises and interpersonal relations between national leaders and their advisers. To the extent that there was theorization, the emphasis was more on the *foreign* element than on the *policy*. That is to say, the actions of US foreign policymakers were understood largely in reference to the constraints and 'rules' of the international system. These are, of course, important ideas that we have explored in this book. But, as someone interested fundamentally in how policy interacts with social divisions and political inequalities, it felt a bit unsatisfactory.

I soon realized that I had too hastily cast US foreign policy askance. There was much more to this subject than elite-focused curios, technocratic insights and hackneyed theoretical concepts. Domestic institutions and voters were inescapably part of the story. As Milner and Tingley rightly observe, 'All foreign policies have material consequences since they require resources' (2015: 40). Foreign policies create winners and losers – not just in the international arena, but at home as well. Some foreign policy choices have broad impacts, affecting many people, perhaps sometimes in rather modest, barely discernible ways; others have large impacts on small constituencies. In a democracy, these impacts will inherently inspire political contestation.

Too often, IR theorists and commentators in the media have regarded these domestic political considerations as unwanted intrusions. Foreign policy, it is thought, is the preserve of careful experts, with years of experience and qualifications from elite institutions. The view that domestic politics should avoid the complicated terrain of foreign policy has been treated in some corners as 'a sacred cow of American politics'

(Preston, 2015: 220). Politicians who take political considerations into account when dealing with foreign policy are sometimes viewed as endangering the 'national interest' and putting party before country. It is simply not credible to think that politicians can simply put aside domestic political considerations when making foreign policy decisions; nor is it reasonable, in a democracy, to expect them to do so.

When scholars and commentators detect the role of partisanship in foreign policy, 'it really does not advance our understanding to lament its presence' (Schwartz, 2009: 189). The relative silence on the domestic implications of foreign affairs conceals more than it reveals. Bill Clinton's National Security Advisor Anthony Lake once likened the way US policymakers spoke about the domestic implications of foreign policy to the Victorians' approach to sex: 'Nobody talks about it, but it's on everybody's mind' (Miller, 2008: 77). It is time for students of US foreign policy to cast aside these outdated pretensions. Donald Trump's acting Chief of Staff Mick Mulvaney became the unlikely spokesperson for this liberation movement when he told reporters in 2019, 'I have news for everybody: Get over it. There's going to be political influence in foreign policy' (Rogers, 2019). On this point, at least, he was right.

The agenda of US foreign policy has arguably expanded in recent decades. US foreign policy of the 19th and early 20th centuries focused on resource extraction, imperial conquest, security and trade. These objectives, in some form or another, have not disappeared, but they have been added with other US foreign policy objectives, such as climate change, human rights and social concerns. As the remit of US foreign policy has increased, so, too, have the incentives for more domestic groups to take an interest. This book emphasizes the *policy* dimension of US foreign policy. The focus is less on the specific details of any particular event or on the grand paradigms of IR theory. Instead, the focus is on the key elements of political life that affect the construction, content and implementation of US foreign policy: political institutions; elected officials and bureaucrats; organized interest groups and parties; elections and campaigns; social movements; race, class and ethnicity; and the role of money and power.

This book is by no means the first to stress the intimate linkages between the public and US foreign policy (Johnstone and Laville, 2010; Milner and Tingley, 2015), but it has done so with perhaps a more unapologetically critical tone. The book has avoided IR labels as best as possible, sometimes explaining them only as a form of critique. This book is from an historical institutionalist perspective: one which brings the state, its institutions and domestic politics 'back in' to the study of foreign policy. Historical patterns, institutional incentive structures, cultural inheritances, reinforcing legal and policy legacies, and ideological blind spots and pathologies have been the focus of this book.

Should the labels of 'realist', 'liberal' or 'constructivist' need to be applied to this book, James Dunkerley's (2017) category of 'left realist' probably best applies. Such a person is 'essentially uninterested in theorizing about international politics' (2017: 19) and treats the ideas of international norms with deep suspicion. Noam Chomsky, to whom Dunkerley applies the label, explains that in the international realm, 'Norms are established by the powerful, in their own interests, and with the acclaim of responsible intellectuals' (2005: 7). They are endowed with a mythology and an air of legitimacy. Foreign policy is said to be too technical or too dangerous for the ordinary citizen. This book rejects such arrogance. Determined to knock out such haughtiness, Chomsky bluntly said, 'there's nothing in the social sciences or history or whatever that is beyond the intellectual capacity of an ordinary fifteen year old' (quoted in Mitchell and Schoffel, 2002: 137). Politics makes policy, and policy makes politics. In a democratic society, the policymakers are ultimately only as good as the electorates who endow them with their authority to govern. It can be no other way.

Further Reading

Introduction

McDougall (1997a) provides an excellent historical overview of the development of US foreign policy to the end of the Cold War. McMahon (2005) and Logevall (2009) emphasize the linkage between domestic politics and US foreign policy. Johnstone and Priest (2017b) provide a wide-ranging set of case studies. Preston (2015) emphasizes the electoral dimension. Dueck (2015) argues that former President Barack Obama prioritized domestic over foreign policy. Schwartz (2009) argues that foreign policy can be used as a tool of domestic politics. Kriner and Shen (2020) show how foreign policy can have sizeable and unexpected electoral consequences.

Chapter 1: The Study of US Foreign Policy

Seminal works of realist IR theory include Carr (1939), Morgenthau (1973 [1948]) and Kennan (1951). Ettinger (2019) explores whether the Trump Doctrine lives up to label of 'principled realism'. Desch (2007) suggests that the liberal tradition in America has been used to justify illiberal practices abroad. Taking a different perspective, Dueck (2006) argues that the US's liberal foreign policy has caused the country to be 'crusaders', but he believes that they are 'reluctant' ones because they are often concerned about the costs. McDougall (1997b) contends that the attempt to synthesize US foreign policy into two competing traditions – realism and idealism – has been misconceived. Henderson (2013), Vitalis (2015) and Anievas et al (2015) dissect the racist history of the discipline, including 'liberalism' and 'realism'. Dunn (2005) challenges the teleological narrative of the US trajectory from 'isolationism' to 'globalism' (see also Ambrose and Brinkley, 2012 [1971]). Wallerstein (2003) examines the limits of American power, framed very much in the context of the Bush Administration and the impact of the September 11 attacks.

Chapter 2: The Ideology of American Exceptionalism

The classic 'liberal' thesis of American exceptionalism was most famously articulated by Hartz (1955). In the present context, Deudney and Meiser (2012) provide the conventional account of American exceptionalism as indicative of some kind of 'special' mission. Lieven (2005) offers a staunch critique of the myths of American exceptionalism. There are ways, nonetheless, in which America is different. Hodgson (2010) draws the distinction between the normative and empirical claims of American exceptionalism. There is a rich debate on the question of weakness of the US socialist movement, one of the oldest questions in the American exceptionalism debate (Foner, 1984). We should always ask, 'exceptional compared to whom?' Traditionally, scholars have compared the US to Western European countries. Fabbrini (1999) draws comparisons between the development of the US and the EU, and suggests that the two polities are becoming increasingly similar in form. Lipset (1990) thought much was to be learned by comparing the US and Canada systematically.

Chapter 3: The Executive Branch: The President, Defense and State

Wildavsky (1966) offered the classic 'two presidencies' thesis defence, and even though he later came to question his own work, this thesis was once more revived by Canes-Wrone et al (2008). Saunders (2014) and Costigliala (2012) emphasize the personal role of the president. Halberstam (1972) and Mann (2004) emphasize the role of advisers. Clinton (2012) explains the many different duties taken on by the State Department today, while Krenn (1999) reflects on the historic role played by African Americans in and out of the State Department. There is a rich literature on the military-industrial complex (Singer, 2003; Hartung, 2010). Stuart (2008) and Hogan (1998) provide detailed insights into the history of the important National Security Act of 1947. Ledbetter (2011) does an excellent job at contexualizing Eisenhower's 1961 warning. On the intimate linkage between social science and the US military, see Jones (1982), Schrecker (1986), Ernst (1998), Amadae (2003), Isaac (2007) and Rohde (2009). Friedberg (2000) argues that a culture of anti-statism in the US acted as brake on even further integration of military and economic life.

Chapter 4: The Legislative Branch

Lindsay (2012) provides a good overview of the relationship between the executive and legislative branch. One of Congress's most important functions is oversight of the executive branch, which Colaresi (2014) and Fowler (2015) explore with respect to intelligence and veterans affairs. Scott and Carter (2002) offer a theoretical framework by which to understand congressional assertiveness. The power to declare war has been seemingly eroded in recent years, yet declarations of its demise have possibly been exaggerated. Deering (2005) and Howell and Pevehouse (2005) engage in this discussion. Hendrickson (2015) analyses the relationship between Obama and Congress, as Obama inherited an array of military challenges from his predecessor George W. Bush. For those who argue that foreign policy doesn't matter in congressional elections, Trumbore and Dulio (2013) offer a partial reply.

Chapter 5: Public Opinion, the Media and Partisanship

It is sometimes said that the general American public are apathetic about foreign policy except in periods of crisis. Baum and Groeling (2009) and Berinsky (2009) explore the public's relationship with war. Nincic (2012) sketches the relationship between elections, partisanship and foreign policy. Shefter (2002) offers a fantastic history of the role of trade in US party politics from the founding to the present. At a closer level, Walter Russell Mead (2012) writes about the Tea Party and its attitudes on foreign policy. In many ways, the voters whom Mead describes, in the context of Obama's first term, could be seen to overlap quite substantially with the core of Donald Trump's electorate at the end of Obama's second term. Mead is mystified by the Tea Party, whom he argues have an incoherent belief system that expresses deep scepticism about America's ability to keep order abroad but also has a firm belief in American exceptionalism. McCormick (2014) provides insights into wider public opinion on foreign policy during this time. Baum (2002) offers a useful perspective on the role of 'soft' media and public information about foreign affairs. Sobel (2001) provides an overview of the public's influence on US foreign policy.

Chapter 6: Interest Groups, Religion and Money

On the role of lobbying and money in US foreign policy, see Jacobs and Page (2011). Broz (2005) has studied the link between campaign donations from international financial institutions and government policy. Newhouse (2009) does an excellent job at outlining the privatization of diplomacy, as international actors increasingly turn to lobby shops in Washington, DC for representation rather than through foreign ministries and embassies. Abelson (2009) highlights the role of think tanks and the 'revolving door' between government and consultancy. Jeffreys-Jones (2010), Barnard (1982) and Narizny (2003) reflect on the power organized labour once had in shaping foreign policy outcomes, now mostly supplanted. Baumgartner et al (2008) provide evidence of the continued influence of religion in perceptions about the US's role in the world.

Chapter 7: Race, Diasporas and Ethnic Politics

There is a fascinating (if sometimes uneven) literature on the role of ethnic groups, diasporas and race in US foreign policy. For overviews, take a look at Ahrari (1987), Gates (1998), Smith (2000), McCormick (2008). On the question of size, see Saideman (2002). Rubenezer and Redd (2010) examine the role diasporic groups have played in US sanctions policy, a key terrain of contestation. Guelke (1996) provides excellent insight into the Irish lobby. On the Cuban lobby, much has been written, including by Haney and Vanderbush (1999, 2008), Gibbs (2010), Rytz (2013) and LeoGrande (2013). The most influential writing on the Israeli lobby comes from Mearsheimer and Walt (2007, 2014). Lieberman (2009) offers a methodical and trenchant critique. Rynhold (2015) and Waxman (2017) emphasize variation in attitudes towards Israel among American Jews. Anderson Paul (2007) and Zarifian (2014) offer insights into the Armenian lobby. The literature on African-American influence in US foreign policy is rich. Tillery (2011) stands out among a crowded field of high-level work, including by Plummer (1996), von Eschen (1997), Janken (1998), Meriwether (2002), Watts (2010) and Ledwidge (2012). On African Americans and the anti-apartheid movement, see Walters (1987) and Grant (2017). On pan-Africanism, see Weisbord (1973). On US–Africa trade, see Blanton and Blanton (2001).

Chapter 8: Realism: Order, Security and Prosperity

Theoretical and historical overviews of US global leadership can be found in Paterson (2001), Gaddis (2005 [1982]), Zelizer (2010), Mearsheimer (2014) and Khong (2014). Being a nuclear power was a core component of US international power in the post-Second

World War era. Herken (1988) offers an insight into the development of the US's nuclear arsenal. Alperovitz (1994) provides a fascinating and compelling argument about the realist motivation behind the dropping of the first nuclear bombs on civilian targets in 1945. Bernstein (1974) critically assesses some of Alperovitz's claims. On the problems of US disarmament, see Lieber and Press (2006) and Tertrais (2010). In the post-Cold War era, scholars have worried that the US has failed to reorient its dominant (and expensive) posture in world defence spending (see, for example, Daalder and Lindsay, 2005; Bacevich, 2010). Chamberlain (2016) explains why the US has been so *unsuccessful* at using its military might to compel behaviour in ostensibly weaker countries in the past several decades. Assertions of the US's declining leadership in the world have been made for some time now, after the initial triumphalism of the immediate post-Cold War years. Examples include Nye (2010) and Sing (2012). In this vein, there is an ever-growing literature on the threat China poses to US primacy. Among these are Goh (2005), Mahapatra (2010) and Allison (2017).

Chapter 9: Idealism: Democracy Promotion and the Paradoxes of US Foreign Policy

Smith (1994) and Bouchet (2013) offer thorough accounts of the US tradition of 'democracy promotion'. A growing number of scholars argue that the 'growth' of the US must be understood on imperial and colonial terms, including Frymer (2017). On US wars and conquest, see Boot (2014 [2002], Chapters 14, 16). On the fascinating role international pressure played in the US civil rights movement of the mid-20th century, see Noer (1985), Fraser (2000), Borstelmann (2001), Dudziak (2000), Perry (2015) and Snyder (2018). On the self-image of the US as a 'nation of immigrants' – and the deficiencies in this assertion – see King (2005).

Glossary

Beijing Consensus   A model of development which includes a combination of authoritarian politics, state-directed domestic economic management and capitalistic international economic engagement; characterized by a muscular state hand on the levers of production, political authoritarianism guided by an unchallenged ruling party, and population control, including family planning.

Bush Doctrine   George W. Bush's foreign policy outlook. Summarized by four elements: pre-emption of terrorist threats, military primacy, new multilateralism ('coalitions of the willing'), and the spread of democracy.

Caucuses (congressional)   Clubs, groupings or membership organizations that (only) members of Congress join (often for a fee) to express their support for particular causes.

Compliance   When Congress accedes to a president's request with little protest.

Constructivism   A catch-all term for international relations theories which, influenced by post-modernism, emphasize the socially and politically manufactured nature of the international system. Constructivism emphasizes the importance of 'self-image' in relation to other actors in explaining foreign policy choices.

Containment   Creating geopolitical counterweights to prevent the expansion of hostile forces and to deter aggression.

Contractarian political theory   The branch of political theory that holds that political legitimacy is based on a usually unspoken (and often non-historical) agreement between the governed and their governors, usually manifested through political norms and understandings. It holds that political legitimacy is ultimately contingent on consent rather than on, for example, raw power or divine authority.

Democratic peace theory   The assumption that democratic states do not go to war with each other.

Diaspora   A population that live in a location that is different from the one in which they originated; includes not only immigrants and their descendants, but also refugees and descendants of slavery, deportation and forced migration.

Ethnic lobby   A loose coalition of individuals and organizations representing a particular diasporic community that actively works to move US foreign policy in a more sympathetic direction to the diasporic community's country of origin or country of affection.

Ethnicity   Operates within racial groups; is often determined by cultural markers such as national origin, language or religion.

Executive-centred partisanship   The orientation of modern party politics around the presidency and the use by the president of the powers and tools of the federal executive branch to advance political and policy goals on behalf of their party for its electoral advantage.

Hegemony   When an actor with overwhelming capabilities in the international system uses its power to provide leadership that underwrites a particular international ordering.

Hispanics   Spanish-speaking people and their descendants.

Howard School of International Relations   A loose grouping of African-American scholars at the prestigious Howard University in Washington, DC, active in the early and mid-20th century. These scholars produced works that challenged the 'liberal' benevolence of the US's international role, depicting the US as a colonial and imperial power.

Ideal type   A deliberate simplification, a heuristic used to highlight the most important and critical elements of an idea. Famously deployed by Max Weber in his work on bureaucracy.

Integration   A liberal form of engagement that entails achieving goals through inclusion in international institutions.

Interest groups   The coalitions by which people with common material aspirations organize collectively to pursue their goals through politics.

Iraq syndrome   A perceived reluctance among the US public to fight further preventative wars due to the unpopularity of the War in Iraq.

Latinos/as   People who hail from Latin America.

Liberalism   A paradigm within international relations theory used to describe the character of foreign policy action by key actors and states. Liberalism regards the nation-state as only one among many participants in foreign policy. It holds that universal values should be the basis of action. It sees it as important to improve overall global conditions, rather than simply focusing on one state. Liberal US foreign policymakers regard free society and free markets as inherent goods, and believe that it is important for other countries to embrace a liberal political and economic model facilitated by global institutions that promote such values. It is sometimes called 'idealism'.

Linked fate   The degree to which people feel that what happens to a group as a whole will also affect them individually due to their membership in that group.

Manhattan Project   The secret US research project during the Second World War that developed the first nuclear weapons.

Marxism   In international relations, Marxism regards foreign policy as a product of the economic needs of those who control its means of production. In the case of the US, a Marxist scholar would argue that American foreign policy tends to serve the economic interests of the elites who occupy the offices of power in Washington, capitalists on Wall Street and business elites.

Military-industrial-academic complex   The intimate relationship between military, industry and research institutions (both universities and private research foundations) to the extent that researchers become reliant on defence investment and, therefore, shape their research agendas according to defence sector priorities.

Military-industrial complex   The military-industrial complex refers to the intimate relationship between US policymakers and those who have a material interest in the perpetuation of the outsized US defence budget. President Dwight Eisenhower used the term in his farewell address in January 1961.

Offshore balancing   Relying on local powers to achieve policy aims while preventing any one power from dominating; a kind of semi-detached leadership, 'stepping in' to solve international conflicts on an ad hoc basis.

Power   The ability to get others to do something you would like them to do.

Primacy   The condition of a country being 'first' compared to all global competitors in a number of key indicators, including military might, economic prosperity and soft power.

Public diplomacy   Efforts that aim to promote America's image abroad and to engage with local populations in order to help explain the work that the US is doing in their country and to educate citizens of other countries about the US's foreign policy mission. It can involve doing television interviews, going to schools, organizing community meetings or student exchange programmes.

Race   A contested concept that refers to broad socially and politically constructed categories structured (imperfectly) according to certain inherited physical characteristics and geographic origin.

Realism   A paradigm within international relations theory used to describe the character of foreign policy action by key actors and states. Realism is based on several key assumptions. First, the nation-state is the primary actor in world politics. Second, national interest is the key concern that states must address and protect. Third, that the distribution of power, especially security, is the primary concern of foreign policymakers. And fourth, the quality of state-to-state relations, not the character of domestic politics within a state, should be what matters to foreign policymakers.

Realism, defensive   A form of realist thought which asserts that security is best found in a fortified posture. Defensive realism discourages unnecessary international engagement.

Realism, offensive   A form of realist thought which contends that security comes through power and power comes through maximizing control over or relative to other countries.

Retrenchment   The reduction of international and military commitments and costs (for example, withdrawing from alliances, reducing expenditures on the military and to international organizations).

Searing effect   When public support for military action runs 'hot' (high enthusiasm) but as the military campaign fails, the public is 'burned' by the negative experience and becomes reluctant to support future military action.

Security dilemma   A paradox that arises in realist international theory. In the anarchic international system, each state must secure itself from others, but each state's pursuit of its own security can lead to greater instability in the overall system.

Think tanks   Not-for-profit research bodies that exist to inform policy debate.

Truman Doctrine   A commitment to contain the spread of communism throughout the world through the guarantee that the US would offer aid and support to any nation that was in a struggle to protect a liberal democratic constitution from communist takeover.

Trump Doctrine   The view that international liberalism no longer serves the interests of the United States and that the liberal international order established in the post-Second World War period imposes its highest costs on the US and greatest benefits on rising powers seeking to challenge the US.

Unipolarity   When one state enjoys an overwhelming advantage in relative capabilities to all other states in the international system.

US Food Administration   An executive agency led, for some of its history, by future President Herbert Hoover during the First World War and its immediate aftermath. The agency oversaw the production and distribution of food in the US, with the goal of increasing US agricultural exports to its allies in Europe, whose domestic production had been severely hit by the war.

Vietnam Syndrome   A perceived reluctance among the US public to engage troops abroad to contain the spread of communism due to the unpopularity of the failed war in Vietnam.

Washington Consensus   The preference for free markets and free political systems with very little state interference, often prescribed as a set of 'reforms' for developing countries.

Notes

Chapter 1

1 For simplicity, this book will not draw a distinction too sharply between 'classical' realism and neorealism. There is enough dancing on pinheads in the field as it is.

2 Remarks by US President Donald Trump to the 73rd Session of the UN General Assembly, New York, 25 September 2018.

3 The US Food Administration was an executive agency led, for some of its history, by future President Herbert Hoover during the First World War and its immediate aftermath. The agency oversaw the production and distribution of food in the US, with the goal of increasing US agricultural exports to its allies in Europe, whose domestic production had been severely hit by the war. The period 1917–19, when Hoover led the Administration, saw a 345 per cent increase in US agricultural exports (Dickson, 1942: 95).

4 The premise has since been disproven by the wars between India and Pakistan (1999), Israel and Lebanon (2006) and Russia and Georgia (2008).

5 Immanuel Kant, one of the heroes of liberal IR theory, drew a sharp distinction between white and non-white diplomacy (Eze, 1995). Kant argued that 'the Negroes of Africa have by nature no feeling that rises above the trifling' (*Observations on the Feeling of the Beautiful and the Sublime*). Kant's theory works only if one accepts the moral distinction he draws between 'persons' and 'sub-persons'. As Charles Mills writes, 'Modern moral theory and modern racial theory have the same father' in Kant (1997: 72).

6 Although it should be said that there is a growing body of excellent critical scholarship, including work by Anievas et al (2015), Manchanda (2018), Vitalis (2015), Acharya (2018) and Parmar (2018).

Chapter 2

1 Public Papers of the Presidents of the United States, Barack Obama, 2009, Book 1, p 417. Available at: www.govinfo.gov/app/collection/PPP/3

2 Sometimes called 'neoconservative' to distinguish it from the domestic understanding of liberal as 'left wing'.

3 The full sentence is, 'La situation des Américains est donc entièrement exceptionnelle, et il est à croire qu'aucun peuple démocratique n'y sera jamais placé' ['The situation of the Americans is thus entirely exceptional, and it is believable that no democratic people will ever be situated as such'] (my translation; *Democracy in America*, vol II, 1840, Chapter 9).

4 'Je ne puis consentir à séparer l'Amérique de l'Europe, malgré l'Océan qui les divise' (*Democracy in America*, vol II, 1840, Chapter 9).

5 www.rev.com/blog/transcripts/democratic-national-convention-dnc-2020-night-2-transcript

6 https://1997-2001.state.gov/statements/1998/980219a.html

Chapter 3

1 Known as the 'foreign secretary' in other systems.

2 The 24th Amendment (1964) implicitly acknowledged parties when it protected the right to vote in primary elections.

3 The State Department is equivalent to the 'Foreign Ministry' in many other political systems.

4 Thomas Jefferson, James Madison, James Monroe, John Quincy Adams, Henry Clay, Martin van Buren, Daniel Webster, James Buchanan, James Blaine, William Jennings Bryan and Charles Evans Hughes.

5 The seven other uniformed services are the Army, Navy, Marine Corps, Air Force, Coast Guard, Public Health Service Commissioned Corps (PHSCC) and National Oceanic and Atomsopheric Administration (NOAA) Officer Corps.

6 Transcript of President Dwight D. Eisenhower's Farewell Address (1961). Available at: www.ourdocuments.gov/doc.php?flash=false&doc=90&page=transcript

7 President John F. Kennedy's Inaugural Address (20 January 1961). Available at: www.jfklibrary.org/learn/about-jfk/historic-speeches/inaugural-address

8 Kennedy won Hawaii by just 115 votes, Illinois by 8,588 and Missouri by 9,980. These states gave Kennedy 43 electoral votes and with them, victory over Nixon.

9 It is worth noting that the Nixon campaign did its best to deflect from the 'soft' on defence spending attack. At the Republican Convention, Nixon abandoned Eisenhower's balanced approach to defence spending, adding to the party platform, 'The US can afford and must provide the increased expenditures to implement fully this necessary program for strengthening our defense posture. There must be no price ceiling on America's security.'

10 Letter in protest of SORO (Special Operations Research Office) (1960). Available at: http://auomeka.wrlc.org/letter-in-protest-of-soro

11 Congress has also delegated broad authority to presidents in their ability to impose sanctions. The legal authority by which presidents impose sanctions is contained in the Trading with the Enemy Act of 1917, the UN Participation Act of 1945, the International Emergency Economic Powers Act of 1977 (the most important), and the Export Administration Act of 1979.

Chapter 4

1 Republican Party Platform of 1960. Available at: www.presidency.ucsb.edu/documents/republican-party-platform-1960

2 Democratic Party Platform. Available at: www.presidency.ucsb.edu/documents/1960-democratic-party-platform

3 H.J.Res. 117 (85th): Joint resolution to promote peace and stability in the Middle East (1957). Available at: www.govtrack.us/congress/bills/85/hjres117/text

4 Transcript of Tonkin Gulf Resolution (1964). Available at: www.ourdocuments.gov/doc.php?flash=false&doc=98&page=transcript

5   S.J.Res. 23 (107th): Authorization for use of military force. Available at: www.govtrack.us/congress/bills/107/sjres23/text

6   War Powers Resolution, Joint Resolution Concerning the War Powers of Congress and the President. Available at: https://avalon.law.yale.edu/20th_century/warpower.asp

7   Public Law 91-652. Available at: www.govinfo.gov/content/pkg/STATUTE-84/pdf/STATUTE-84-Pg1942.pdf#page=1

8   A grant paid by the federal government to support low-income students in higher education. About 5.5 million students receive such grants each year.

Chapter 5

1   US Department of State Bureau of Consular Affairs, US passports. Available at: https://travel.state.gov/content/travel/en/about-us/reports-and-statistics.html

2   A similar tendency occurred during the Obama Administration, where voters' views on the president had a direct bearing on their views about a range of policy issues, including those with no obvious ideological content (Tesler, 2016).

3   On 18 December 2019, 299 House Democrats voted to impeach the president for abuse of power, with just two voting 'No' and two abstaining or not voting.

4   These two statements appear somewhat contradictory, leading us to wonder if the critics who say that the US public is 'incoherent' on foreign policy might have had a point.

5   CNN US Politics, Exit polls. Available at: https://edition.cnn.com/election/2016/results/exit-polls

6   CNN Politics, Exit polls. Available at: https://edition.cnn.com/election/2020/exit-polls/president/national-results

7   Abramowitz (1995) argued that it was social/cultural concerns that drove Clinton to the White House in his memorably titled *Journal of Politics* article 'It's abortion, stupid'.

8   *House Documents, Nos 36–40*, United States Congressional Serial Set, 1981, p 14.

Chapter 6

1   OpenSecrets.org, Cost of election. Available at: www.opensecrets.org/overview/cost.php

2   www.squirepattonboggs.com/en/professionals/b/boehner-john

3   US Department of Justice, Short Form Registration Statement. Available at: https://efile.fara.gov/docs/6280-Short-Form-20170118-26.pdf

4   There are four to five veto players in the US lawmaking process: the US House of Representatives, the US Senate, the US president, the US Supreme Court and (depending on the type of policy) state governments. For example, Barack Obama's Medicaid expansion was passed by large congressional majorities (veto players 1 and 2) and signed into law by the president (veto player 3), but the Supreme Court (veto player 4) made the expansion optional, handing discretion to State governments (veto player 5).

5   https://projects.propublica.org/represent/lobbying/r/300929929

6   https://projects.propublica.org/represent/lobbying/search?search=human+AND+rights+AND+accountability+AND+global+AND+initiative+AND+foundation

7   US Department of State, Global Magnitsky Act. Available at: www.state.gov/global-magnitsky-act/

8   https://projects.propublica.org/represent/lobbying/r/300929724

9   Subsequent reporting has suggested that Trump officials believed that the Russian contacts would provide damaging information about Hillary Clinton (Becker et al, 2017).

10 Senate Judiciary Committee (2017) 'Interview of: Donald J. Trump.' Available at: www.judiciary.senate.gov/imo/media/doc/Trump%20Jr%20Transcript_redacted.pdf

11 See https://fara.us/criminal-enforcement-summaries/

12 US Bureau of Labor Statistics, Economic News Release. Available at: www.bls.gov/news.release/union2.nr0.htm

13 US House Committee on Appropriations, Volume 4, 85th Congress, 1st Session, 1957, 74.

14 US Bureau of Labor Statistics, Economic News Release. Available at: www.bls.gov/news.release/union2.nr0.htm

15 About 35.5 million voters were evangelical/born-again (26 per cent) in 2016, according to the national exit poll. Eighty per cent of these voted for Trump (about 28.5 million). Trump won just under 63 million votes, meaning that evangelicals made up about 45 per cent of his voters.

16 http://lifewayresearch.com/wp-content/uploads/2020/09/Report-Americans-Sept-2020-Election.pdf

17 *The Daily Show with Jon Stewart*. Available at: www.cc.com/video-clips/kj9zai/the-daily-show-with-jon-stewart-martin-gilens---benjamin-page

Chapter 7

1   Michael Omi and Howard Winant's work on racial formation is one of the most important in the field in establishing that racial identity is socially and political constructed and enforced (see Omi and Winant, 2014).

2   Public Law 94-311. Available at: https://uscode.house.gov/statutes/pl/94/311.pdf

3   However, it is sometimes argued that not all countries in the geographic region of Central and South America are considered Latin American. 'Latin' American also has a linguistic basis: speakers of Romance (Latin descendant) languages. In Belize and Guyana, the official language is English. In Suriname, residents speak Dutch and Sranan Tongo. None of these languages originate from a Romance (Latin-based) language, such as Spanish, French or Portuguese. Jamaica is considered Caribbean, not Latin American, because residents speak English, whereas Haiti is considered both Caribbean and Latin American because residents speak French.

4   www.pewresearch.org/hispanic/2017/12/20/hispanic-identity-fades-across-generations-as-immigrant-connections-fall-away/#describe-identity

5   https://imsvintagephotos.com/presidential-candidate-jimmy-carter-is-shown-wearing-a-button-saying-england-get-out-of-ireland-while-marching-in-new-york-s-st-patricks-s-day-parade-1548131

6   Harris is the second non-white vice president. Herbert Hoover's Vice President Charles Curtis (1929–33) was Native American, a member of the Kaw Nation.

7   www.oireachtas.ie/en/debates/debate/dail/1921-08-17/6/

8   https://cain.ulster.ac.uk/sutton/tables/Location.html

9   *Attorney General v Irish Northern Aid Committee*, 530 Supp 24 (SDNY 1981).

10 Democratic National Committee Membership Roster 2016–2020. Available at: https://cdn0.vox-cdn.com/uploads/chorus_asset/file/7977435/2016-2020_DNC_MEMBER_ROSTER_SIMPLE.0.pdf

11 'Biden suffers foot-in-mouth syndrome as he hosts Irish PM – Daily Mail', YouTube. Available at: momentwww.youtube.com/watch?v=_S3Z3lYwfu0

12 This is about the same distance as between Scotland and Northern Ireland.

13 https://knowledge.wharton.upenn.edu/article/the-hispanic-vote-and-the-u-s-presidential-election/

14 US Department of Homeland Security (2017) 'Fact Sheet: Changes to parole and expedited removal policies affecting Cuban nationals'. Available at: www.dhs.gov/sites/default/files/publications/DHS%20Fact%20Sheet%20FINAL.pdf

15 Statement by the President on Cuban Immigration Policy (2017). Available at: https://obamawhitehouse.archives.gov/the-press-office/2017/01/12/statement-president-cuban-immigration-policy

16 'Venezuelan Dictator Nicolás Maduro Praises "Comrade Biden"', YouTube. Available at: www.youtube.com/watch?v=DgLxjp8ylCA

17 *The New York Times* Election Needles. Available at: www.nytimes.com/interactive/2020/11/03/us/elections/forecast-president.html

18 https://twitter.com/ANCA_DC/status/1343943518495137792

19 https://explorer.usaid.gov/cd/ARM

20 https://anca.org/assets/pdf/102220_Pallone_Artsakh_Recognition.pdf

21 https://twitter.com/bradsherman/status/1314724517755924480?lang=en-gb

22 http://armeniansforobama.com/common/pdf/Obama_letter_to_Rice_July_26_2008.pdf

23 The text of the resolution is as follows: 'This resolution states that it is US policy to (1) commemorate the Armenian Genocide, the killing of 1.5 million Armenians by the Ottoman Empire from 1915 to 1923; (2) reject efforts to associate the US government with efforts to deny the existence of the Armenian Genocide or any genocide; and (3) encourage education and public understanding about the Armenian Genocide.'

24 In 1980, the Jewish vote split 45 per cent for Jimmy Carter, 39 per cent for Ronald Reagan and 15 per cent for John Anderson.

25 For overviews, see King (2007 [1995]) and Thompson (2015). On Asians in America, see Loewen (1971) and Kim (1999). On Latinos, see Haney Lopez (2000) and Fox and Guglielmo (2012).

26 See, for example, Sanchez Gibau (1997) on Cape Verdeans, Waters (1999) on West Indians and Stoller and McConatha (2001) on West Africans.

Chapter 8

1 Truman was aware of the Soviet plans, writing in his diary on 17 July 1945 after a meeting with Stalin, 'He'll be in the Jap War on August 15th' (quoted in Alperovitz, 1994: 24).

2 Edwin Pauley, who negotiated for the US at the July 1945 Potsdam Conference, later revealed that Truman stated that the recent successful nuclear test in New Mexico 'would keep the Russians straight' (quoted in Alperovitz, 1994: 54).

3 The US has, of course, inconsistently enforced these objectives, especially with regard to non-white nations.

4 www.bbc.co.uk/news/business-56036245

Chapter 9

1   Declaration of Independence: A Transcription (1776). Available at: www.archives. gov/founding-docs/declaration-transcript
2   US–China Institute (1901). Available at: https://china.usc.edu/us-senator-albert-j-beveridge-speaks-philippine-question-us-senate-washington-dc-january-9-1900
3   *The Congressional Record*, House, 55th Congress, 2nd Session, 11 June 1898, 5792.
4   Secretary of State Madeleine K. Albright interview (1998). Available at: https://1997-2001.state.gov/statements/1998/980219a.html
5   Speech to the 2012 Republican National Convention.
6   *The New York Times*, Obama's Speech in Cairo (2009). Available at: www.nytimes. com/2009/06/04/us/politics/04obama.text.html
7   Remarks by President Obama in Address to the United Nations General Assembly (2011). Available at: https://obamawhitehouse.archives.gov/the-press-office/2011/09/21/remarks-president-obama-address-united-nations-general-assembly
8   US National Security Strategy (2010). Available at: https://obamawhitehouse. archives.gov/sites/default/files/rss_viewer/national_security_strategy.pdf
9   *Telegraph* Reporters (2017) 'Donald Trump's Saudi Arabia speech: Eight key points', *The Telegraph*, 21 May. Available at: www.telegraph.co.uk/news/2017/05/21/donald-trumps-saudi-arabia-speech-eight-key-points/
10 Remarks by President Trump on the policy of the United States towards Cuba (2017). Available at: https://trumpwhitehouse.archives.gov/briefings-statements/remarks-president-trump-policy-united-states-towards-cuba/
11 Remarks by President Trump on the policy of the United States towards Cuba (2017). Available at: https://trumpwhitehouse.archives.gov/briefings-statements/remarks-president-trump-policy-united-states-towards-cuba/
12 On South Carolina, see Mickey (2015: 149).
13 This prohibition was particularly devastating because black teachers were the backbone of NAACP membership in many states. Private sector black workers, such as agricultural labourers, were already informally barred from joining such organizations by the white capitalists on whom they were economically dependent.
14 Native Americans on reservations did not get the right to vote in Arizona, New Mexico, Idaho, Maine, Mississippi or Washington until the 1940s. They did not get the right to vote in Utah until 1957 or in Colorado until 1970. Alaska banned Native Alaskans who were not proficient in English from voting until the 1970s (National Commission on Voting Rights, 2014: 14).
15 Christopher Thorne (1998) writes about the awkwardness of US troop segregation in the UK where many segregated units were stationed.
16 www.trumanlibrary.gov/library/to-secure-these-rights
17 www.trumanlibrary.gov/library/to-secure-these-rights
18 www.supremecourt.gov/publicinfo/speeches/viewspeech/sp_10-25-04
19 Secretary of State John Foster Dulles to Attorney General Herbert Brownell, 24 September 1957, quoted in Fraser (2000: 247).

References

Abelson, Donald (2004) 'The Business of Ideas: The Think Tank Industry in the USA', in D. Stone and A. Denham (eds) *Think Tank Traditions: Policy Research and the Politics of Ideas*, Manchester: Manchester University Press.

Abelson, Donald (2006) *A Capitol Idea: Think Tanks and US Foreign Policy*, Montreal: McGill-Queen's University Press.

Abelson, Donald (2009) 'What Were They Thinking? Think Tanks, the Bush Presidency, and US Foreign Policy', in M. Ledwidge, I. Parmar and L. Miller (eds) *New Directions in US Foreign Policy*, New York: Routledge.

Abramowitz, Alan (1995) 'It's abortion, stupid: Policy voting in the 1992 presidential election', *Journal of Politics*, 57(1), 176–86.

Acharya, Amitra (2018) *Constructing Global Order: Agency and Change in World Politics*, Cambridge: Cambridge University Press.

Adler, David and Ben Judah (2019) 'Traditional foreign policy no longer', *The Guardian*, 2 December.

Ahrari, Mohammed E. (1987) *Ethnic Groups and US Foreign Policy*, Westport, CT: Greenwood Publishing Group.

Albright, Jonathan (2017) 'Welcome to the era of fake news', *Media & Communication*, 5(2), 87–9.

Aldous, Richard (2012) *Reagan and Thatcher: The Difficult Relationship*, London: Hutchinson.

Aldrich, John, John Sullivan and Eugene Borgida (1989) 'Foreign affairs and issue voting', *American Political Science Review*, 83(1), March, 123–41.

Allen, Theodore (1975) *The Invention of the White Race*, London: Verso.

Allison, Graham (2017) *Destined for War: Can America and China Escape Thucydides' Trap?*, New York: Houghton Mifflin.

Almond, Gabriel (1962 [1950]) *The American People and Foreign Policy*, New York: Harcourt, Brace, & Co.

Alperovitz, Gar (1994) *Atomic Diplomacy: Hiroshima and Potsdam*, London: Pluto Press.

Amadae, Sonja (2003) *Rationalizing Capitalist Democracy: The Cold War Origins of Rational Choice Liberalism*, Chicago, IL: University of Chicago Press.

Ambrose, Stephen and Douglas Brinkley (2012 [1971]) *Rise to Globalism: American Foreign Policy since 1938* (9th edn), London: Penguin.

Ambrosius, Lloyd (1996) 'Dilemmas of National Self-Determination: Woodrow Wilson's Legacy', in C. Baechler and C. Fink (eds) *The Establishment of European Frontiers after the Two World Wars*, Bern: Peter Lang.

Andelic, Patrick (2019) *Donkey Work: Congressional Democrats in Conservative America, 1974–1994*, Lawrence, KS: University of Kansas Press.

Anderson, Benedict (2006) *Imagined Communities: Reflecting on the Origins and Spread of Nationalism* (2nd edn), London: Verso.

Anderson, Perry (2017) *American Foreign Policy and Its Thinkers*, London: Verso.

Anderson Paul, Rachel (2007) 'Grassroots mobilization and diaspora politics: Armenian interest groups and the role of collective memory', *Nationalism and Ethnic Politics*, 6(1), 24–47.

Anievas, Alexander, Nivi Manchanda and Robbie Shilliam (eds) (2015) *Race and Racism in International Relations: Confronting the Global Colour Line*, New York: Routledge.

Anton, Michael (2019) 'The Trump Doctrine', *Foreign Policy*, 20 April.

Archibugi, Danielle (1995) 'Immanuel Kant, cosmopolitan law and peace', *European Journal of International Relations*, 1(4), 429–56.

Armacost, Michael (2015) *Ballots, Bullets, and Bargains: American Foreign Policy and Presidential Elections*, New York: Columbia University Press.

Arnsdorf, Isaac and Benjamin Oreskes (2016) 'Putin's favorite congressman', *POLITICO*, 23 November.

Arrow, Kenneth (1963 [1951]) *Social Choice and Individual Values*, New York: John Wiley & Sons, Inc.

Bacevich, Andrew (2010) *Washington Rules: America's Path to Permanent War*, New York: Metropolitan Books.

Baldwin, James and Margaret Mead (1971) *A Rap on Race*, Philadelphia, PA: J.B. Lippincott & Co.

Barnard, John (1982) 'Workers, the Labor Movement, and the Cold War, 1945–1960', in R. Bremmer and G. Reichard (eds) *Reshaping America: Society and Institutions, 1945–1960*, Columbus, OH: Ohio State University Press.

Barrow, Bill (2019) 'Biden calls Sanders' pitch to leverage Israel aid bizarre', Associated Press, 8 December.

Bartels, Larry (2016) *Unequal Democracy: The Political Economy of the New Gilded Age* (2nd edn), Princeton, NJ: Princeton University Press.

Baum, Matthew (2002) 'Sex, lies, and war: How soft news brings foreign policy to the inattentive public', *American Political Science Review*, 96(1), March, 91–109.

Baum, Matthew and Tim Groeling (2009) *War Stories: The Causes and Consequences of Public Views of War*, Princeton, NJ: Princeton University Press.

Baumgartner, Jody, Peter Francia and Jonathan Morris (2008) 'A clash of civilizations? The influence of religion on public opinion of US foreign policy in the Middle East', *Political Research Quarterly*, 61(2), 171–9.

BBC News (2014) 'Study: US is an oligarchy, not a democracy', 17 April. Available at: www.bbc.co.uk/news/blogs-echochambers-27074746

Becker, Jo, Matt Apuzzo and Adam Goldman (2017) 'Trump's son met with Russian lawyer after being promised damaging information on Clinton', *The New York Times*, 9 July.

Beckert, Sven (2014) *Empire of Cotton: A New History of Global Capitalism*, New York: Alfred Knopf.

Beckwith, Ryan T. (2016) 'Read President Obama's speech to the Cuban people', *Time*, 22 March. Available at: https://time.com/4267933/barack-obama-cuba-speech-transcript-full-text

Bell, Derrick (1980) '*Brown v Board of Education* and the interest-convergence dilemma', *Harvard Law Review*, 93(3), January, 518–33.

Berggen, D. Jason and Nicol Rae (2006) 'Jimmy Carter and George W. Bush: Faith, foreign policy, and an evangelical presidential style', *Presidential Studies Quarterly*, 36(4), 606–32.

Berinsky, Adam J. (2009) *In Time of War: Understanding American Public Opinion from World War II to Iraq*, Chicago, IL: University of Chicago Press.

Bernstein, Barton (1974) 'The atomic bomb and American foreign policy, 1941–1945: An historiographical controversy', *Peace & Change*, 2(1), 1–16.

Blanton, Robert and Shannon Blanton (2001) 'Democracy, human rights, and US–Africa trade', *International Interactions*, 27(3), 275–95.

Bobo, Lawrence and Cybelle Fox (2003) 'Race, racism, and discrimination: Bridging problems, methods, and theory in social psychological research', *Social Psychology Quarterly*, 66(4), 319–32.

Boot, Max (2014 [2002]) *The Savage Wars of Peace: Small Wars and the Rise of American Power*, New York: Basic Books.

Booth, Ken and Nicholas Wheeler (2007) *The Security Dilemma: Fear, Cooperation, and Trust in World Politics*, Basingstoke: Palgrave Macmillan.

Borstelmann, Thomas (2001) *The Cold War and the Color Line*, Cambridge, MA: Harvard University Press.

Bouchet, Nicholas (2013) 'The democracy tradition in US foreign policy and the Obama presidency', *International Affairs*, 89(1), 31–51.

Bowles, Nigel and Robert McMahon (2014) *Government and Politics of the United States* (3rd edn), New York: Palgrave Macmillan.

Boyle, Kevin (1995) *The UAW and the Heyday of American Liberalism, 1945–1968*, Ithaca, NY: Cornell University Press.

Bremmer, Ian (2019) 'How Americans view foreign policy in the Trump era', *Time*, 19 February.

Brinkley, Douglas (1992) *Dean Acheson: The Cold War Years*, New Haven, CT: Yale University Press.

Brinkley, Douglas (1997) 'Democratic enlargement: The Clinton Doctrine', *Foreign Policy*, 106, Spring, 110–27.

Brooks, Stephen and William Wohlforth (2008) *World Out of Balance: International Relations and the Challenge of American Primacy*, Princeton, NJ: Princeton University Press.

Brown, Chris, Terry Nardin and Nicholas Rengger (2002) 'Augustine of Hippo', in C. Brown, T. Nardin and N. Rengger (eds) *International Relations in Political Thought*, Oxford: Oxford University Press.

Brown, Michael (1997) 'Bargaining for social rights: Unions and the reemergence of welfare capitalism, 1945–1952', *Political Science Quarterly*, 112(4), Winter, 645–74.

Broz, Lawrence (2005) 'Congressional politics of international financial rescues', *American Journal of Political Science*, 49(3), July, 479–96.

Bull, Hedley (1977) *The Anarchical Society: A Study of Order in World Politics*, New York: Columbia University Press.

Bunche, Ralph (1936) *A World View of Race*, Washington, DC: Associates in Negro Folk Education.

Bunche, Ralph (1995 [1929]) 'Marxism and the Negro Question', in C. Henry (ed) *Ralph J. Bunche: Selected Speeches and Writings*, Ann Arbor, MI: University of Michigan Press.

Burke, John (1992) *The Institutional Presidency*, Baltimore, MD: Johns Hopkins University Press.

Burns, Sarah (2020) 'Ancestors of Biden, Obama, JFK, Reagan left Ireland within some 10 years of each other', *Irish Times*, 22 November.

Buzzanco, Robert (1996) *Masters of War: Military Dissent and Politics in the Vietnam Era*, Cambridge: Cambridge University Press.

Caesar, James (2012) 'The origins and character of American exceptionalism', *American Political Thought*, 1(1), Spring, 3–28.

Calhoun, Frederick (1993) *Uses of Force and Wilsonian Foreign Policy*, Kent, OH: Kent State University Press.

Canes-Wrone, Brandice, William Howell and David Lewis (2008) 'Toward a broader understanding of presidential power: A reevaluation of the two presidencies thesis', *Journal of Politics*, 70(1), January, 1–18.

Carpenter, Daniel (2001) *The Forging of Bureaucratic Autonomy: Reputations, Networks, and Policy Innovation in Executive Agencies, 1862–1928*, Princeton, NJ: Princeton University Press.

Carr, E.H. (1939) *The Twenty Years' Crisis, 1919–1939: An Introduction to the Study of International Relations*, London: Macmillan.

Carter, Jimmy (1977) 'Address at commencement exercises at the University of Notre Dame', The American Presidency Project, 22 May. Available at: www.presidency.ucsb.edu/documents/address-commencement-exercises-the-university-notre-dame

Carter, Jimmy (2005) *Our Endangered Values: America's Moral Crisis*, New York: Simon & Schuster.

Cassidy, John (2014) 'Is America an oligarchy?', *The New Yorker*, 18 April.

Cater, Douglass (1964) *Power in Washington*, New York: Random House.

Chadwick, Stephen (2009) 'John Locke, the state of nature, and terrorism', *Critical Studies on Terrorism*, 2(3), 438–52.

Chaffee, Steven and Stacey Kanihan (1997) 'Learning about politics from the mass media', *Political Communication*, 14(4), 421–30.

Chamberlain, Dianne Pfundstein (2016) *Cheap Threats: Why the United States Struggles to Coerce Weak States*, Washington, DC: Georgetown University Press.

Cheeseman, Abbie (2020) 'Jonathan Pollard welcomed home by Netanyahu', *The Telegraph*, 30 December.

Chomsky, Noam (ed) (1997) *The Cold War and the University: Toward an Intellectual History of the Postwar Years*, New York: New Press.

Chomsky, Noam (2005) 'Simple truths, hard problems: Some thoughts on terror, justice, and self-defence', *Philosophy*, 80(1), 5–28.

Churchill, Winston (1899) *The River War: An Account of the Reconquest of the Sudan*, London: Longmans, Green & Co.

Clark, Michael (1993) 'Realism ancient and modern: Thucydides and international relations', *PS: Political Science & Politics*, 26(3), 491–4.

Clinton, Bill (1994) 'The Budget message of the President', Office of Management and Budget.

Clinton, Bill (2000) 'Expanding trade, projecting values: Why I'll fight to make China's trade status permanent', *The New Democrat*, January.

Clinton, Hillary (2007) 'Security and opportunity for the twenty-first century', *Foreign Affairs*, 86(6), November/December, 2–18.

Clinton, Hillary (2012) 'Leading through Civilian Power', in J. McMcormick (ed) *The Domestic Sources of American Foreign Policy*, Lanham, MD: Rowman & Littlefield.

Coates, Ta-Nehisi (2015) *Between the World and Me*, New York: Spiegel & Grau.

Cobbs, Elizabeth (1996) 'Decolonization, the Cold War, and the foreign policy of the Peace Corps', *Diplomatic History*, 20(1), Winter, 79–105.

Cohen, Bernard (1957) *The Political Process and Foreign Policy*, Princeton, NJ: Princeton University Press.

Colaresi, Michael (2014) *Democracy Declassified: The Secrecy Dilemma in National Security*, Oxford: Oxford University Press.

Converse, Philip (1964) 'The nature of belief systems in mass publics', *Critical Review*, 18, 1–74.

Costigliala, Frank (2012) *Roosevelt's Lost Alliances: How Personal Politics Helped Start the Cold War*, Princeton, NJ: Princeton University Press.

Cotton, Timothy (1986) 'War and American democracy: Electoral costs of the last five wars', *Journal of Conflict Resolution*, 30(4), December, 616–35.

Cox, Michael and Doug Stokes (2012) 'Introduction', in M. Cox and D. Stokes (eds) *US Foreign Policy* (2nd edn), Oxford: Oxford University Press.

Cox, Robert W. (1987) *Production, Power and World Order: Social Forces in the Making of History*, New York: Columbia University Press.

Cox, Robert W. (2002) 'Reflections and Transitions', in R. Cox and M. Schechter (eds) *The Political Economy of a Plural World*, London: Routledge.

Curran, James, Shanto Iyengar and Anker Brink Lund (2009) 'Media system, public knowledge, and democracy', *European Journal of Communication*, 24(1), 5–26.

Cushing, Lincoln (2011) 'San Francisco Bay Area Posters, 1968–1978', in C. Carlsson (ed) *Ten Years that Shook the City*, San Francisco, CA: City Light Books.

Daalder, Ivo and James Lindsay (2005) *America Unbound: The Bush Revolution in Foreign Policy*, New York: Wiley.

Dahl, Robert (1950) *Congress and Foreign Policy*, New York: Harcourt.

Dahl, Robert (2003) *How Democratic Is the American Constitution?*, New Haven, CT: Yale University Press.

Dark, Taylor (1999) *The Unions and the Democrats: An Enduring Alliance*, Ithaca, NY: Cornell University Press.

Davidson, Helen (2020) 'Hong Kong activist Joshua Wong jailed for 13 and a half months over protest', *The Guardian*, 2 December.

Davis, Nancy and Robert Robinson (1996) 'Are rumors of the war exaggerated?', *The American Journal of Sociology*, 102(3), 756–87.

Davis, Vincent (1967) *The Admirals Lobby*, Chapel Hill, NC: University of North Carolina Press.

Dawson, Michael (1994) *Behind the Mule: Race and Class in African American Politics*, Princeton, NJ: Princeton University Press.

De Conde, Alexander (1971) *Half Bitter, Half Sweet: An Excursion into Italian American History*, New York: Charles Scribner's Sons.

Deering, Christopher (2005) 'Foreign Policy and War', in P. Quirk and S. Binder (eds) *The Legislative Branch*, Oxford: Oxford University Press.

Department of Defense (1997) 'Selected Manpower Statistics', Directorate for Information Operations and Reports, Table 2.13. www.alternatewards.com/BBOW/Stats/DOD_SelectedStats_FY97.pdf

Desch, Michael (2007) 'America's liberal illiberalism: The ideological origins of overreaction in US foreign policy', *International Security*, 32(3), Winter, 7–45.

Desilver, Drew (2014) '5 facts about Indian Americans', Pew Research Center, 30 September. Available at: www.pewresearch.org/fact-tank/2014/09/30/5-facts-about-indian-americans/

Deudney, Daniel and G. John Ikenberry (2017) 'Realism, liberalism, and the Iraq War', *Survival*, 59(4), 7–26.

Deudney, Daniel and Jeffrey Meiser (2012) 'American Exceptionalism', in M. Cox and D. Stokes (eds) *US Foreign Policy* (2nd edn), Oxford: Oxford University Press.

Dewey, John (1954 [1927]) *The Public and Its Problems: An Essay in Political Inquiry*, University Park, PA: Pennsylvania State University Press.

Dickinson, G. Lowes (1916) *The European Anarchy*, New York: Macmillan.

Dickson, Maxcy (1942) 'The food administration: Educator', *Agricultural History*, 16(2), April, 91–6.

Dinlersoz, Emin and Jeremy Greenwood (2016) 'The rise and fall of unions in the United States', *Journal of Monetary Economics*, 83, October, 129–46.

Dione, E.J. (2003) 'Inevitably, the politics of terror', *The Washington Post*, 25 May.

Divine, Robert (1974) *Foreign Policy and US Presidential Elections*, New York: New Viewpoints.

Dodge, Toby (2010) 'The ideological roots of failure: The application of kinetic neo-liberalism to Iraq', 86(6), November, 1269–86.

Doherty, Brendan (2012) *The Rise of the President's Permanent Campaign*, Lawrence, KS: University of Kansas Press.

Domhoff, G. William (2015) 'Is the corporate elite fractured, or is there continuing corporate dominance?', *Class, Race, and Corporate Power*, 3(1), 1–42.

Doyle, Michael (1990) 'Thucydidean realism', *Review of International Studies*, 16(3), 223–37.

Doyle, Michael (2005) 'Three pillars of democratic peace', *American Political Science Review*, 99(3), August, 463–6.

Drezner, Daniel (2018) 'Thank you, Jimmy Carter', *Foreign Policy*, July.

Du Bois, W.E.B. (1915) 'The African roots of war', *The Atlantic Monthly*, 115(May), 707–14.

Du Bois, W.E.B. (1946) *The World and Africa: An Inquiry into the Part which Africa Has Played in World History*, New York: International Publishers.

Dudziak, Mary (2000) *Cold War Civil Rights: Race and the Image of American Democracy*, Princeton, NJ: Princeton University Press.

Dueck, Colin (2006) *Reluctant Crusaders: Power, Culture, and Change in American Grand Strategy*, Princeton, NJ: Princeton University Press.

Dueck, Colin (2015) *The Obama Doctrine: American Grand Strategy Today*, Oxford: Oxford University Press.

Duffin, Erin (2021) 'Percentage of educational attainment in the United States in 2018, by ethnicity', Statista, 8 January. Available at: www.statista.com/statistics/184264/educational-attainment-by-enthnicity/

Dunkerley, James (2017) 'Introduction: Thinking about America in the World in the Longer Run', in J.-F. Drolet and J. Dunkerley (eds) *American Foreign Policy: Studies in Intellectual History*, Manchester: Manchester University Press.

Dunn, David (2005) 'Isolationism revisited: Seven persistent myths in the contemporary American foreign policy debate', *Review of International Studies*, 31, 237–61.

Eckel, Mike (2016) 'Russian "gun for hire" lurks in shadows of Washington's lobbying world', RadioFreeEurope, RadioLiberty, 17 July. Available at: www.rferl.org/a/rinat-akmetshin-russia-gun-for-hire-washington-lobbying-magnitsky-browder/27863265.html

Edozien, Frankie (2001) 'Fuming Schumer: Yasser = Taliban', *The New York Post*, 3 December.

Edsall, Thomas (1985) *The New Politics of Inequality*, New York: Norton.

Edwards, George (2003) *On Deaf Ears: The Limits of the Bully Pulpit*, New Haven, CT: Yale University Press.

Emerson, Michael and J. Russell Hawkins (2007) 'Viewed in Black and White', in M. Noll and L. Harlow (eds) *Religion and American Politics* (2nd edn), Oxford: Oxford University Press.

Engerman, David (2004) 'The romance of economic development and new histories of the Cold War', *Diplomatic History*, 28(1), January, 23–54.

Ernst, John (1998) *Forging a Fateful Alliance: Michigan State University and the Vietnam War*, East Lansing, MI: Michigan State University Press.

Ettinger, Aaron (2019) 'Principled realism and populist sovereignty in Trump's foreign policy', *Cambridge Review of International Affairs*, 33, 410–31.

Evans, Peter, Dietrich Rueschemeyer and Theda Skocpol (eds) (1985) *Bringing the State Back In*, Cambridge: Cambridge University Press.

Eze, Emmanuel (1995) 'The Color of Reason', in K. Faull (ed) *Anthropology and the German Enlightenment*, Lewisburg, PA: Bucknell University Press.

Fabbrini, Sergio (1999) 'American democracy from a European perspective', *Annual Review of Political Science*, 2, 465–91.

Falaky, Faycal (2014) 'A foresaken and foreclosed utopia: Rousseau and international relations', *European Journal of Political Theory*, 15(1), 61–76.

Fall, Bernard (1961) *Street without Joy: Indochina at War, 1946–54*, Harrisburg, PA: Stackpole Co.

Farkas, Johan and Jannick Schou (2019) *Post-Truth, Fake News, and Democracy: Mapping the Politics of Falsehood*, London: Taylor & Francis.

Fatton, Robert (1984) 'The Reagan foreign policy toward South Africa: The ideology of the new Cold War', *African Studies Review*, 27(1), 57–82.

Ferguson, Niall (2004) *Colossus: The Price of America's Empire*, New York: Penguin Press.

Finnemore, Martha (1996) *National Interests in International Society*, Ithaca, NY: Cornell University Press.

Fleisher, Richard, Jon R. Bond, Glen S. Krutz and Stephen Hanna (2000) 'The demise of the two presidencies', *American Politics Research*, 28(1), 3–25.

Foner, Philip (1984) *US Labor and the Vietnam War*, New York: International Publishers.

Forde, Steven (1995) 'International realism and the science of politics: Thucydides, Machiavelli, and neorealism', *International Studies Quarterly*, 39(2), June, 141–60.

Form, William (1995) *Segmented Labor, Fractured Politics: Labor Politics in American Life*, New York: Plenum Press.

Forsythe, David and Patrice McMahon (2016) *American Exceptionalism Reconsidered: US Foreign Policy, Human Rights, and World Order*, New York: Routledge.

Fowler, Linda (2015) *Watchdogs on the Hill: The Decline of Congressional Oversight of US Foreign Relations*, Princeton, NJ: Princeton University Press.

Fox, Cybelle and Thomas Guglielmo (2012) 'Defining America's racial boundaries: Blacks, Mexicans, and European immigrants', *American Journal of Sociology*, 118(2), 327–79.

Frank, Andre (1971) 'On the Mechanisms of Imperialism', in K. Fann and D. Hodges (eds) *Readings in US Imperialism*, Boston, MA: Porter Sargeant.

Franke, Mark (2001) *Global Limits: Immanuel Kant, International Relations, and Critique of World Politics*, Albany, NY: State University of New York Press.

Franklin, John Hope (1993) *The Color Line: Legacy for the Twenty-First Century*, Columbia, MO: University of Missouri Press.

Fraser, Cary (2000) 'Crossing the color line in Little Rock: The Eisenhower administration and the dilemma of race for US foreign policy', *Diplomatic History*, 24(2), April, 233–64.

Fredrickson, George M. (2002) *Racism: A Short History*, Princeton, NJ: Princeton University Press.

Freedman, Lawrence (2005) 'The age of liberal wars', *Review of International Studies*, 31, December, 93–107.

Freeman, J. Leiper (1955) *The Political Process: Executive Bureau–Legislative Committee Relations*, New York: Random House.

Friedberg, Aaron (2000) *In the Shadow of the Garrison State: America's Anti-Statism and Its Cold War Strategy*, Princeton, NJ: Princeton University Press.

Friedberg, Aaron (2011) *A Contest for Supremacy: China, America, and the Struggle for Mastery in Asia*, New York: W.W. Norton.

Friedberg, Aaron (2012) 'Bucking Beijing: An alternative US China policy', *Foreign Affairs*, 91(5), 48–58.

Friedberg, Aaron (2020) 'An answer to aggression: How to push back against Beijing', *Foreign Affairs*, September/October.

Friedman, Thomas (1999) *The Lexus and the Olive Tree: Understanding Globalization*, New York: Farrar, Straus & Giroux.

Frymer, Paul (2017) *Building an American Empire: The Era of Territorial and Political Expansion*, Princeton, NJ: Princeton University Press.

Fukuyama, Francis (1989) 'The end of history?', *The National Interest*, 16, Summer, 3–18.

Fukuyama, Francis (1992) *The End of History and the Last Man*, New York: Free Press.

Fullam, Kevin and Alan Gitelson (2009) 'A Lasting Republican Majority? George W. Bush's Electoral Strategy', in A. Wroe and J. Herbert (eds) *Assessing the George W. Bush Presidency*, Edinburgh: Edinburgh University Press.

Fullmer, Elliott (2015) 'Early voting: Do more sites lead to higher turnout?', *Election Law Journal*, 14(2), 81–96.

Gaddis, John Lewis (2005 [1982]) *Strategies of Containment: A Critical Appraisal of American National Security Policy During the Cold War* (2nd edn), Oxford: Oxford University Press.

Gartner, Scott and Gary Segura (2008) 'All politics is still local: The Iraq War and the 2006 midterm elections', *PS: Political Science & Politics*, 41(1), January, 95–100.

Gartner, Scott, Gary Segura and Bethany Barratt (2004) 'War casualties, policy positions, and the fate of legislators', *Political Research Quarterly*, 57(3), September, 467–77.

Garton Ash, Timothy (1993) *In Europe's Name: Germany and the Divided Continent*, New York: Random House.

Gates, E. Nathaniel (ed) (1998) *Race and US Foreign Policy from 1900 through World War II*, New York: Routledge.

Gerber, Larry (1997) 'Shifting perspectives on American exceptionalism: Recent literature on American labor relations and labor politics', *Journal of American Studies*, 31(2), August, 253–74.

Gerstle, Gary (2015) *Liberty and Coercion: The Paradox of American Government, from the Founding to the Present*, Princeton, NJ: Princeton University Press.

Geselbracht, Raymond (ed) (2019 [1955]) *The Memoirs of Harry S. Truman: A Reader's Edition*, Columbia, MO: University of Missouri Press.

Gettelfinger, Ron (no date) 'Proposed US–Korea Treaty has many holes', Reliable Plant. Available at: www.reliableplant.com/Read/5767/viewpoint-proposed-us-korea-treaty-has-many-holes

Gibbs, Jessica (2010) 'The Cuba Lobby and US Policy Toward Cuba', in A. Johnstone and H. Laville (eds) *The US Public and American Foreign Policy*, London: Routledge.

Gibson, Edward and Desmond King (2016) 'Federalism and Subnational Democratization in the United States', in J. Behrend and L. Whitehead (eds) *Illiberal Practices: Territorial Variance within Large Federal Democracies*, Baltimore, MD: Johns Hopkins University Press.

Gilens, Martin and Benjamin Page (2014) 'Testing theories of American politics: Elites, interest groups, and average citizens', *Perspectives on Politics*, 12(3), 564–81.

Gingrich, Newt (2011) *A Nation Like No Other: Why American Exceptionalism Matters*, New York: Simon & Schuster.

Giroux, Henry (2007) *The University in Chains: Confronting the Military-Industrial-Academic Complex*, Boulder, CO: Paradigm Publishers.

Glaser, Charles (1997) 'The security dilemma revisited', *World Politics*, 50(1), October, 171–201.

Global Times (2016) 'Candidates will embrace pragmatism over populism', 16 March.

Goh, Evelyn (2005) *Meeting the China Challenge*, Washington, DC: East–West Center.

Goldfield, Michael (1987) *The Decline of Organized Labor in the United States*, Chicago, IL: University of Chicago Press.

Golub, Grant (2020) 'History exposes the problem with Biden's Defense Secretary nominee: Civilian control over the military is no given', *The Washington Post*, 17 December.

Gonzalez, Francisco and Desmond King (2004) 'The state and democratization: The United States in comparative perspective', *British Journal of Political Science*, 34(2), 193–210.

Goulden, Joseph (1969) *Truth is the First Casualty: The Gulf of Tonkin Affair*, Chicago, IL: Rand McNally.

Graham, Thomas (1994) 'Public Opinion and US Foreign Policy Decision Making', in D. Deese (ed) *The New Politics of American Foreign Policy*, New York: St Martin's Press.

Grann, David (2017) *Killers of the Flower Moon: The Osage Murders and the Birth of the FBI*, New York: Doubleday.

Grant, Colin (2008) *Negro with a Hat: The Rise and Fall of Marcus Garvey*, London: Jonathan Cape.

Grant, Nicholas (2017) *Winning Our Freedoms Together: African Americans and Apartheid, 1945–1960*, Chapel Hill, NC: University of North Carolina Press.

Gray, Rosie (2017) 'Bill Browder's testimony to the Senate Judiciary Committee', *The Atlantic*, 25 July. Available at: www.theatlantic.com/politics/archive/2017/07/bill-browders-testimony-to-the-senate-judiciary-committee/534864/

Grieco, Joseph (1997) 'Realist International Theory and the Study of World Politics', in M. Doyle and J. Ikenberry (eds) *New Thinking in International Relations Theory*, Boulder, CO: Westview Press.

Grieco, Joseph, R. Powell and Duncan Snidal (1993) 'The relative-gains problem for international cooperation', *American Political Science Review*, 87(3), 727–43.

Grose, Christian and Bruce Oppenheimer (2007) 'The Iraq War, partisanship, and candidate attributes: Variation in partisan swing in the 2006 US House elections', *Legislative Studies Quarterly*, 32(4), 531–57.

Gross, Ariela (2008) *What Blood Won't Tell: A History of Race on Trial in America*, Cambridge, MA: Harvard University Press.

Guelke, Adrian (1996) 'The United States, Irish Americans, and the Northern Ireland peace process', *International Affairs*, 72(3), July, 521–36.

Haas, Lawrence (2016) *Harry and Arthur: Truman, Vandenberg, and the Partnership that Created the Free World*, Omaha, NE: University of Nebraska Press.

Hacker, Jacob and Paul Pierson (2010) 'Winner-take-all politics: Public policy, political organization, and the precipitous rise of top incomes in the United States', *Politics & Society*, 38(2), 152–204.

Hacker, Jacob and Paul Pierson (2020) *Let Them Eat Tweets: How the Right Rules in an Age of Extreme Inequality*, New York: Norton.

Hagee, John (2007) *In Defense of Israel*, Lake Mary, FL: FrontLine.

Halberstam, David (1972) *The Best and the Brightest*, New York: Random House.

Halbfinger, David M. (2020) 'For Netanyahu, Trump's gifts kept on coming', *The New York Times*, 21 November.

Hall Kindervater, Katharine (2017) 'Drone strikes, ephemeral sovereignty, and changing conceptions of territory', *Territory, Politics, Governance*, 5(2), 207–21.

Haney, Patrick (2002) *Organizing for Foreign Policy Crises*, Ann Arbor, MI: University of Michigan Press.

Haney, Patrick and Walt Vanderbush (1999) 'The role of ethnic interest groups in US foreign policy: The case of the Cuban American National Foundation', *International Studies Quarterly*, 43(2), June, 341–61.

Haney, Patrick and Walt Vanderbush (2008) 'The Helms–Burton Act: Congress and Cuba Policy', in R. Carter (ed) *Contemporary Cases in US Foreign Policy: From Terrorism to Trade*, Washington, DC: CQ Press.

Haney Lopez, Ian (2000) *White by Law: The Legal Construction of Race*, New York: New York University Press.

Harrison, Ewan (2002) 'Waltz, Kant, and systemic approaches to international relations', *Review of International Studies*, 28(1), January, 143–62.

Hartford Courant (2004) 'Workers and war', 4 September.

Hartung, William (2010) *Prophets of War: Lockheed Martin and the Making of the Military-Industrial Complex*, New York: Nation Books.

Hartz, Louis (1955) *The Liberal Tradition in America: An Interpretation of American Political Thought*, New York: Harcourt Brace & Co.

Heater, Derek (1994) *National Self-Determination: Woodrow Wilson and His Legacy*, Basingstoke: Macmillan.

Heer, Jeet (2018) 'Trump's disdain for democracy promotion', *New Republic*, 6 March.

Heer, Jeet (2020) 'At liberalism's crossroads', *The Nation*, 6 October.

Heinze, Eric (2008) 'The new utopianism: Liberalism, American foreign policy, and the War in Iraq', *Journal of International Political Theory*, 4(1), 105–25.

Henderson, Errol (2013) 'Hidden in plain sight: Racism in international relations theory', *Cambridge Review of International Affairs*, 26(1), 71–92.

Henderson, Errol (2017) 'The revolution will not be theorised: Du Bois, Locke, and the Howard School's challenge to White supremacist IR theory', *Millennium*, 45(3), 492–510.

Hendrickson, Ryan (2015) *Obama at War: Congress and the Imperial Presidency*, Lexington, KY: University of Kentucky Press.

Herbert, Jon (2011) 'The toxic presidency of George W. Bush', *Representation*, 47(3), 265–80.

Herken, Gregg (1988) *The Winning Weapon: The Atomic Bomb in the Cold War, 1945–1950*, Princeton, NJ: Princeton University Press.

Herring, George (1987) 'The Executive, Congress, and the Vietnam War, 1965–1975', in M. Barnart (ed) *Congress and United States Foreign Policy*, Albany, NY: State University of New York Press.

Hersh, Eitan and Brian Schaffner (2016) 'The GOP's Jewish donors are abandoning Trump', FiveThirtyEight, 21 September. Available at: https://fivethirtyeight.com/features/the-gops-jewish-donors-are-abandoning-trump/

Hertel-Fernandez, Alexander, Theda Skocpol and Jason Sclar (2018) 'When political mega-donors join forces: How the Koch Network and the Democracy Alliance influence organized US politics on the right and left', *Studies in American Political Development*, 32, October, 127–65.

Heumann, Stefan (2011) 'State, nation, and empire: The formation of the US', *Journal of Political Power*, 4(3), 375–93.

Hibbs, Douglas (2000) 'Bread and peace voting in US elections', *Public Choice*, 104, 149–80.

Hinckley, Barbara (1994) *Less than Meets the Eye: Foreign Policy Making and the Myth of the Assertive Congress*, Chicago, IL: University of Chicago Press.

History in Pieces (no date) 'US military personnel 1954–2014.' Available at: https://historyinpieces.com/research/us-military-personnel-1954-2014

Hodgson, Godfrey (2010) *The Myth of American Exceptionalism*, New Haven, CT: Yale University Press.

Hoetink, Harry (1967) *The Two Variants of Caribbean Race Relations*, Oxford: Oxford University Press.

Hoffmann, Stanley (1963) 'Rousseau on war and peace', *American Political Science Review*, 57(2), June, 317–33.

Hofstadter, Richard (1948) *The American Political Tradition and the Men Who Made It*, New York: Alfred A. Knopf.

Hofstadter, Richard (1960) *The Idea of a Party System: The Rise of Legitimate Opposition in the United States, 1780–1840*, Berkeley, CA: University of California Press.

Hogan, Michael (1998) *A Cross of Iron: Harry S. Truman and the Origins of the National Security State, 1945–54*, Cambridge: Cambridge University Press.

Holmes, Oliver (2020) 'Will Trump's major foreign policy legacy be Israel and Palestine?', *The Guardian*, 19 November.

Hoock, Holger (2017) *Scars of Independence: America's Violent Birth*, New York: Crown Publishing Group.

Hopkins, Daniel (2018) *The Increasingly United States: How and Why American Political Behavior Nationalized*, Chicago, IL: University of Chicago Press.

Horne, Gerald (2001) *From the Barrel of a Gun: The United States and the War Against Zimbabwe, 1965–1980*, Chapel Hill, NC: University of North Carolina Press.

Horwitz, Tony (2014) 'The horrific Sand Creek massacre will be forgotten no more', *Smithsonian Magazine*, December. Available at: www.smithsonianmag.com/history/horrific-sand-creek-massacre-will-be-forgotten-no-more-180953403/

Howard, Michael (2002) 'What's in a name? How to fight terrorism', *Foreign Affairs*, 81(1), 8–13.

Howe, Irving (1985 [1977]) *Socialism and America*, Fort Washington, PA: Harvest Books.

Howell, William (2003) *Power without Persuasion: The Politics of Presidential Direct Action*, Princeton, NJ: Princeton University Press.

Howell, William (2013) *Thinking about the Presidency: The Primacy of Power*, Princeton, NJ: Princeton University Press.

Howell, William and Jon Pevehouse (2005) 'Presidents, Congress, and the use of force', *International Organization*, 59(1), 209–32.

Hughes, Thomas (2004) *Human-Built World: How to Think about Technology and Culture*, Chicago, IL: University of Chicago Press.

Hunt, Michael (2009) *Ideology and US Foreign Policy* (Revised edn), New Haven, CT: Yale University Press.

Huntington, Samuel P. (1981) *American Politics: The Promise of Disharmony*, Cambridge, MA: Belknap Press of Harvard University Press.

Hurrell, Andrew (1990) 'Kant and the Kantian paradigm in international relations', *Review of International Studies*, 16(3), July, 183–205.

Hurwitz, Jon and Mark Peffley (1987) 'How are foreign policy attitudes structured? A hierarchical model', *American Political Science Review*, 81(4), December, 1099–120.

Hutchinson, William (1987) *Errand to the World: American Protestant Thought and Foreign Missions*, Chicago, IL: University of Chicago Press.

Ignatiev, Noel (1995) *How the Irish Became White*, New York: Routledge.

Ikenberry, G. John (2001) *After Victory: Institutions, Strategic Restraint, and the Rebuilding of Order after Major Wars*, Princeton, NJ: Princeton University Press.

Ikenberry, G. John (2004a) 'Illusions of empire: Defining the new American order', *Foreign Affairs*, March/April, 83(2), 144–54.

Ikenberry, G. John (2004b) 'Liberalism and empire: Logics of order in the American unipolar age', *Review of International Studies*, 30, 609–30.

Ikenberry, G. John (2009) 'Liberal internationalism 3.0: America and the dilemmas of liberal world order', *Perspectives on Politics*, 7(1), March, 71–87.

Ikenberry, G. John (2011) *Liberal Leviathan: The Origins, Crisis, and Transformation of the American World Order*, Princeton, NJ: Princeton University Press.

Ikenberry, G. John (2018) 'The end of the liberal international order?', *International Affairs*, 94(1), January, 7–23.

Immerwahr, Daniel (2019) *How to Hide an Empire: A Short History of the Greater United States*, London: Vintage.

Isaac, Joel (2007) 'The human sciences in Cold War America', *The Historical Journal*, 50(3), 725–46.

Ismay, Hastings (1960) *The Memoirs of Lord Ismay*, New York: Viking Press.

Jackson, Robert, Georg Sørensen and Jørgen Møller (2016) *Introduction to International Relations: Theories and Approaches* (7th edn), Oxford: Oxford University Press.

Jacobs, Frank (2013) 'Where do babies come from?', *Foreign Policy*, 11 January.

Jacobs, Lawrence and James Druckman (2011) 'Segmented Representation', in P. Enns and C. Wlezien (eds) *Who Gets Represented?*, New York: Russell Sage.

Jacobs, Lawrence and Benjamin Page (2005) 'Who influences US foreign policy?', *American Political Science Review*, 99(1), February, 107–23.

Jacobs, Lawrence and Benjamin Page (2011) 'Business Versus Public Influence in US Foreign Policy', in G. Ikenberry (ed) *American Foreign Policy: Theoretical Essays* (6th edn), New York: Oxford University Press.

Jacobs, Nicholas and Sidney Milkis (2020) 'Donald Trump, the Republican Party, and Executive-Centered Partisanship', Paper presented at the Annual Meeting of the American Political Science Association, 10–13 September.

Jacobson, Matthew (1995) *Special Sorrows: The Diasporic Imagination of Irish, Polish, and Jewish Immigrants in the United States*, Cambridge, MA: Harvard University Press.

Jacobson, Matthew (1998) *Whiteness of a Different Color: European Immigrants and the Alchemy of Race*, Cambridge, MA: Harvard University Press.

Jakes, Lara and David M. Halbfinger (2019) 'In shift, US says Israeli settlements in West Bank do not violate international law', *The New York Times*, 18 November.

James, Scott (2005) 'The evolution of the presidency', *Institutions of American Democracy*, 3–40.

Janis, Irving (1972) *Victims of Groupthink: A Psychological Study of Foreign-Policy Decisions and Fiascos*, New York: Houghton Mifflin.

Janken, Kenneth (1998) 'From colonial liberation to Cold War liberalism: Walter White, the NAACP, and foreign affairs, 1941–1955', *Ethnic and Racial Studies*.

Jeffreys-Jones, Rhodri (2010) 'Organized Labor and the Social Foundations of American Diplomacy, 1898–1920', in A. Johnstone and H. Laville (eds) *The US Public and American Foreign Policy*, London: Routledge.

Jervis, Robert (1978) 'Cooperation under the security dilemma', *World Politics*, 30(2), January, 167–214.

Johnson, Chalmers (2004) *The Sorrows of Empire: Militarism, Secrecy, and the End of the Republic*, New York: Metropolitan Books.

Johnson, Kimberley (2007) *Governing the American State: Congress and the New Federalism, 1877–1929*, Princeton, NJ: Princeton University Press.

Johnson, Loch (2008) 'The Church Committee investigation of 1975 and the evolution of modern intelligence accountability', *Intelligence and National Security*, 23(2), April, 198–225.

Johnson, Richard (2017) 'Hamilton's deracialization: Barack Obama's racial politics in context', *Du Bois Review*, 14(2), Fall, 621–38.

Johnson, Richard (2020a) 'Low-Resource Candidates and Fundraising Appeals', in E. Suhay, B. Grofman and A. Trechsel (eds) *The Oxford Handbook of Electoral Persuasion*, Oxford: Oxford University Press.

Johnson, Richard (2020b) *The End of the Second Reconstruction*, Cambridge: Polity Press.

Johnson, Robert (2006) *Congress and the Cold War*, Cambridge: Cambridge University Press.

Johnstone, Andrew and Helen Laville (eds) (2010) *The US Public and American Foreign Policy*, London: Routledge.

Johnstone, Andrew and Andrew Priest (2017a) 'Introduction', in A. Johnstone and A. Priest (eds) *US Presidential Elections and Foreign Policy*, Lexington, KY: University of Kentucky Press.

Johnstone, Andrew and Andrew Priest (eds) (2017b) *US Presidential Elections and Foreign Policy*, Lexington, KY: University of Kentucky Press.

Jones, Charles (1994) *The Presidency in a Separated System*, Washington, DC: Brookings Institution.

Jones, Kenneth (1982) 'The Government-Science Complex', in R. Bremner and G. Reichard (eds) *Reshaping America: Society and Institutions, 1945–60*, Columbus, OH: Ohio State University Press.

Kagan, Frederick W. (2011) *Choosing Victory: A Plan for Success in Iraq, Phase I Report*, A Report of the Iraq Planning Group at the American Enterprise Institute. Available at: www.aei.org/wp-content/uploads/2011/11/20070111_ChoosingVictoryupdated.pdf?x88519

Kammen, Michael (1972) *People of Paradox*, New York: Alfred Knopf.

Karol, David and Edward Miguel (2007) 'The electoral cost of war: Iraq casualties and the 2004 US presidential election', *Journal of Politics*, 69(3), 633–48.

Katzenstein, Peter (1996) *The Culture of National Security: Norms and Identity of World Politics*, New York: Columbia University Press.

Kazmi, Zaheer (2019) 'Contesting the State of Nature: Anarchism and International Relations', in C. Levy and S. Newman (eds) *The Anarchist Imagination*, New York: Routledge.

Kelly, George Armstrong (1992) *The Humane Comedy: Constant, Tocqueville, and French Liberalism*, Cambridge: Cambridge University Press.

Kennan, George (1951) *American Diplomacy, 1900–1950*, Chicago, IL: University of Chicago Press.

Kennedy, Stetson (1990) *Jim Crow Guide to the USA*, Tuscaloosa, AL: University of Alabama Press.

Kernell, Samuel (1986) *Going Public: New Strategies of Presidential Leadership*, Washington, DC: Congressional Quarterly Press.

Khong, Yuen Foong (1992) *Analogies at War*, Princeton, NJ: Princeton University Press.

Khong, Yuen Foong (2014) 'Primacy or world order? The United States and China's rise', *International Security*, 38(3), 153–75.

Kim, Claire (1999) *Bitter Fruit: The Politics of Black-Korean Conflict in New York*, New Haven, CT: Yale University Press.

Kindleberger, Charles (1989) 'Commercial Policy Between the Wars', in P. Matthias and S. Pollard (eds) *The Cambridge Economic History of Europe*, vol 8, Cambridge: Cambridge University Press.

King, Bob (2011) 'UAW backs Korea trade agreement', The USTR Archives, October. Available at: https://ustr.gov/about-us/policy-offices/press-office/blog/2011/october/uaw-backs-korea-trade-agreement

King, Desmond S. (2000) *Making Americans: Immigration, Race, and the Origins of Diverse Democracy*, Cambridge, MA: Harvard University Press.

King, Desmond S. (2005) *The Liberty of Strangers: Making the American Nation*, Oxford: Oxford University Press.

King, Desmond S. (2007 [1995]) *Separate and Unequal: Black Americans and the US Federal Government*, Oxford: Oxford University Press.

King, Desmond S. and Rogers M. Smith (2005) 'Racial orders in American political development', *American Political Science Review*, 99(1), 75–92.

Kinsella, David (2005) 'No rest for democratic peace', *American Political Science Review*, 99(3), August, 453–7.

Kissinger, Henry (2003) *Ending the Vietnam War: A History of America's Involvement in and Extrication from the Vietnam War*, New York: Simon & Schuster.

Klein, Morton A. (2009) 'ZOA to President Obama: Don't appoint anti-Israel, pro-Arab lobbyist Chas Freeman to head National Intelligence Council', Zionist Organization of America (ZOA), 25 February. Available at: https://zoa.org/2009/02/102383-zoa-to-president-obama-dont-appoint-anti-israel-pro-arab-lobbyist-chas-freeman-to-head-national-intelligence-council/

Knutsen, Torbjorn (1994) 'Re-reading Rousseau in the post-Cold War World', *Journal of Peace Research*, 31(3), 247–62.

Kotz, Nick (1988) *Wild Blue Yonder: Money, Politics, and the B-1 Bomber*, New York: Pantheon Books.

Kraig, Robert (2002) 'The tragic science: The uses of Jimmy Carter in foreign policy realism', *Rhetoric & Public Affairs*, 5(1), Spring, 1–30.

Krasner, Stephen (1978) *Defending the National Interest: Raw Materials Investments and US Foreign Policy*, Princeton, NJ: Princeton University Press.

Krenn, Michael (1999) *Black Diplomacy: African Americans and the State Department, 1945–1969*, Armonk, NY: M.E. Sharpe.

Kriner, Douglas (2010) *After the Rubicon: Congress, Presidents, and the Politics of Waging War*, Chicago, IL: University of Chicago Press.

Kriner, Douglas and Francis Shen (2016) 'Invisible inequality: The two Americas of military sacrifice', *Memphis Law Review*, 46, 545–635.

Kriner, Douglas and Francis Shen (2020) 'Battlefield casualties and ballot-box defeat: Did the Bush–Obama wars cost Clinton the White House?', *PS: Political Science & Politics*, 53(2), 248–52.

Kuo, Lily and Verna Yu (2020) 'Controversial Hong Kong national security law comes into effect', *The Guardian*, 30 June.

Kuzmarov, Jeremy (2012) *Modernizing Repression: Police Training and Nation Building in the American Century*, Amherst, MA: University of Massachusetts Press.

Laffey, Mark and Jutta Weldes (2008) 'Decolonizing the Cuban Missile Crisis', *International Studies Quarterly*, 52(3), 555–77.

Lake, Anthony (1976) *The Tar Baby Option: American Policy Toward Southern Rhodesia*, New York: Columbia University Press.

Landler, Mark and David M. Halbfinger (2017) 'US to recognize Jerusalem as Israel's capital', *The New York Times*, 5 December.

Landler, Mark and David M. Halbfinger (2019) 'Trump, with Netanyahu, formally recognizes Israel's authority over Golan Heights', *The New York Times*, 25 March.

Layne, Christopher (1994) 'Kant or Cant: The myth of democratic peace', *International Security*, 19(2), Fall, 5–49.

Leahy, William (1950) *I Was There*, New York: Whittlesey House.

Lebergott, Stanley (1957) 'Annual Estimates of Unemployment in the United States, 1900–1954', Table 1: Bureau of the Budget, in National Bureau of Economic Research, *The Measurement and Behavior of Unemployment*, NBER. Available at: www.nber.org/system/files/chapters/c2644/c2644.pdf

Ledbetter, James (2011) *Unwarranted Influence: Dwight D. Eisenhower and the Military-Industrial Complex*, New Haven, CT: Yale University Press.

Ledwidge, Mark (2012) *Race and US Foreign Policy: The African-American Foreign Affairs Network*, London: Routledge.

Lenin, V.I. (1917 [2010]) *Imperialism: The Highest Stage of Capitalism*, New York: Penguin Classics.

Lens, Sidney (1959) *The Crisis of American Labor*, Champaign, IL: Sagamore Press.

LeoGrande, William (2013) 'The Cuba Lobby', *Foreign Policy*, April.

Leslie, Stuart (1993) *The Cold War and American Sciences: The Military-Industrial-Academic Complex at MIT and Stanford*, New York: Columbia University Press.

Levendusky, Matthew (2009) *The Partisan Sort: How Liberals Became Democrats and Conservatives Became Republicans*, Chicago, IL: University of Chicago Press.

Levi, Margaret (2002) 'The State of the Study of the State', in I. Katznelson and H. Milner (eds) *Political Science: State of the Discipline*, New York: W.W. Norton & Company.

Lewis, David (1997) 'The two rhetorical presidencies: An analysis of televised presidential speeches, 1947–1991', *American Politics Quarterly*, 25(3), 380–95.

Lewontin, Richard (1997) 'The Cold War and the Transformation of the Academy', in N. Chomsky (ed) *The Cold War and the University*, New York: New Press.

Lieber, Keir and Daryl Press (2006) 'The end of MAD? The nuclear dimension of US primacy', *International Security*, 30(4), 7–44.

Lieberfeld, Daniel (2005) 'Theories of conflict and the Iraq War', *International Journal of Peace Studies*, 10(2), Autumn/Winter, 1–21.

Lieberman, Robert (2009) 'The Israel Lobby and American politics', *Perspectives on Politics*, 7(2), 235–57.

Lieven, Anatol (2005) *America Right or Wrong: An Anatomy of American Nationalism*, London: HarperCollins.

Lieven, Anatol (2012) *America Right or Wrong: An Anatomy of American Nationalism* (2nd edn), Oxford: Oxford University Press.

Lijphart, Arend (1997) 'Unequal participation: Democracy's unresolved dilemma', *American Political Science Review*, 91(1), 1–14.

Lindsay, James (2012) 'The Shifting Pendulum of Power: Executive-Legislative Relations on American Foreign Policy', in J. McCormick (ed) *The Domestic Sources of US Foreign Policy* (6th edn), Lanham, MD: Rowman & Littlefield.

Lippmann, Walter (1920) *Liberty and the News*, Princeton, NJ: Princeton University Press.

Lippmann, Walter (1922) *Public Opinion*, New York: Harcourt, Brace, & Company.

Lippmann, Walter (1925) *The Phantom Public*, Piscataway, NJ: Transaction Publishers.

Lippmann, Walter (1955) *The Public Philosophy*, Boston: Little, Brown, & Co.

Lipset, Seymour Martin (1990) *Continental Divide: The Values and Institutions of the United States and Canada*, New York: Routledge.

Lipset, Seymour Martin and Gary Marks (2000) *It Didn't Happen Here: Why Socialism Failed in the United States*, New York: W.W. Norton.

Locke, Alain (1992 [1916]) 'Race Contacts and Interracial Relations', in J. Stewart (ed) *Race Contacts and Interracial Relations*, Washington, DC: Howard University Press.

Loewen, James (1971) *The Mississippi Chinese: Between Black and White*, Cambridge, MA: Harvard University Press.

Logevall, Fredrick (2009) 'Politics and foreign relations', *Journal of American History*, 95(4), March, 1074–8.

Loop, Emma, Anthony Cormier, Jason Leopold, Tanya Kozyreva and John Templon (2019) 'A lobbyist at the Trump Tower meeting received half a million dollars in suspicious payments', BuzzFeed News, 17 April. Available at: www.buzzfeednews.com/article/emmaloop/trump-tower-meeting-russian-lobbyist-akhmetshin-suspicious-p

Lopez, Mark Hugo, Jens Manuel Krogstad and Jeffrey S. Passel (2020) 'Who is Hispanic?', Pew Research Center, Fact Tank, 15 September. Available at: www.pewresearch.org/fact-tank/2020/09/15/who-is-hispanic/

Loriaux, Michael (1992) 'The realist and Saint Augustine: Skepticism, psychology, and moral action in international relations thought', *International Studies Quarterly*, 36(4), 401–20.

Lowell, A. Lawrence (1899) 'Colonial expansion of the United States', *The Atlantic*, February.

Lowi, Theodore (1969) *The End of Liberalism: The Second Republic of the United States*, New York: Norton.

Lowi, Theodore (1984) 'Why is there no socialism in the United States? A federal analysis', *International Political Science Review*, 5(4), 369–80.

Lubell, Samuel (1952) *The Future of American Politics*, New York: Doubleday.

Lucas, Scott (2010) 'You Don't Launch a Marketing Campaign in August: The Bush Administration and the Public Before and After the Iraq Invasion', in A. Johnstone and H. Laville (eds) *The US Public and American Foreign Policy*, London: Routledge.

Luconi, Stefano (2002) 'The impact of World War II on the political behavior of the Italian-American electorate in New York City', *New York History*, 83(4), Fall, 404–17.

Lynch, Allen (2002) 'Woodrow Wilson and the principle of national self-determination: A reconsideration', *Review of International Studies*, 28(2), 419–36.

Lynch, Colum and Robbie Gramer (2017) 'State Department reorganization eliminates climate, Muslim, and Syria envoys', *Foreign Policy*, 29 August.

McCormick, James (2008) 'Ethnic Groups in American Foreign Policy', in E. Witkopf and J. McCormick (eds) *The Domestic Sources of US Foreign Policy* (6th edn), New York: Rowman & Littlefield.

McCormick, James (2011) 'American Foreign Policy During the Obama Administration: Insights from the Public', in M. Ledwidge, I. Parmar and L. Miller (eds) *Obama and the World: New Directions in US Foreign Policy*, London: Routledge.

McCormick, James (2014) 'American Foreign Policy During the Obama Administration: Insight from the Public', in I. Parmar, L. Miller and M. Ledwidge (eds) *Obama and the World: New Directions in US Foreign Policy* (2nd edn), London: Routledge.

McCubbins, Matthew and Thomas Schwartz (1987) 'Congressional Oversight Overlooked: Police Patrol Versus Fire Alarms', in M. McCubbins and T. Sullivan (eds) *Congress: Structure and Policy*, Cambridge: Cambridge University Press.

McDougall, Walter (1997a) *Promised Land, Crusader State: The American Encounter with the World since 1776*, Boston, MA: Mariner Books.

McDougall, Walter (1997b) 'Back to bedrock: The eight traditions of American statecraft', *Foreign Affairs*, 76(2), March/April, 134–46.

McMahon, Robert (2005) 'Diplomatic history and policy history: Finding common ground', *Journal of Policy History*, 17(1), 93–109.

Magleby, David, J. Quinn Monson and Kelly Patterson (2007) *Dancing without Partners: How Candidates, Parties, and Interest Groups Interact in the Presidential Campaign*, Lanham, MD: Rowman & Littlefield.

Mahapatra, Chintamani (2010) 'Fairy tale of American decline and China's rise', *Strategic Analysis*, 34(4), 519–21.

Malcolm, Noel (2002) *Aspects of Hobbes*, Oxford: Oxford University Press.

Mallinson, Samuel and Richard Johnson (2021: under review) 'Race, rights, and realism: The discourses of the anti-apartheid sanctions movement in the United States, 1972–86', *Human Rights Quarterly*.

Manchanda, Nivi (2018) 'Security and Postcolonialism', in P. Williams and M. McDonalds (eds) *Security Studies: An Introduction*, London: Routledge.

Manela, Erez (2007) *The Wilsonian Moment*, Oxford: Oxford University Press.

Mann, Jim (2004) *Rise of the Vulcans: The History of Bush's War Cabinet*, New York: Penguin.

Mansbridge, Jane (1999) 'Should Blacks represent Blacks and women represent women? A contingent yes', *Journal of Politics*, 61(3), August, 628–57.

Mansfield, Edward, Diana Mutz and Devon Brackill (2019) 'Effects of the Great Recession on American attitudes toward trade', *British Journal of Political Science*, 49(1), 37–58.

Manson, Katrina (2007) 'Russian lobbyist Rinat Akhmetshin on that notorious meeting at Trump Tower', *Financial Times*, 1 September.

Marsden, Lee (2008) *For God's Sake: The Christian Right and US Foreign Policy*, London: Zed Books.

Marsden, Lee (2018) *Lessons from Russia: Clinton and US Democracy Promotion*, London: Taylor & Francis.

Marshall, Bryan and Richard Pacelle (2005) 'Revisiting the two presidencies: The strategic use of Executive Orders', *American Politics Research*, 33(1), 81–105.

Marty, Martin (2002) 'Introduction', in E. Blumhofer (ed) *Religion, Politics, and the American Experience*, Tuscaloosa, AL: University of Alabama Press.

Massey, Douglas (2007) *Categorically Unequal: The American Stratification System*, New York: Russell Sage.

May, Christopher (2017) 'Contract as Normative Regulation and Its Relation to the Rule of Law', in A.C. Cutler and T. Dietz (eds) *The Politics of Private Transactional Governance by Contract*, London: Routledge.

May, Ernest (1961) *Imperial Democracy: The Emergence of America as a Great Power*, New York: Harcourt, Brace, & World.

Mayhew, David (1974) *Congress: The Electoral Connection*, New Haven, CT: Yale University Press.

Mead, Walter Russell (2012) 'The Tea Party, Populism, and the Domestic Culture of Foreign Policy', in J. McCormick (ed) *The Domestic Sources of American Foreign Policy*, Philadelphia, PA and Plymouth: Rowman & Littlefield.

Meaney, Thomas (2020) 'Warfare state', *London Review of Books*, 5 November.

Mearsheimer, John (2001) *The Tragedy of Great Power Politics*, New York: W.W. Norton & Company.

Mearsheimer, John and Stephen Walt (2007) *The Israel Lobby and US Foreign Policy*, New York: Farrar, Straus, & Giroux.

Mearsheimer, John and Stephen Walt (2011) 'The Israel Lobby', in G.J. Ikenberry (ed) *American Foreign Policy: Theoretical Essays* (6th edn), Boston, MA: Wadsworth.

Mearsheimer, John (2014) *The Tragedy of Great Power Politics*, New York: Norton.

Mearsheimer, John and Stephen Walt (2014) 'The Israel Lobby', in G.J. Ikenberry and P. Trubowitz (ed) *American Foreign Policy: Theoretical Essays* (7th edn), Boston, MA: Wadsworth.

Medhurst, Martin (1997) 'Eisenhower and the crusade for freedom: The rhetorical origins of a Cold War campaign', *Presidential Studies Quarterly*, 27(4), Fall, 646–61.

Meernik, James (1994) 'Presidential decision making and the political use of military force', *International Studies Quarterly*, 38(1), March, 121–38.

Meier, August and Elliott Rudwick (1979) *Black Detroit and the Rise of the UAW*, Ann Arbor, MI: University of Michigan Press.

Melanson, Richard (1996) *American Foreign Policy Since the Vietnam War: The Search for Consensus* (2nd edn), New York: Routledge.

Melanson, Richard (2000) *American Foreign Police since the Vietnam War* (4th edn), New York: Routledge.

Meriwether, James (2002) *Proudly We Can Be Africans: Black Americans and Africa, 1935–1961*, Chapel Hill, NC: University of North Carolina Press.

Messer, Robert (1982) *The End of an Alliance: James F. Byrnes, Roosevelt, Truman, and the Origins of the Cold War*, Chapel Hill, NC: University of North Carolina Press.

Mickey, Robert (2015) *Paths out of Dixie: The Democratization of Authoritarian Enclaves in America's Deep South, 1944–1972*, Princeton, NJ: Princeton University Press.

Miliband, Ralph (1969) *The State in Capitalist Society: An Analysis of the Western System of Power*, London: Quartet Books.

Milkis, Sidney and Nicholas Jacobs (2017) 'I alone can fix it: Donald Trump, the administrative presidency, and the hazards of executive-centered partisanship', *The Forum*, 15(3), 583–613.

Milkis, Sidney and Jesse Rhodes (2007) 'George W Bush, the party system, American federalism', *Publius*, 37(3), 478–503.

Milkis, Sidney and Daniel Tichenor (2019) *Rivalry and Reform: Presidents, Social Movements, and the Transformation of American Politics*, Chicago, IL: University of Chicago Press.

Milkis, Sidney and John York (2017) 'Barack Obama, organizing for America, and executive-centered partisanship', *Studies in American Political Development*, 31(1), 1–23.

Miller, Aaron (2008) *The Much Too Promised Land: America's Elusive Search for Arab–Israeli Peace*, New York: Random House.

Miller, Benjamin (2010) 'Explaining change in US grand strategy: 9/11, the rise of offensive liberalism, and the War in Iraq', *Security Studies*, 19(1), 26–65.

Miller, David (2020) *Is Self-Determination a Dangerous Illusion?*, Cambridge: Polity.

Mills, C. Wright (1956) *The Power Elite*, Oxford: Oxford University Press.

Mills, Charles (1997) *The Racial Contract*, Ithaca, NY: Cornell University Press.

Milne, David (2008) *America's Rasputin: Walt Rostow and the Vietnam War*, New York: Farrar, Straus & Giroux.

Milner, Helen and Dustin Tingley (2015) *Sailing the Water's Edge: The Domestic Politics of American Foreign Policy*, Princeton, NJ: Princeton University Press.

Mitchell, Peter and John Schoffel (eds) (2002) *Understanding Power: The Indispensible Chomsky*, New York: The New Press.

Molloy, Sean (2017) *Kant's International Relations*, Ann Arbor, MI: University of Michigan Press.

Montgomery, David (1967) *Beyond Equality: Labor and the Radical Republicans, 1862–1872*, New York: Alfred Knopf.

Moody, Kim (1988) *An Injury to All: The Decline of American Unionism*, London: Verso.

Moore, Peter and Will Dahlgreen (2014) 'In travel, Britannia rules the waves', YouGov, 21 November. Available at: https://yougov.co.uk/news/2014/11/21/british-people-far-more-well-travelled-americans

Morgenthau, Hans (1973 [1948]) *Politics Among Nations: The Struggle for Power*, New York: Knopf.

Morris, Dick (1997) *Behind the Oval Office: Winning the Presidency in the Nineties*, New York: Random House.

Morrison, Toni (1993) 'On the back of blacks', *Time*, 2 December.

Morrow, James (1989) 'Capabilities, uncertainties, and resolve', *American Journal of Political Science*, 33(4), November, 941–72.

Mueller, John (2005) 'The Iraq Syndrome', *Foreign Affairs*, 84(6), 44–54.

Myrdal, Gunnar (1944) *An American Dilemma: The Negro Problem and Modern Democracy*, New York: Harper & Row.

Naftali, Timothy (2020) 'Trump hijacked US foreign policy during his impeachment', *Foreign Affairs*, 23 March.

Narizny, Kevin (2003) 'Both guns and butter, or neither: Class interest in the political economy of rearmament', *American Political Science Review*, 97(2), 203–20.

Nasr, Vali (2013) *Dispensable Nation: American Foreign Policy in Retreat*, New York: Doubleday.

Nathan, Richard (1975) *The Plot that Failed: Nixon and the Administrative Presidency*, New York: Wiley.

National Commission on Voting Rights (2014) *Protecting Minority Voters: Our Work is Not Done.*

National Geographic, Gallup and Council on Foreign Relations (2019) *US Adults' Knowledge About the World.* Available at: https://cdn.cfr.org/sites/default/files/report_pdf/NatGeo_CFR_US%20Knoweldge.pdf

Naughtie, James (2004) *The Accidental American: Tony Blair and the Presidency*, New York: Public Affairs.

Neuberger, Benyamin (1995) 'National self-determination: Dilemmas of a concept', *Nations and Nationalism*, 1(3), 297–325.

Neustadt, Richard (1990) *Presidential Power and the Modern Presidents*, New York: Free Press.

Newhouse, John (2009) 'Diplomacy Inc: The influence of lobbies on US foreign policy', *Foreign Affairs*, 88(3), 73–92.

Newsweek (1963) 62, 11 November, p 107.

Niedermayer, Oskar (2020) 'Staatliche Parteienfinanzierung', *Bundeszentrale für politische Bildung*, 22 June. Available at: www.bpb.de/politik/grundfragen/parteien-in-deutschland/zahlen-und-fakten/42240/staatliche-parteienfinanzierung

Nincic, Miroslav (2012) 'External Affairs and the Electoral Connection', in J. McCormick (ed) *Domestic Sources of American Foreign Policy*, New York: Rowman & Littlefield.

Noer, Thomas (1985) *Cold War and Black Liberation: The United States and White Rule in Africa*, Columbia, MO: University of Missouri Press.

Noll, Mark and Luke Harlow (2007) *Religion and American Politics* (2nd edn), Oxford: Oxford University Press.

Nuruzzaman, Mohammed (2006) 'Beyond the realist theories: Neo-conservative realism and the American invasion of Iraq', *International Studies Perspectives*, 7(3), August, 239–53.

Nye, Joseph (2010) 'The future of American power: Dominance and decline in perspective', *Foreign Policy*, 89(6), 2–12.

Oldfield, Duane and Aaron Wildavsky (1989) 'Reconsidering the two presidencies', *Society*, 26, 54–9.

Oliphant, J. Baxter (2018) 'The Iraq War continues to divide the US public, 15 years after it began', Pew Research Center, 19 March. Available at: www.pewresearch.org/fact-tank/2018/03/19/iraq-war-continues-to-divide-u-s-public-15-years-after-it-began

Omi, Michael and Howard Winant (2014) *Racial Formation in the United States* (3rd edn), Abingdon: Routledge.

ONS (Office for National Statistics) (2013) *Detailed Country of Birth and Nationality Analysis from the 2011 Census of England and Wales*, Newport: ONS. Available at: https://webarchive.nationalarchives.gov.uk/20160107124139/http://www.ons.gov.uk/ons/dcp171776_310441.pdf

Onuf, Nicholas (1989) *World of Our Making*, Columbia, SC: University of South Carolina Press.

OpenSecrets.org (2018) 'Cost of 2018 election to surpass $5 billion, CRP projects', 17 October. Available at: www.opensecrets.org/news/2018/10/cost-of-2018-election/

OpenSecrets.org (2020) '2020 election to cost $14 billion, blowing away spending records', 28 October. Available at: www.opensecrets.org/news/2020/10/cost-of-2020-election-14billion-update

Orren, Karen and Stephen Skowronek (2004) *The Search for American Political Development*, Cambridge: Cambridge University Press.

O'Sullivan, John (2006) *The President, the Pope, and the Prime Minister: Three Who Changed the World*, Washington, DC: Regenery Publishing.

Pach, Chester and Elmo Richardson (1991) *The Presidency of Dwight D. Eisenhower* (Revised edn), Lawrence, KS: University of Kansas Press.

Page, Benjamin and Robert Shapiro (1992) *The Rational Public: Fifty Years of Trends in American Policy*, Chicago, IL: University of Chicago Press.

Parmar, Inderjeet (2004) 'Institutes of International Affairs: Their Roles in Foreign Policy-Making, Opinion Mobilization, and Unofficial Diplomacy', in D. Stone and A. Denham (eds) *Think Tank Traditions: Policy Research and the Politics of Ideas*, Manchester: Manchester University Press.

Parmar, Inderjeet (2018) 'The US-led liberal order: Imperialism by another name?', *International Affairs*, 94(1), January, 151–72.

Parsi, Vittorio E. (2003) 'The global political system: From one to many?', *Irish Studies in International Affairs*, 14, 205–19.

Paterson, Thomas (2001) 'An Exaggerated Threat and the Rise of American Globalism', in R. Griffith and P. Baker (eds) *Major Problems in American History since 1945*, New York: Houghton Mifflin.

Pelosi, Nancy (2019) Pelosi remarks at address to Irish Parliament, 17 April. Available at: www.speaker.gov/newsroom/41719

Perry, Kennetta Hammond (2015) 'US Negroes, Your Fight is Our Fight: Black Britons and the 1963 March on Washington', in R. Kelley and S. Tuck (eds) *The Other Special Relationship: Race, Rights, and Riots in Britain and the United Kingdom*, New York: Palgrave Macmillan.

Persaud, Randolph B. and R.B.J. Walker (2001) 'Race in international relations', *Alternatives*, 26, 373–6.

Peterson, Mark (2004) 'Bush and Interest Groups', in C. Campbell and B. Rockman (eds) *The George W. Bush Presidency*, Washington, DC: CQ Press.

Pew Research Center (2013) *A Portrait of Jewish Americans*, Chapter 5. Available at: www.pewforum.org/2013/10/01/chapter-5-connection-with-and-attitudes-towards-israel/

Phillips, Kevin (2006) *American Theocracy: The Perils and Politics of Radical Religion, Oil, and Borrowed Money in the 21st Century*, London: Viking.

Pletcher, David (1998) *The Diplomacy of Trade: American Economic Expansion in the Hemisphere, 1865–1900*, Columbia, MO: University of Missouri Press.

Plummer, Brenda (1996) *Rising Wind: Black Americans and US Foreign Affairs, 1935–1960*, Chapel Hill, NC: University of North Carolina Press.

Porter, Patrick (2018) 'Iraq: A liberal war after all', *International Politics*, 55(2), 334–48.

Porter, Patrick (2020) *The False Promise of Liberal Order: Nostalgia, Delusion, and the Rise of Trump*, Cambridge: Polity Press.

Powell, Lynda and Clyde Wilcox (2010) 'Money and American Elections', in J. Leighley (ed) *Oxford Handbook of American Elections and Political Behavior*, Oxford: Oxford University Press.

Preston, Andrew (2010) 'Religion and World Order at the Dawn of the American Century', in A. Johnstone and H. Laville (eds) *The US Public and American Foreign Policy*, London: Routledge.

Preston, Andrew (2015) 'Beyond the Water's Edge: Foreign Policy and Electoral Politics', in G. Davies and J. Zelizer (eds) *America at the Ballot Box: Elections and Political History*, Philadelphia, PA: University of Pennsylvania Press.

Preston, Julia (2016) 'Tensions simmer as Cubans breeze across US border', *The New York Times*, 12 February.

Price, David (2016) *Cold War Anthropology*, Durham, NC: Duke University Press.

Price, Richard and Christian Reus-Smit (1998) 'Dangerous liaisons? Critical international theory and constructivism', *European Journal of International Relations*, 4(3), September, 259–94.

Prins, Brandon and Bryan Marshall (2001) 'Congressional support of the President: A comparison of foreign, defense, and domestic policy decision making during and after the Cold War', *Presidential Studies Quarterly*, 31(4), December, 660–78.

Protess, Ben, Danielle Ivory and Steve Eder (2017) 'Where Trumps' hands-off approach to governing does not apply', *The New York Times*, 10 September. Available at: www.nytimes.com/2017/09/10/business/trump-regulations-religious-conservatives.html

Rabin, Yitzhak (1979) *The Rabin Memoirs*, Boston, MA: Little, Brown, & Company.

Rapkin, David (2005) 'Empire and its discontents', *New Political Economy*, 10(3), 389–411.

Rathbun, Brian (2007) 'Hierarchy and community at home and abroad: Evidence of a common structure of domestic and foreign policy beliefs in American elites', *Journal of Conflict Resolution*, 51(3), June, 379–407.

Raymond, Jack (1964) *Power at the Pentagon*, Portsmouth, NH: Heinemann.

Reagan, Ronald (1989) 'Farewell Address to the Nation', 11 January. Available at: www.reaganfoundation.org/media/128652/farewell.pdf

Reeves, Julie (2004) *Culture and International Relations: Narratives, Natives, and Tourists*, New York: Routledge.

Rich, Andrew (2004) *Think Tanks, Public Policy, and the Politics of Expertise*, Cambridge: Cambridge University Press.

Riley, Patrick (1973) 'Rousseau as a theorist of national and international federalism', *Publius*, 3(1), Spring, 5–17.

Risse-Kappen, Thomas (1991) 'Public opinion, domestic structure, and foreign policy in liberal democracies', *World Politics*, 43(4), July, 479–512.

Rockman, B. (1994) 'Presidents, Opinion, and Institutional Leadership', in D. Deese (ed) *The New Politics of American Foreign Policy*, New York: St Martin's Press.

Roediger, David (2005) *Working Toward Whiteness: How America's Immigrants Became White*, New York: Basic Books.

Rogers, Katie (2019) 'Get over it? Why political influence matters in foreign policy matters', *The New York Times*, 21 October.

Rogin, Josh (2020) 'Trump's foreign policy is all politics, no policy', *The Washington Post*, 7 February.

Rohde, Joy (2009) 'Gray matters: Social scientists, military patronage, and democracy in the Cold War', *Journal of American History*, 96(1), 99–122.

Romney, Mitt (2010) *No Apology: The Case for American Greatness*, New York: St Martin's Press.

Roosevelt, Grace (2006) 'Rousseau versus Rawls on international relations', *European Journal of Political Theory*, 5(3), 301–20.

Rosato, Sebastian (2003) 'The flawed logic of democratic peace theory', *American Political Science Review*, 97(4), November, 585–602.

Rostow, Eugene (1993) *A Breakfast for Bonaparte: US Security Interests from the Heights of Abraham to the Nuclear Age*, Washington, DC: National Defense University Press.

Rothman, Adam (2007) *Slave Country: American Expansion and Origins of the South*, Cambridge, MA: Harvard University Press.

Rubenezer, Trevor and Steven Redd (2010) 'Ethnic minority groups and US foreign policy: Examining congressional decision making and economic sanctions', *International Studies Quarterly*, 54(3), 755–77.

Rubin, Jennifer (2011) 'Hillary Clinton: Why did we do nothing in Syria?', *The Washington Post*, 8 November.

Rueschemeyer, Dietrich, Evelyne H. Stephens and John D. Stephens (1992) *Capitalist Development and Democracy: The Importance of Social Class in Historical Comparative Perspective*, Chicago, IL: University of Chicago Press.

Ruggie, John (1996) *Winning the Peace: America and World Order in the New Era*, New York: Columbia University Press.

Ryan, Missy, Anne Geeran and Karen DeYoung (2018) 'US to close Palestinian office in Washington', *The Washington Post*, 10 September.

Rynhold, Jonathan (2015) *The Arab–Israeli Conflict in American Political Culture*, Cambridge: Cambridge University Press.

Rytz, Henriette (2013) *Ethnic Interest Groups in US Foreign Policy-Making: A Cuban Story of Success and Failure*, New York: Palgrave Macmillan.

Saideman, Stephen (2002) 'The power of small: The impact of ethnic minorities on foreign policy', *SAIS Review*, 22(2), Summer/Fall, 93–105.

Sanchez Gibau, Gina (1997) 'The politics of Cape Verdean American identity', *Transforming Anthropology*, 6(1–2), 54–71.

Sandbrook, Dominic (2008) 'Salesmanship and Substance', in F. Lovegall and A. Preston (eds) *Nixon in the World*, Oxford: Oxford University Press.

Santiago, Fabiola (2014) '20 years ago, 35,000 balseros fled Castro's Cuba on anything that would float', *Miami Herald*, 18 August.

Sarotte, Mary E. (2001) *Dealing with the Devil: East Germany, Détente, and Ostpolitik*, Chapel Hill, NC: University of North Carolina Press.

Saunders, Elizabeth (2014) *Leaders at War: How Presidents Shape Military Interventions*, Ithaca, NY: Cornell University Press.

Sawer, Patrick (2020) 'Joe Biden angered British government over US visa for Gerry Adams', *The Telegraph*, 7 November.

Schafer, Amy (2017) *Generations of War: The Rise of the Warrior Caste and the All Volunteer Force*, Washington, DC: Center for a New American Security.

Schattschneider, Elmer E. (1960) *The Semi-Sovereign People: A Realist's View of Democracy in America*, New York: Holt, Rinehart & Winston.

Scherer, Michael and John Wagner (2019) 'Former vice president Joe Biden jumps into White House race', *The Washington Post*, 25 April.

Schiffrin, Harold (1968) *Sun Yat-sen and the Origins of the Chinese Revolution*, Berkeley, CA: University of California Press.

Schlesinger, Arthur (1973) *The Imperial Presidency*, New York: Houghton Mifflin.

Schlesinger, Arthur (1986) *The Cycles of American History*, New York: Houghton Mifflin.

Schmidt, Brian (2012) 'Theories of US Foreign Policy', in M. Cox and D. Stokes (eds) *US Foreign Policy* (2nd edn), Oxford: Oxford University Press.

Schmidt, Brian and Michael Williams (2008) 'The Bush Doctrine and the Iraq War: Neoconservatives versus realists', *Security Studies*, 17(2), 191–220.

Schmitt, Eric (1995) 'Senators query US role in Bosnia', *The New York Times*, 18 October.

Schmitz, David and Vanessa Walker (2004) 'Jimmy Carter and the foreign policy of human rights: The development of a post-Cold War foreign policy', *Diplomatic History*, 28(1), January, 113–43.

Schneider, Howard (2010) 'Obama, Lee outlined US–Korea trade deal in Seoul', *The Washington Post*, 6 December.

Schneider, William (2001) 'Elián González defeated Al Gore', *The Atlantic*, 1 May.

Schraufnagel, Scot and Stephen Shellman (2001) 'The two presidencies, 1984–98: A replication and extension', *Presidential Studies Quarterly*, 31(4), December, 699–707.

Schrecker, Ellen (1986) *No Ivory Tower: McCarthyism and the Universities*, Oxford: Oxford University Press.

Schwartz, Thomas (2009) 'Henry, winning an election is terribly important: Partisan politics in the history of US foreign relations', *Diplomatic History*, 33(2), April, 173–90.

Schwartz, Thomas (2017) 'The Peace Candidate: Richard Nixon, Henry Kissinger, and the Election of 1972', in A. Johnstone and A. Priest (eds) *US Presidential Elections and Foreign Policy*, Lexington, KY: University of Kentucky Press.

Schwarz, Benjamin and Christopher Layne (2002) 'A new grand strategy', *The Atlantic*, January.

Schweller, Randall (1996) 'Neorealism's status–quo bias: What security dilemma?', *Security Studies*, 3, 90–121.

Scigliano, Eric (2018) 'The university that launched a CIA front operation in Vietnam', *POLITICO*, 25 March.

Scigliano, Robert and Guy Fox (1965) *Technical Assistance in Vietnam: The Michigan State University Experience*, New York: Praeger.

Scott, James and Ralph Carter (2002) 'Acting on the Hill: Congressional assertiveness in US foreign policy', *Congress & the Presidency*, 9(2), 151–69.

Seagrave, Sterling (1985) *The Soong Dynasty*, New York: Perennial.

Shafer, Byron (1991) 'Introduction', in B. Shafer (ed) *Is America Different? A New Look at American Exceptionalism*, Oxford: Oxford University Press.

Sharp, Jeremy (2020) *US Foreign Aid to Israel*, Washington, DC: Congressional Research Service.

Shawcross, William (2004) *Allies: Why the West Had to Remove Saddam*, New York: Public Affairs.

Shear, Michael D. and Katie Rogers (2019) 'Mulvaney says, then denies, that Trump held back Ukrainian aid as quid pro quo', *The New York Times*, 5 November.

Shefter, Martin (2002) 'War, Trade, and US Party Politics', in I. Katznelson and M. Shefter (eds) *Shaped by War and Trade: International Influences on American Political Development*, Princeton, NJ: Princeton University Press.

Shepardson, David (2019) 'Trump declares some auto imports pose national security threat', Reuters, 17 May. Available at: www.reuters.com/article/us-autos-tariffs-usa-idUSKCN1SN1FY

Shergold, Peter (1983) *Working-Class Life: The American Standard in Comparative Perspective*, Pittsburgh, PA: University of Pittsburgh Press.

Shilliam, Robbie (2011) *International Relations and Non-Western Thought: Imperialism, Colonialism, and Investigations of Global Modernity*, New York: Routledge.

Sing, Robert (2012) *Barack Obama's Post-American Foreign Policy*, London: Bloomsbury.

Singer, Peter W. (2003) *Corporate Warriors: The Rise of the Privatized Military Industry*, Ithaca, NY: Cornell University Press.

SIPRI (Stockholm International Peace Research Institute) (2018) *SIPRI Yearbook 2018: Armaments, Disarmament, and International Security*, Oxford: Oxford University Press.

Skidmore, David (1993) 'Carter and failure of foreign policy reform', *Political Science Quarterly*, 108(4), Winter, 699–729.

Skidmore, David (1996) *Reversing Course: Carter's Foreign Policy, Domestic Politics, and the Failure of Reform*, Nashville, TN: Vanderbilt University Press.

Small, Melvin (1991) 'Public Opinion', in M. Hogan and T. Paterson (eds) *Explaining the History of American Foreign Relations*, Cambridge: Cambridge University Press.

Smeltz, Dina, Marshall Bouton, Craig Kafura, Benjamin Page, Steven Kull and Gregory Holyk (2012) *Chicago Council Survey on American Public Opinion and Foreign Policy*, Ann Arbor, MI: Inter-university Consortium for National and Social Research, 2015-12-07. Available at: https://doi.org/10.3886/ICPSR36230.v.1

Smetak, Jacqueline (1994) 'Review of Philip Foner, *US Labor and the Vietnam War* (1989)', *Nobody Get Off the Bus*, 5(1–4), March. Available at: www2.iath.virginia.edu/sixties/HTML_docs/Texts/Reviews/Smetak_US_Labor_01.html

Smith, Hedrick (1988) *The Power Game: How Washington Works*, New York: Random House.

Smith, Jordan Michael (2011) 'The weakness of Obama's strength', *Salon*, 23 November.

Smith, Joseph (2010) 'From Coast Defense to Embalmed Beef: The Influence of the Press and Public Opinion on McKinley's Policymaking During the Spanish–American War', in A. Johnstone and H. Laville (eds) *The US Public and American Foreign Policy*, London: Routledge.

Smith, Rogers (1993) 'Beyond Tocqueville, Mydral, and Hartz: The multiple traditions in America', *American Political Science Review*, 87(3), September, 549–66.

Smith, Tony (1994) *America's Mission: The United States and the Worldwide Struggle for Democracy in the Twentieth Century*, Princeton, NJ: Princeton University Press.

Smith, Tony (2000) *Foreign Attachments: The Power of Ethnic Groups in the Making of American Foreign Policy*, Cambridge, MA: Harvard University Press.

Sneh, Itai (2008) *The Future Almost Arrived: How Jimmy Carter Failed to Change US Foreign Policy*, New York: Peter Lang.

Snyder, Alvin (1995) *Warriors of Disinformation: American Propaganda, Soviet Lies, and the Winning of the Cold War: An Insider's Account*, New York: Arcade Publishing.

Snyder, Glenn (1984) 'The security dilemma in alliance politics', *World Politics*, 36(4), July, 461–95.

Snyder, Jack (1991) *Myths of Empire: Domestic Politics and International Ambition*, Ithaca, NY: Cornell University Press.

Snyder, Sarah (2018) *From Selma to Moscow: How Human Rights Activists Transformed US Foreign Policy*, New York: Columbia University Press.

Sobel, Richard (1989) 'Public opinion about United States intervention in El Salvador and Nicaragua', *Public Opinion Quarterly*, 53(1), Spring, 114–28.

Sobel, Richard (2001) *The Impact of Public Opinion on US Foreign Policy since Vietnam*, Cambridge: Cambridge University Press.

Solovey, Mark (2001) 'Science and the state during the Cold War: Blurred boundaries and contested legacy', *Social Studies of Science*, 31(2), April, 165–70.

Sombart, Werner (1962 [1906]) quoted in Daniel Bell, *The End of Ideology*, New York: Collier Books.

Sondergaard, Ramus (2015) 'Bill Clinton's democratic enlargement and the securitization of democracy promotion', *Diplomacy & Statecraft*, 26(3), 534–51.

Spengler, Oswald (1926 [1918]) *The Decline of the West*, London: Unwin Hyman.

Steel, Ronald (1995) 'The domestic core of foreign policy', *The Atlantic*, June.

Stepan, Alfred and Juan Linz (2011) 'Comparative perspectives on inequality and the quality of democracy in the United States', *Perspectives on Politics*, 9(4), December, 841–56.

Stephens, Elizabeth (2010) 'The American Public and the US–Israel Special Relationship', in A. Johnstone and H. Laville (eds) *The US Public and American Foreign Policy*, London: Routledge.

Stoddard, Lothrop (1920) *The Rising Tide of Color Against White World Supremacy*, New York: Charles Scribner's Sons.

Stoller, Paul and Jasmin Tahmaseb McConatha (2001) 'City life: West African communities in New York', *Journal of Contemporary Ethnography*, 30(6), 651–77.

Stone, Diane and Andrew Denham (2004) *Think Tank Traditions: Policy Research and the Politics of Ideas*, Manchester: Manchester University Press.

Stuart, Douglas (2008) *Creating the National Security State: A History of the Law that Transformed America*, Princeton, NJ: Princeton University Press.

Summers, Mark (2003) *Rum, Romanism, and Rebellion: The Making of a President, 1884*, Chapel Hill, NC: University of North Carolina Press.

Taliaferro, Jeffrey, Steven Lobell and Norin Ripsman (2009) 'Introduction', in S. Lobell, N. Ripsman and J. Taliaferro (eds) *Neoclassical Realism, the State, and Foreign Policy*, Cambridge: Cambridge University Press.

Tang, S. (2010) *A Theory of Security Strategy for Our Time: Defensive Realism*, New York: Palgrave Macmillan.

Taylor, Alan (2016) *American Revolutions: A Continental History, 1750–1804*, New York: W.W. Norton & Co.

Tertrais, Bruno (2010) 'The illogic of zero', *The Washington Quarterly*, 33(2), 125–38.

Tesler, Michael (2016) *Post-Racial or Most-Racial? Race and Politics in the Obama Era*, Chicago, IL: University of Chicago Press.

Thatcher, Margaret (1991) 'Speech at Hoover Institution Lunch', 8 March. Available at: www.margaretthatcher.org/document/108264

The Congressional Record, 11 June 1898, 5792.

The Economist (2008) 'After Bush', 27 March.

The Economist (2009) 'Beware the Beijing Model', *The Economist*, 26 May.

The Economist Intelligence Unit (1963) *The Economic Effects of Disarmament*, Toronto: University of Toronto Press.

The Electoral Commission (2019) 'Campaign spending: Political parties and non-party campaigners', 11 July. Available at: www.electoralcommission.org.uk/find-information-by-subject/political-parties-campaigning-and-donations/political-party-spending-at-elections/details-of-party-spending-at-previous-elections

The New York Times (1893) 'Time enough', 30 January.

The New York Times (1975) 'Year of Intelligence', 8 February.

The New York Times (1980) 'Weicker says Castro seems to want better US ties', 19 October.

The New York Times (2016) '2016 Presidential election results'. Available at: www.nytimes.com/elections/2016/results/president

The New York Times (2020) 'Presidential election results'. Available at: www.nytimes/com/interactive/2020/11/03/us/elections/results-president.html

The President's Committee on Administrative Management (1937) *Report of the Committee with Studies of Administrative Management in the Federal Government (The Brownlow Committee Report)*, Washington, DC: US Government Printing Office.

Therborn, Göran (1977) 'The rule of capital and the rise of democracy', *New Left Review*, 103, May/June, 3–41.

The Telegraph (2018) 'The truth about how Americans travel', 4 July.

Thompson, Debra (2015) 'What lies beneath: Equality and the making of racial classifications', *Social Philosophy & Policy*, 31(2), 114–36.

Thompson, John (1992) 'The exaggeration of American vulnerability: The anatomy of a tradition', *Diplomatic History*, 16(1), Winter, 23–43.

Thorne, Christopher (1998) 'Britain and the Black GIs', in E.N. Gates (ed) *Race and US Foreign Policy from 1900 through World War II*, New York: Routledge.

Throntveit, Trygve (2011) 'The fable of the Fourteen Points: Woodrow Wilson and national self-determination', *Diplomatic History*, 35(3), June, 445–81.

Tiewes, Frederick (1987) 'Carter's foreign policy: The perception of failure', *Australian Outlook*, 41, 53–5.

Tillery, Alvin (2011) *Between Homeland and Motherland: Africa, US Foreign Policy, and Black Leadership in America*, Ithaca, NY: Cornell University Press.

Tocqueville, Alexis de (1835/40) *Democracy in America*, London: Saunders and Otley.

Tocqueville, Alexis de and F. Mélonio (eds) (2001 [1856]) *The Old Regime and the Revolution*, Chicago, IL: University of Chicago Press.

Trager, Frank (ed) (1960) *Marxism in South East Asia: A Study of Four Countries*, Oxford: Oxford University Press.

Truman, Harry (1948) 'Special message to Congress on civil rights', 2 February, Washington, DC.

Trumbore, Peter F. and David A. Dulio (2013) 'Running on foreign policy? Examining the role of foreign policy issues in the 2000, 2002, and 2004 congressional campaigns', *Foreign Policy Analysis*, 9(3), 267–86.

US Census Bureau (2012) *2010 Census of Population and Housing, Population and Housing Unit Counts*, CPH-2-1, United States Summary. Washington, DC: US Government Printing Office. Available at: www.census.gov/prod/cen2010/cph-2-1.pdf

US Congress (2019–20) *United States–Mexico–Canada Agreement Implementation Act*, HR 5430, 116th Congress. Available at: www.congress.gov/bill/116th-congress/house-bill/5430/all-info

US Department of State Historical Division (1957) *American Foreign Policy, Current Documents*, Washington, DC: Bureau of Public Affairs.

US Government (2015) *Historical Tables, Budget of the US Government, Fiscal Year 2015*, Table 5.1. Available at: www.govinfo.gov/app/details/BUDGET-2015-TAB/BUDGET-2015-TAB-5-1/summary

US House of Representatives Permanent Select Committee on Intelligence (2019) *The Trump–Ukraine Impeachment Inquiry: Full Testimonies of Yovanovitch, McKinley, Sondland, Volker, Taylor & Kent*. Available at: www.justsecurity.org/wp-content/uploads/2019/12/impeachment-report-majority-schiff-intelligence-december-3-2019.pdf

USA Today (2015) 'Selma', 5 March.

van Cleve, George (2010) *A Slaveholders' Union: Slavery, Politics, and the Constitution in the Early American Republic*, Chicago, IL: University of Chicago Press.

van Evera, S. (1999) *Causes of War: Power and the Roots of Conflict*, Ithaca, NY: Cornell University Press.

van Rythoven, Eric (2015) 'The perils of realist advocacy and the promise of securitization theory: Revisiting the tragedy of the Iraq War debate', *European Journal of International Relations*, 22(3), 487–511.

Vitalis, Robert (2000) 'The graceful and generous liberal gesture: Making racism invisible in American international relations', *Milennium*, 29(2), 331–56.

Vitalis, Robert (2015) *White World Order, Black Power Politics: The Birth of American International Relations*, Ithaca, NY: Cornell University Press.

von Eschen, Penny (1997) *Race Against Empire: Black Americans and Anticolonialism, 1937–1957*, Ithaca, NY: Cornell University Press.

von Ranke, Leopold (1981) 'The Great Powers', in R. Wines (ed) *The Secret of World History*, New York: Fordham University Press.

Wallerstein, Immanuel (1993) 'The world system after the Cold War', *Journal of Peace Research*, 30(1), February, 1–6.

Wallerstein, Immanuel (2003) *The Decline of American Power*, New York: New Press.

Walt, Stephen (1987) *The Origins of Alliances*, Ithaca, NY: Cornell University Press.

Walt, Stephen (2000) 'Two cheers for Clinton's foreign policy', *Foreign Affairs*, 79(2), March/April, 63–79.

Walters, Ronald (1987) 'African American Influence on US Foreign Policy Toward South Africa', in M. Ahrari (ed) *Ethnic Groups and US Foreign Policy*, New York: Greenwood Press.

Waltz, Kenneth (1996) 'International politics is not foreign policy', *Security Studies*, 6(1), 54–7.

Ward, Lee (2006) 'Locke on the moral basis of international relations', *American Journal of Political Science*, 50(3), July, 691–705.

Waterman, Richard (2009) 'The administrative presidency, unilateral power, and the unitary executive theory', *Presidential Studies Quarterly*, 39(1), 5–9.

Waters, Mary (1999) *Black Identities*, Cambridge, MA: Harvard University Press.

Watts, Carl (2010) 'African Americans and US Foreign Policy: The American Negro Leadership Conference on Africa and the Rhodesian Crisis', in A. Johnstone and H. Laville (eds) *The US Public and American Foreign Policy*, London: Routledge.

Waxman, Dov (2017) 'Young American Jews and Israel: Beyond birthright and BDS', *Israel Studies*, 22(3), Fall, 177–99.

Weiner, Tim (2006) 'F Mark Wyatt, 86, CIA Officer, is dead', *The New York Times*, 6 July.

Weisbord, Robert (1973) *Ebony Kinship: Africans and Afro-Americans*, Westport, CT: Greenwood Press.

Welch, David (2003) 'Why international relations theorists should stop reading Thucydides', *Review of International Studies*, 29(3), July, 301–19.

Wendt, Alexander (1995) 'Constructing international politics', *International Security*, 20(1), Summer, 71–81.

Wendt, Alexander (1999) *Social Theory of International Politics*, Cambridge: Cambridge University Press.

Western, Bruce and Jake Rosenfeld (2011) 'Unions, norms, and the rise in US wage inequality', *American Sociological Review*, 76(4), 513–37.

White, Hugh (2012) *The China Choice: Why America Should Share Power*, Oxford: Oxford University Press.

White House (2020) 'President Donald J. Trump is protecting America's founding ideals by promoting patriotic education', 2 November. Available at: www.whitehouse.gov/briefings-statements/president-donald-j-trump-protecting-americas-founding-ideals-promoting-patriotic-education/

Wildavsky, Aaron (1966) 'The two presidencies', *Trans-Action*, 4, 7–14.

Wilkins, Burleigh T. (2007) 'Kant on international relations', *The Journal of Ethics*, 11(2), June, 147–59.

Williams, Michael (1989) 'Rousseau, realism, and *Realpolitik*', *Millennium: Journal of International Studies*, 182(2), 185–203.

Williams, Michael (1996) 'Hobbes and international relations: A reconsideration', *International Organization*, 50(2), Spring, 213–36.

Williams, William Appleman (1959) *The Tragedy of American Diplomacy*, Cleveland, OH: World Publishing Company.

Wills, Garry (2007) *Head and Heart: American Christianities*, New York: Penguin Books.

Wilson, Charles E. (ed) (1947) *To Secure these Rights: The Report of the President's Committee on Civil Rights*. Available at: www.trumanlibrary.gov/library/to-secure-these-rights

Wilson, Megan R. (2016) 'Tom Daschle registers as a lobbyist', The Hill, 29 March. Available at: https://thehill.com/business-a-lobbying/business-a-lobbying/274569-tom-daschle-registers-as-a-lobbyist

Winters, Jeffrey A. (2011) *Oligarchy*, Cambridge: Cambridge University Press.

Wong, Edward (2018) 'US to end funding to UN Agency that helps Palestinian refugees', *The New York Times*, 31 August.

Woodward, Bob (2004) *Plan of Attack: The Definitive Account of the Decision to Invade Iraq*, New York: Simon & Schuster.

Woodward, Bob (2006) *State of Denial*, New York: Simon & Schuster.

World Economic Forum (2017) 'Joe Biden's last major speech as Vice President in full', 18 January. Available at: www.weforum.org/agenda/2017/01/joe-bidens-last-major-speech-in-full/

Wylie, Paul (2016) *Blood on the Marias: The Baker Massacre*, Norman, OK: University of Oklahoma Press.

Yates, Jeff and Andrew Whitford (1998) 'Presidential power and the United States Supreme Court', *Political Research Quarterly*, 51(2), 539–50.

Yordan, Carlos (2006) 'America's quest for hegemony: Offensive realism, the Bush Doctrine, and the 2003 Iraq War', *Theoria*, 53(110), 125–57.

Young, John and John Kent (2013) *International Relations since 1945: A Global History* (3rd edn), Oxford: Oxford University Press.

Yurdusev, A. Nuri (2006) 'Thomas Hobbes and international relations: From realism to rationalism', *Australian Journal of International Affairs*, 60(2), 305–21.

Zarifian, Julien (2014) 'The Armenian-American lobby and its impact on US foreign policy', *Society*, 51, 503–12.

Zelizer, Julian (2010) *Arsenal of Democracy: The Politics of National Security from World War II to the War on Terrorism*, New York: Basic Books.

Zeller, Belle (1948) 'American government and politics: The Federal Regulation of Lobbying Act', *American Political Science* Review, 42(2), April, 244.

Zielinski, Rosella (2018) 'US wars abroad increase inequality at home', *Foreign Affairs*, October.

Zimmerman, Warren (2002) *First Great Triumph: How Five Americans Made Their Country a World Power*, Boston, MA: Farrar, Straus & Giroux.

Zimmern, Alfred (1926) *The Third British Empire*, Oxford: Oxford University Press.

Index

References to tables and figures are in *italics*

Printed in the USA
CPSIA information can be obtained
at www.ICGtesting.com
JSHW011924090124
55096JS00007B/222